THE IMMIGRANT CHURCH

The Immigrant Church

NEW YORK'S IRISH AND GERMAN
CATHOLICS, 1815–1865

803620

JAY P. DOLAN

Foreword by Martin E. Marty

BALTIMORE AND LONDON

THE JOHNS HOPKINS
UNIVERSITY
PRESS

J.D.R.H.S.

This book has been brought to publication with the generous assistance of the Andrew W. Mellon Foundation.

Grateful acknowledgment is made to *The Review of Politics* for permission to use material from a previously published article, "A Critical Period in American Catholicism," *The Review of Politics* 35, 4 (October 1973): 523–36, in chapter nine.

The Johns Hopkins University Press, Baltimore, Maryland 21218
The Johns Hopkins University Press Ltd., London

Library of Congress Catalog Card Number 75–12552
ISBN 0–8018–1708–0
Library of Congress Cataloging in Publication data will be found on the last printed page of this book.

To my mother and to the memory of my father

Contents

Maps and Tables

Foreword

"IT IS A GOOD MOMENT to be a social historian." This assessment by
the British Marxist historian E. J. Hobsbawm would receive enthusiastic seconding, just as it is elaborately illustrated here, by Jay P.
Dolan. Hobsbawm, writing in *Daedalus* (Winter 1971), noted that
"social history is at present in fashion" and that "writing the history
of society" is a valid enterprise. Dolan, one senses, would pursue his
subject the same way whether or not it were in fashion. He has a
story to tell, and the way to do that is to sidle up as close as possible
to the people who enacted it, people who have often been overlooked by those who concentrate only on leadership and elites.

This is not to say that other approaches to writing history are
neglected here. *Social* history is sometimes posed over against intellectual history. It happens that there was not much formal theological construction going on among the new immigrant Roman Catholics of nineteenth-century New York, and they are the subject of
this inquiry. But Dolan does not despair: he studies the preaching
and the ideas that formed or bonded the religious communities of
the time. He is beginning to contribute to a different way of looking
at Catholic ideas in America.

If this is an essay in social history, it should also be of interest—as
the previous paragraph implied—to those who study American
Roman *Catholic* history. One is always reluctant to make extrava-
gant claims for freshness or novelty in the writing of history. The
terrain is too cluttered with past efforts, the landscape too crowded

with previous achievements, to warrant the proclamation of newness whenever an overlooked aspect of older times is discovered and discussed. To those schooled in social history, there would be reasons to stifle yawns in the face of announcements that Catholics have decided to tell the story of their people, their lay members, ordinary men and women in the American past.

The student of Catholic historiography, however, will not yawn. He or she has reason these days to be alert to the excitements occurring on many fronts—and Dolan is an illustration of one of these—as inquiry into the past of the Roman Catholic community transgresses old boundaries. The beginnings had been promising. A century ago "The Father of American Catholic History," John Gilmary Shea, had set it on a course that included the story of Catholic people in their social environments. While he has had great impact on subsequent historical writing, certainly in respect to the weight of numbers most subsequent authors departed from his approach.

The volumes on the American Catholic past are preponderantly ecclesiastical in tone. They concentrate on the people who rose to positions of leadership or on institutions in apparent isolation from their environments. One always asks who pays a scholar's grocery bills. In the case of Catholic history, most subsidy or support for chronicling the past has come from dioceses, religious orders, or other institutions that have an interest in presenting the best face of the most important people.

Whoever scans, then, extensive bibliographies such as John Tracy Ellis's *A Guide to American Catholic History* will find chiefly the following topics: diocesan and sectional history (203 items); biographies, correspondence, and memoirs of Catholic dignitaries and leaders (301 items); religious communities (70 items); education— chiefly institutional (64 items). They all leave casual traces of reference to the lived experience of the faithful, but these tend to be incidental, and the newcoming reader has to reach past many formal elements that are of interest to few outside the institutions under study in order to grasp a sense of the "feel" of the people's lives.

There are some more promising books in the older Ellis bibliography, including twenty-two parish histories, some of them attentive to the people's experience and, best of all, over ninety books on colonization, journalism, law, missions, nationalism, nativism, social studies, wars, and the like. Whoever has worked with that miscellaneous literature will often be disappointed, however, by the official tone or institutional awe that marks much of it. Thanks in part to Ellis, who might most plausibly be conceived to be Shea's twentieth-century successor, numbers of newer-style histories have been written since his guide was published in 1959. Ellis's achievement was to see Catholicism in the context of American political history, as many of his older contemporaries did not.

Now a new generation is on the scene, one that is impatient with a mere address to the old questions. Catholicism is now, after the Second Vatican Council, wholly exposed to the American environment. To use a linguistic barbarism of the times, it has been "de-ghettoized," and so, progressively, has been its history. Dolan helps bring this process to a new stage, precisely by examining the walls of the old ghettos, as well as the fissures in them. Here is no church history that sees the church protected as if lead-encased in a hostile environment but, instead, the story of people in the incipient pluralism of an expanding metropolis.

Metropolis: this book should also interest *urban* historians. Here again, one can claim no novelty for Dolan's work. Urban history with its story of ethnic groups in the cities is a familiar theme in at least the recent past. But the urban theme has only occasionally been employed in the study of Catholicism, the major urban religious group, a population element without which the story of New York and similar cities cannot be understood.

I have also just mentioned the *ethnic* motif. Inevitably that is strong in a study of New York Catholicism during the crucial decades of institutional formation. Dolan concentrates on the two major clusters, the Germans and the Irish. The story of the Irish has been frequently told; the Germans have received less attention. This book will help correct the balance and serve as a model in a study of comparative ethnic history. Hobsbawm could as well have said that history of ethnicity is now in fashion. In that sense, Dolan rides a wave of interest rather than helping to fashion it. But his concern, once again, is to tell the story and not to be in vogue.

The concern here has been, not to anticipate the story, but to locate it and its importance and to point to audiences for it. Looking over the author's shoulder during the years when he was researching old parish archives, newspaper files, and the like, and then looking on as he put his research in the order of the story, I have great confidence in his ability to make a contribution to understanding a decisive moment in the history of American cities. Best of all, he will help readers come as close as possible to sensing what it must have been like to be involved in the brick and mortar, the rhetoric and reality, the sweat and the dreams of life in those years.

Martin E. Marty
The University of Chicago

Acknowledgments

SCORES OF PEOPLE have helped me in the research and writing of this work, and my gratitude to them has been expressed many times in the past. To a special few, however, I owe a particular debt.

To Martin E. Marty I am especially indebted. His lively mind and buoyant spirit stimulated me in my work and inspired me throughout the years as this study progressed from a seminar paper to a dissertation and finally to a finished manuscript. Richard C. Wade taught me to appreciate the importance of the city in history and offered continued encouragement. His advice and counsel were always appreciated, and I hope that his demands for excellence and scholarship are met in the pages that follow. Henry J. Browne, a friend and scholar, read the manuscript in its early stages and offered many helpful suggestions. He loaned me his unpublished biography of Archbishop John Hughes and shared his hospitality with me on numerous occasions during the course of my work. The late Rev. Michael J. Curley, C.SS.R., aided me in my research on the German Catholics and put at my disposal his extensive collection of material on American Catholic history. Monsignor John Tracy Ellis, Philip Gleason, and David O'Brien were also generous with their time and read the manuscript.

A grant from the O'Brien Fund of the University of Notre Dame enabled me to complete additional research. A fellowship from the Shelby Cullom Davis Center for Historical Studies at Princeton University, under the direction of Lawrence Stone, provided the time and cherished leisure to do additional research and to revise the manuscript for publication.

Brother Barnabas D. Hipkins, C.SS.R., Redemptorist provincial archivist, was especially generous and helpful during my work at the provincial archives in Brooklyn, New York. Rev. Thomas T. Mc-Avoy, C.S.C., archivist at the University of Notre Dame until his death in 1969, and Rev. Lawrence McDonnell, C.S.P., archivist for the Paulist Fathers, were also very cooperative. The pastor of Transfiguration Church, Bishop John W. Comber, M.M., and the pastor of Most Holy Redeemer Church, Rev. George C. Rosenkranz, C.SS.R., were also very gracious in putting the respective parish records at my disposal.

I would also like to thank the library staffs of the New York Historical Society, New York Public Library, Columbia University, Catholic University of America, University of Chicago, University of Notre Dame, and St. Joseph's Seminary for making my work not only easier but possible. I also owe a debt of appreciation to Shirley Schneck, who typed the manuscript.

Finally, to my wife Patricia for her continued support and intelligent criticisms I give thanks. As a wife she could not help but encourage my work, but as an historian she did not fail to criticize it.

THE IMMIGRANT CHURCH

Introduction

AFTER THE WAR OF 1812 the United States stood on the threshold of a new age. A new spirit of democracy emerged, and the people elected as president their new folk hero, Andrew Jackson. Unbridled enthusiasm pushed forward numerous programs of reform, and utopia seemed just around the corner. People crossed the Appalachian Mountains by the wagonload as the frontier moved westward toward the Mississippi and beyond. A revolution in transportation was underway, and a national economy was beginning to emerge. Imports were increasing tenfold, while exports rose at the same accelerated rate. People were moving from the country to the city in unprecedented numbers: by 1860 close to twenty percent of the nation were city dwellers, an increase of almost eight hundred percent in forty years.[1] The social, economic, and political landscape of America was changing, and a new chapter was being written in the history of the young nation.

During this age of newness religion was also in the process of relocation. With a new "social contract," wrote Martin E. Marty, "religion acquiesced in the assignment to address itself to the personal, familial and leisured sectors of life while the public dimension —political, social, economic, cultural—were to become autonomous or pass under the control of other hands of tutelage."[2] No denomination was immune to this change, least of all the Roman Catholic church.

In 1815 the Catholic church was chiefly an Anglo-American community, and Baltimore was the Rome of the United States. The Maryland Catholic resembled his old English counterpart: both wanted "no fuss and no extremes in anything especially in religion."[3] One young contemporary admiringly described the archbishop of Baltimore, John Carroll, as "a polished gentleman" who delighted everyone with his conversation.[4] John Cheverus, the French-born bishop of Boston, mingled so gracefully with Yankee Protestants that many of Boston's prominent citizens judged him "to be a blessing and a treasure in our social community."[5] Catholics generally enjoyed polite relationships with their neighbors, and for the moment the church did not pose any serious threat to American institutions or values. Less visible than the polite gentleman were the poor immigrant Catholics who were beginning to crowd into cities along the Atlantic coast. Their presence had swelled the population of the church in the United States: in 1815 Catholics numbered somewhere in the vicinity of one hundred thousand; no one knew for sure how many there were or might have been.[6] Comparatively speaking, the Catholic church was a small and insignificant denomination scattered across the religious landscape of the country. But the United States was about to undergo a transformation; fifty years later, when the sounds of Civil War had died out, Americans could take time out to look around and assess the changes that had taken place in the last half-century. There were more railroads, more factories, more cities, and yes, even more Catholics. In fact, the Catholic church was the single largest denomination in the country, numbering more than three and one-half million members.[7]

During this half-century of transformation the church had undergone important changes. The Anglo-American predominance had faded into the background, and the church became a decidedly immigrant community with a heavy Irish flavor. Militancy had replaced the polite gentility of earlier years, and Catholics did not hesitate to challenge American customs and institutions. As large numbers of newcomers settled in the cities the church became increasingly more concentrated along the urban frontier. Large gothic cathedrals symbolized its presence in the city, while wooden chapels recalled nostalgic memories of an agrarian past. The city is the most visible arena from which to view this change and the most representative as well, since Catholics throughout the nineteenth century were predominantly an urban people. Indeed, Catholics lived in the heartland of Indiana or Minnesota along with many other Americans, but for the large majority the city was their homestead.

One major chapter in this period of transformation was the administrative expansion of the church. The number of Catholic dioceses increased, and there was a corresponding rise in the number of bishops and priests. John Gilmary Shea, a pioneer Catholic historian, focused on this expansion in his work, *The History of the Catholic Church in the United States*.[8] But the story of Catholicism in this period was more than just a record of administrative expansion and a multiplication of clergy. Catholicism drew its strength from the people, and this concern for the man in the pew was absent from Shea's work. This study seeks to correct the imbalance by focusing on the people and not the prelates.

Another theme of this period was the bitter anti-Catholic prejudice that erupted in town and city. Ray Allen Billington wrote of this in *The Protestant Crusade, 1800–1860*.[9] Anti-Catholicism was unquestionably a major factor in the nativist crusade, and according to Billington, "the advent of foreign immigration on a large scale was probably the most important causal force leading to this revival [of nativism]."[10] American historians cannot ignore the Protestant crusade, but large-scale immigration posed problems for the church, as well as for the rest of American society, and Billington's study does not enter into this realm. American Protestants were worried about foreign-born immigrants, but so were American Catholics. How they resolved this problem comprises a large part of this book.

Oscar Handlin in his acclaimed work, *Boston's Immigrants, 1790–1865*, focused on the group-consciousness of Irish immigrants and the subsequent conflict that emerged when the newcomers challenged the old social order and values of Yankee Boston.[11] Handlin's use of the concepts of group-consciousness and acculturation have provided the historian with a useful framework to study the history of immigrant communities in the New World. But strange as it may seem, Boston's Catholics were not all Irish, and the sons of Erin were almost as much of a problem to Boston's Yankee Catholics as they were to their Protestant neighbors. Handlin found a militant Irish community, but in setting up the lines of cultural conflict, he skimmed over the conflict and diversity present within the Catholic community. This study will focus on the diversity present in an urban Catholic community and the allied problem of conflict and consensus in the church.

Anti-Catholicism and group-consciousness were both operative in American Catholicism during the ante-bellum period. One does not exclude the other; in fact, anti-Catholic prejudice sharpened the lines of group-consciousness as far as Catholics were concerned. But with or without this discrimination group-consciousness would have certainly emerged both in the church and in the nation. The reason for this seems clear: large-scale immigration brought people of varying cultures and backgrounds to the United States, and they began to live as they best knew how—as Irishmen or as Germans. For many of the newcomers the church was the one institution they recognized in the New World, and they wanted it to be a replica of what they had known in the old country.

Historians generally recognize the importance of the church in the immigrant community, but the church the immigrant knew was not an abstract entity; it was localized and represented in the neighborhood parish church. Built of wood or stone, it occupied space in the neighborhood; people could see it, touch it, and enter inside it to pray or simply to get out of the cold. The church building was the religious center of the neighborhood: it is here that one can discover the piety, or the expression of religious beliefs, of Catholic immigrants.

In the nineteenth century the parish was the focal point of Catholic life in Western Europe, and the church transplanted this parochial structure to the United States. Ideally, geographical boundaries defined the size of the parish, but in American cities it was not that simple. Germans could not understand English preachers any more than the Irish could fathom the subtleties of French sermons. Because of this ethnic diversity, intensified with each successive wave of immigrants, the concept of a national parish emerged, based more on language than on geography. Later, as parishes of one national group multiplied, fixed boundaries were established, but only in terms of the particular language group. Thus, a German parish could have Irish parishes within its territory and vice versa, but church law said that Germans could only attend their national parish, and the Irish were to avoid the German church. It seemed simple enough in theory, but in reality the urban neighborhood did not lend itself to such neat delineation. Neighborhoods were not homogeneous; over the years they changed their ethnic configuration, and parish communities reflected this. The national parish served as a buffer zone between different ethnic groups, but as the numerical balance of power in the neighborhood shifted from one group to the other, conflict became more real. If the priests chose to cater to the parish newcomers by preaching in English, as was the case with the Irish, then the Germans for whom the church was originally designated expressed their ire. Even within the same community conflict over parish loyalties was evident, frequently resulting in parish schisms. The aftermath was often a new parish established a few blocks from the old one, and the people made the decision as to where they would worship and what church they would support. In other words, the Catholic parish in the city ideally served the needs of a community located in a particular neighborhood, but in fact language as well as geography defined the parish boundaries.

Occasionally economic class best described the neighborhood parish for the simple reason that some neighborhoods were socially more homogeneous than others. But in ante-bellum cities few neighborhoods enjoyed such distinction; if they did, it was a safe bet that Catholic immigrants did not live there. Upper-class Catholics might have had a residence in the area, and if they were numerous enough, they had their own parish church. Otherwise, and this was generally the case, they had to worship alongside their greenhorn coreligionists.

In this study the parish is the point of departure, and New York

City is the environment that I have chosen to study. By focusing on the parish I was able to follow the development of the church in the city and to show the interrelationship of urban and church growth. In this way the diversity of the city and the church becomes apparent. In ante-bellum New York the most significant groups of Catholic immigrants were the Irish and German. They furnish the mainstream of the story, and the relatively smaller groups at the time, the French, Italian, and Negro, are treated only in a peripheral manner to illustrate the ethnic diversity of urban Catholicism.

To study the people who were known as Catholics I have centered on three parish communities, one Irish, one German, and the third a mixed group of Irish and Germans. The two ethnic groups shared a common environment, the urban neighborhood, and the similarities between Little Ireland and Little Germany were striking. In shifting from the neighborhood to the church I was able to study the religious life of the immigrants. It is in this area that one discovers the differences as well as the similarities between the Irish and the Germans.

The Germans in New York City were not only outsiders in a strange new world, they were also foreigners in an Irish-dominated church. For every German parish in New York there were three Irish parishes; for every German Catholic there were as many as six to seven Irishmen, and equally significant, the principal authority figure in the city, the bishop, was an Irishman. To preserve their religious heritage in a Protestant country and an Irish church the Germans placed great emphasis on language and the religious customs they had known in the old country. In things religious they exhibited an intense degree of ethnic consciousness, or nationalism, as one observer described it.[12] As the majority group of Catholics, the Irish were not hard-pressed to preserve their religious traditions. It was only when the host Protestant society challenged them that they got their Irish up. They could certainly argue with the Germans and often did, but as the larger and more powerful of the two communities in New York, they had less reason to do so.

German Catholics transplanted their church and their religion to the United States, and the Irish did the same. Each church was a replica of the church in the old country. They honored their favorite religious heroes and fostered their particular devotions. This link with the old country was very evident in the life of the parish, and

6

yet this point led to another conclusion that was too convincing to ignore: though the communities were different in language and customs, the piety they developed was strikingly similar.

This piety can be described as Tridentine Catholicism. More precisely, it was the type of religion fostered in Europe during the Catholic reform period of the sixteenth and seventeenth centuries. It was centered in the parish and emphasized the sacraments of baptism and confirmation, attending Sunday Mass, receiving communion at least once a year, and annual confession of one's sins. Numerous devotional practices were encouraged, religious confraternities were multiplied, and the catechism became the handbook of faith. Periodic parish revivals or missions attempted to reinforce these patterns with the emphasis always on the salvation of one's soul. The Catholic reform period had ushered in a new type of spiritual rhythm with the result that a more active spiritual life replaced the contemplative, more tranquil style of religion characteristic of medieval monasticism.[13]

This active type of piety was revived in Europe during the nineteenth century as Catholicism underwent a religious renewal after the onslaught of the Enlightenment and the political revolutions of the eighteenth and early nineteenth centuries.[14] It was also the type of piety that became normative in nineteenth-century America and was visibly present in both Irish and German communities. This fact is manifest in catechisms, school books, novels, newspapers, and sermons. The numerous religious societies and institutions that Catholics founded also reflected the spiritual activism associated with Tridentine Catholicism. Through all of these agencies the Church sought not only to preserve the faith of the immigrants but also to bind them together in a united Catholic community.

The expression "to preserve the faith of the immigrants" is frequently found in Catholic historical writing, and with good reason. It was the principal task confronting the church in the United States, and every means was employed to achieve this end. But this raises a question which historians have not adequately treated. What type of faith was the church trying to preserve? Were Catholic immigrants fervent, lukewarm, or indifferent in their religious practice? The question is easily asked, but less readily answered. One fact is certain, however: Catholics in the ante-bellum period were not extraordinarily fervent in their religious practice; in fact, many were ignorant of basic Christian beliefs. This study of parish communities, as well as that of the history of parish missions, confirms this, and a reading of Irish and German religious history reinforces it. When these immigrants were arriving in the United States in the 1830s and 1840s, they were coming from cultures where Catholics were less than fervent in their religious practice. This meant that the task of the church in the United States was not merely to preserve the faith of the newcomers, but in many cases to change nominal Catholics into practicing believers.

The study concludes with an analysis of the change that took place in New York Catholicism over a period of fifty years. Though diversity was present in the urban church, the common bond of religion, coupled with increasing centralization of authority, bound the Catholic community together. Catholics built a citadel in the city and walled themselves off from a hostile Protestant environment. The quest was for unity among Catholics despite their various backgrounds, and the church in its legislation and institutions worked toward this goal.

The period under study, 1815–65, was chosen for several reasons. It marked the first large-scale immigration of Catholics to the United States. As a result the church increased in size and importance. But the change in Catholicism was more than just one of numbers: it was a critical juncture for the church in America, and during this period it developed a style of operation that became normative for its later history. Large-scale immigration pushed the church in this direction; at the same time the diverse backgrounds of the newcomers and their concentration in the city emphasized the need for systematic organization, a need which was not so pronounced in 1815 but which would increase with each new decade. National meetings of the hierarchy multiplied considerably during this period, and through legislation the bishops sought to achieve complete uniformity of church life in the United States.[15] The church also sought to define its relationship with mainline Protestant America, and the position it adopted persisted long after the Civil War. The church was experiencing both internal and external conflicts, and the resolution of these problems set the pattern for the future of American Catholicism.

New York City was chosen as the setting for this study not only because it represented in microcosm what was happening in American Catholicism but also because it was the most important center of the church in the United States. At mid-century New York was the leading metropolis in the nation, and such prominence invested the church with a measure of prestige not found in other locales. The size of the Catholic population reinforced this prominence; and one Catholic booster did not hesitate to rank New York among the great Catholic cities of the world.[16] The importance of New York as the capital of American Catholicism became most evident during the episcopacy of John Hughes, 1838–64. Hughes arrived in New York in 1838 to assist the aging Frenchman John Dubois, who had been bishop since 1826. The young Hughes exercised his leadership from the very beginning, and when Dubois died in 1842, Hughes officially became bishop of New York. His reign in New York spanned the most important years of this period, and he was the acknowledged leader of a new, emerging Catholicism. As one contemporary historian observed, "no prelate of the Catholic Church has ever attained in the United States a position such as his."[17] The gothic magnificence of the Cathedral of St. Patrick on Fifth Avenue still stands as a monument to his bold imagination and the vigor of his day.

An American-born priest, Isaac Hecker, perhaps best described the special importance that the New York church enjoyed during the middle of the nineteenth century. Shortly after the death of Hughes in January 1864, Hecker wrote to an influential friend at the Vatican to impress upon him the importance of choosing the right man to succeed Hughes. In his letter Hecker stated that "the Archdiocese of New York is the largest and in every respect the most influential in this country." As for New York City, he believed that it was "the heart of this country, the Rome of our modern Republic," and if the right person were chosen as archbishop, "the most important act will have been done for the advancement of the interests of our Holy religion in this country."[18]

New York was indeed the Rome of the United States, but it was still a single city, and New York Catholicism was not American Catholicism writ small. Yet, a microcosmic study of one city has its definite advantages. By concentrating on a limited area I was able to know the city and the church more thoroughly than if I had chosen a wider expanse. In this manner I was most able to work toward my principal goal: to write a reliable history of an urban Catholic community looking at it from the level of the street and not just from the level of the bishop's desk. At the same time I believe that this local study can be broadly meaningful. It is a new portrait of urban Catholicism, reflecting in miniature the history of the church in the nineteenth-century city. Catholicism in New York shared common problems with the church in other cities and resorted to similar solutions. What happened in New York was not unique but the most conspicuous example of what was taking place in many cities across the nation.

ONE

The City and the Church

I<small>N</small> M<small>AY</small> 1815 New Yorkers witnessed the dedication of the Catholic Cathedral of St. Patrick. It was located on Mott Street, just south of Houston Street, "at the farther end of the city towards the country," as one observer put it.[1] This was an especially important occasion for the Catholic community, since St. Patrick's was the first visible expansion of the church in New York in thirty years. The first Catholic parish had been organized in 1785, and over the years it served the needs of an increasing population. At the turn of the century Catholics had already recognized the need for another church, but financial difficulties and the War of 1812 delayed the necessary expansion. By 1815 New York Catholics numbered fifteen thousand, and two parishes appeared sufficient for their needs. In the next fifty years, however, the church underwent phenomenal growth as people and parishes multiplied.

The year 1815 also ushered in a period of rapid growth for the city. Once the war with Great Britain was over the city awoke to new life. Within ten years New York had inaugurated a regular transatlantic service to Liverpool, developed a prosperous coastal trade, and celebrated the opening of the Erie Canal. The city had become the gateway to Europe, and by 1860 two thirds of all the nation's imports and one third of its exports passed through the port of New York.[2] Merchants measured their success by the number of ships that passed through the harbor, and Catholics judged their progress by the number of churches that served the city. By 1865 both groups were able to point to impressive achievements.

In 1815 New York was the most populous city in the nation, outdistancing its rival, Philadelphia, for the first time. The built-up area of the city extended north about two miles from the lower end of the island. Since the only city transportation at that time was by private carriage, most New Yorkers lived close to their places of work. Twenty-five years later the population of New York was 312,710, and the city limits extended about one mile beyond the 1815 line of settlement.[3] The great fire of 1835 had caused a movement of business uptown, and the development of regular city transportation in the 1830s aided this expansion. During this period, 1815–40, eight new Catholic parishes were organized in the city, with the result that ten churches served the needs of an estimated eighty to ninety thousand Catholics in 1840.[4] Seven of these parishes were located below Fourteenth Street, the line of settlement in 1840. Catholics living south of this boundary were concentrated on the East Side near the East River shipyards, where many immigrants found employment.

Located beyond Fourteenth Street were the small suburban villages of Harlem, Bloomingdale, and Yorkville. Harlem was located about eight miles from City Hall, and by 1834 it had a sufficient number of Catholics to warrant the organization of a parish. St. Paul's Church in Harlem soon became the center of a missionary apostolate that extended north into Westchester and Long Island.[5] On the West Side was the small settlement of Bloomingdale. The

Church of St. John the Baptist was organized there in 1840 to accommodate the needs of an increasing number of German Catholics.[6] The third parish in the suburbs was St. John the Evangelist, located on Fiftieth Street near Fifth Avenue "for the acommodation of the numerous Catholic families in the neighborhood."[7] Thus, by 1840 the church was visibly present in the many diverse neighborhoods of New York.

TABLE 1. ROMAN CATHOLIC CHURCHES IN NEW YORK CITY, 1865

Church	Date of Foundation	Location
1. St. Peter	1785	Barclay St.
2. St. Patrick	1809[a]	Mott St.
3. St. Mary	1826	Grand St.
4. St. Joseph	1829	6th Ave.
5. St. Nicholas (German)	1833	E. 2d St.
6. St. Paul	1834	E. 117th St.
7. St. James	1836	James St.
8. Transfiguration	1836	Mott St.
9. St. John the Baptist (German)	1840	W. 30th St.
10. St. John the Evangelist	1840	E. 50th St.
11. St. Vincent de Paul (French)	1841	W. 23d St.
12. Nativity	1842	2d Ave. n. 2d St.
13. St. Andrew	1842	Duane St.
14. Most Holy Redeemer (German)	1844	E. 3d St.
15. St. Francis (German)	1844	W. 31st St.
16. St. Columba	1845	W. 25th St.
17. St. Alphonsus (German)	1847	Thompson St.
18. St. Francis Xavier	1847	W. 16th St.
19. St. Stephen	1848	E. 28th St.
20. St. Brigid	1848	Ave. B. n. 8th St.
21. St. Lawrence	1851	4th Ave. at 84th St.
22. Holy Cross	1852	W. 42d St.
23. St. Ann	1852	E. 8th St.
24. Annunciation	1853	W. 131st St.
25. Immaculate Conception	1855	E. 14th St.
26. St. Michael	1857	W. 32d St.
27. Assumption (German)	1858	W. 50th St.
28. St. Boniface (German)	1858	2d Ave. at 47th St.
29. St. Paul	1858	W. 60th St.
30. St. Gabriel	1859	E. 37th St.
31. St. Joseph (German)	1860	W. 125th St.
32. St. Teresa	1863	Rutgers St.

[a] St. Patrick's did not open until 1815.

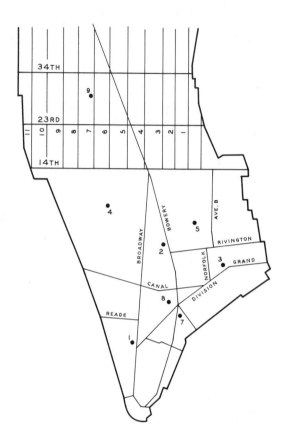

MAP 1

Location of Catholic Churches in New York, 1840. The numbers correspond to those given to churches in table 1.

During the next twenty-five years both the church and the city grew at an unusually rapid rate. The increasing volume of foreign immigration brought many new people to New York, the movement of population from the country to the city added to this number, and the development of more rapid and widespread transportation expanded the city limits. From a population of 312,710 in 1840 New York mushroomed to a population of 726,386 in 1865. Between Fourteenth Street and Forty-second Street, the line of settlement in

14

1865, a new city was built which housed over 190,138 people.[8] Above Forty-second Street streets remained ungraded and unpaved, and between Fifty-ninth Street and 110th Street stretched the hilly terrain of Central Park.[9] As the city expanded so did the church. In 1840 there was only one parish between Fourteenth Street and Forty-second Street. By 1865 nine more were in operation in the new city, and the spires of thirty-two Catholic churches decorated the city's skyline—an increase of twenty-two parishes in twenty-five years. The number of Catholics in New York at that time was estimated to be somewhere between three hundred thousand and four hundred thousand, almost one-half of the city's population. The mission parish of 1785 had become the symbol of another era, and Roman Catholicism was no longer a minority religion in New York City.[10]

An essential factor enabling the city to spread out and accommodate the residents of the new city was the development of mass transportation. The brightly-colored omnibus with seats for twelve passengers was the first step in this transit revolution; shortly after came the street railway, which doubled the seating capacity of the omnibus and provided almost unlimited standing and hanging-on room. With these new modes of travel the city was able to break the old boundaries of the walking city. People could live quite removed from downtown and still work there. New neighborhoods developed along the routes of transportation, and as the city spread out the church was forced to extend its reach. The development of the New York and Harlem Railroad is an example of the relationship between the church and mass transit.

On 14 November 1832 the city's first railroad, the New York and Harlem, made its first trip downtown from Fourteenth Street along the Bowery Road to Prince Street, not far from the Cathedral of St. Patrick. After the inaugural ceremony, construction continued along Fourth Avenue on the East Side of the city. In 1833 the tracks reached the neighborhood of Murray Hill in the vicinity of Thirtieth Street. By 1834 the railroad passed through the village of Yorkville (near Eighty-sixth Street), and four years later the line was fully completed to Harlem. The building of the railroad was an engineering phenomenon in its day. Tunnels had to be cut through solid rock in Murray Hill and Harlem Heights (near Ninetieth Street), while

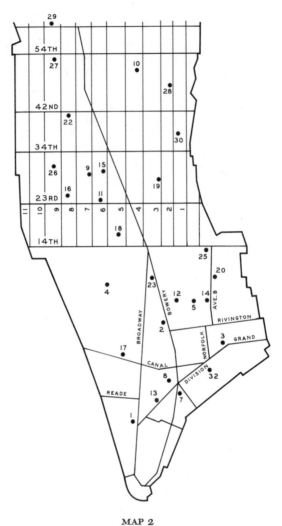

MAP 2

Location of Catholic Churches in New York,
1865. The numbers correspond to those given
to churches in table 1.

16

wooden bridges scaled rivers and ravines. Laborers were in demand, and Harlem and Yorkville began to attract as new residents those who worked on the railroad. The construction of a depot and hotels provided additional employment in both villages.[11]

As Harlem and Yorkville developed, the needs of the church in these areas became more pressing. It is true that with the coming of the railroad neither village experienced a population explosion. In 1846 only 1,500 people lived in Harlem, and Yorkville was still a small hamlet in a sparsely settled region of the city.[12] But because of their strategic positions along the route of transportation they attracted enough new settlers and a sufficient number of Catholics to create the need for a church in each village. St. Paul's, in Harlem, was organized in 1834, two years after construction of the railroad began. St. Lawrence's, in Yorkville, was established in 1851, when the village, situated about two miles beyond the city limits, was still a depot stop for the Harlem Railroad.[13]

While the New York and Harlem Railroad aided the development of suburbs on the East Side of the island, the construction of the Hudson River Railroad had a similar effect on the West Side. About seven miles from City Hall, on the banks of the Hudson, was the village of Manhattanville. In 1846 only five hundred people lived there.[14] By 1851 the Hudson River Railroad reached Manhattanville, and the coming of the railroad encouraged the growth of the area. Midtown Manhattan was no longer a remote destination, and some people could afford the luxury of working in the city while living in Manhattanville. Numbered among the small property holders of the village were many Irish and German Catholics. In 1853, two years after the railroad arrived, the Church of the Annunciation was founded. In 1860 St. Joseph's Parish was organized to accommodate the needs of an increasing number of German Catholics.[15] Before the railroad the population of the village was about five hundred. In 1865, after the arrival of the railroad and additional street railway transportation to the lower city, the population of Manhattanville numbered 2,189.[16]

In later years more rapid transportation and the expansion of the city absorbed the suburban communities of ante-bellum New York. New suburbs were created, and the demand arose once again for more "suburban churches."[17] Yet the pattern of the church in the suburb was established in New York by the mid-nineteenth century.

In addition to the development of suburbs, mass transportation also increased the area of the densely populated city by spreading out the concentration of people. In doing so it inevitably created the need for additional parishes. But in this case the connection between transportation, neighborhood growth, and the organization of new parishes was not as evident, though it was no less real. For the new mode of transportation to succeed, it had to provide regular and frequent service along a fixed and long route for a reasonable fare— the cheaper the better. The twelve-passenger omnibus was able to meet these demands. When this strange looking horse-drawn carriage first appeared on Broadway in 1827, it was one of a kind operating along a single avenue for a costly fare.[18] During the 1830s and 1840s the number of vehicles increased, routes multiplied, and rates became cheaper. By 1855 over one thousand horse-drawn stages rumbled about the city along fixed routes at a single fare of six and a half cents—half the price of 1830.[19]

As the line of settlement stretched uptown the omnibus trailed along providing the necessary transportation for the people living in the new city. Beyond the city limits the omnibus also made connections with suburban communities. In the 1850s, however, the horse-drawn street railway competed for the omnibus trade in New York. In 1855 the street railway was in operation along six avenues above Fourteenth Street, and it soon supplanted the omnibus as the principal means of transit in the upper city. The street railway was faster and more convenient, carried more people, and cost less—five cents rather than six.[20] The street railway enjoyed instant success, and in one year, 1866, the Third Avenue Railroad alone carried twenty million passengers.[21]

The new transit lines encouraged the development of uptown neighborhoods. By 1850 the line of settlement reached Thirty-fourth Street, and in the next ten years the street railway stretched it further north to Forty-second Street and beyond.[22] As new neighborhoods developed, the need for additional parishes increased. Between 1840 and 1865 nine Catholic churches were organized between Fourteenth Street and Forty-second Street, five of them on the West Side, the more densely populated section of the new city. During the same period only three parishes were organized between

Forty-second and Fifty-ninth Streets, a sparsely settled section of the city.[23]

Despite the growth of the city north of Fourteenth Street the bulk of the population still lived downtown, that is, south of Fourteenth Street. In 1840, 278,786 people lived in this area. Twenty-five years later it numbered 420,683 people, and the largest population increase had taken place on the East Side.[24] In 1840 there were seven churches located downtown; by 1865 the number had doubled. The largest parishes in the city were located in this area, especially on the densely populated Lower East Side. St. Peter's, located at the lower end of Manhattan, had "a large Catholic population."[25] Father Gabriel Healy was anxious to establish a second parish in the area because he was convinced that he could gather together a "plentiful congregation."[26] On the Lower East Side St. Mary's attempted to provide for the religious needs of some twenty thousand people. St. James's, situated in the densely populated area near the Catherine Street Ferry, numbered twenty-five thousand Catholics within its boundaries.[27] On Fourteenth Street, the fringe of the Lower East Side, the Church of the Immaculate Conception had a congregation of at least twenty thousand people.[28]

Thus, by 1865 the Catholic church was present in the different areas in the city. Downtown, below Fourteenth Street, there were fourteen churches; the new city, below Fifty-ninth Street, had another fourteen; the suburban communities could claim only four. Each of these parishes was a distinct center of religious life serving its own neighborhood of the city. Within a fifty-year period the church in New York had not only undergone a rapid growth but had acquired a degree of diversity unmatched in the small towns and villages of the United States.

The diversity of New York was visible to all who visited the city. Walt Whitman described the New York of his day as a "city of the world! For all races are here; all the lands of the earth make contributions here."[29] Fundamental to the cosmopolitan quality of the city were its neighborhoods. People did not live in the city, but on a specific block in a given neighborhood. Each neighborhood might exhibit a high degree of homogeneity, but among the neighborhoods there were varying degrees of difference. A characteristic that distinguished one neighborhood from another, and thus one parish from another, was social class. St. Paul's Church was founded in 1858 on West Fifty-ninth Street on the edge of the city in an area noted for its squatter population and their makeshift shanties. The people of the parish were poor, and almost all of them belonged to the class of manual laborers.[30] In the village of Manhattanville lived a large number of small property owners, many of whom belonged to Annunciation Church.[31] Yet, one of the most evident examples of a "class" parish in Catholic New York was St. Ann's, located on Eighth Street near Astor Place, in the fashionable section of Greenwich Village.[32]

St. Ann's was organized in 1852, and the first two pastors were former priests of the fashionable Episcopal Church. The parish was described as "relatively small," and it preserved this elitist size despite the large number of Irish living in the area.[33] In 1869 the parish had only four thousand members, and priests still considered it a "good parish."[34] The parishioners belonged to the upper strata of society that lived in the fine homes of the Washington Square district. Those who attended Solemn Sunday Mass were the class of Catholics who could afford to live in the country in the summer months and have servants to care for them in both their town and country homes.[35]

A more distinctive mark of the neighborhood than social class was the ethnic heritage of the people. New immigrants to the city tended to gather together in separate neighborhoods, and as one New Yorker put it, they "create for themselves distinct communities almost as impervious to American sentiments and influences as [were] the inhabitants of Dublin or Hamburg."[36] Little Germany, Little Ireland, and Little Italy acquired their names and characters as German, Irish, and Italian immigrants began to group together in new urban villages. Each village was set apart by the ethnicity of the residents, and for Catholics an important institution was the local parish. Like the neighborhood itself, the church reflected the nationality of the people. Little Ireland was unlike Little Italy, and to a similar degree St. Patrick's was different from the Church of St. Anthony of Padua. Such variety was characteristic of nineteenth-century urban Catholicism and continues today as new immigrants settle in the city.

The church in the ethnic village has been described as a "trans-

planted church" and as a "national parish." Both descriptions identify the same phenomenon: the institutionalized attempt of an
immigrant group to preserve the religious life of the old country.[37]
Traditionally the American Catholic parish was organized on a territorial basis, with the pastor having jurisdiction and responsibility
for a particular area.[38] But the large influx of immigrants from
various nations, speaking different languages, necessitated the adop-
tion of the national parish to satisfy the religious needs of each
group.[39]

The distinguishing element in the national parish was language
rather than nationality, even though the two are often thought to be
identical. This was especially true in the middle of the nineteenth
century, when the sense of nationality was not very well developed
among European immigrants. A German-speaking church might
have included natives of Austria, Prussia, and Bavaria; French-
speaking parishes had members from Haiti as well as from France;
and an Italian congregation included immigrants from both the
Papal States and northern Italy.

In addition, a national parish was in fact organized territorially,
since the group it served had generally settled in a distinct neighborhood. Thus, in New York City at mid-century English-language
parishes were generally Irish, established on the basis of territory
but serving a distinct ethnic group. They fulfilled the same function
as other "transplanted churches." German, French, and Italian parishes, established on the basis of language, were also territorially
defined by the patterns of settlement of each language group. Since
foreign language was closely identified with a particular neighborhood, the distinction between national and territorial parishes was
more fiction than fact. Almost all the churches in the city were
national parishes, and geographical boundaries were applicable only
within the same language group.

The largest immigrant group among New York Catholics was the
Irish. From the formal beginning of Catholic New York in 1785
down to the Civil War and beyond, Irish-born laity and priests
occupied a dominant position in the Catholic community.[40] In 1830
the Irish community in New York was self-sufficient, with its own
papers, fraternal societies, lawyers, priests, physicians, teachers,
academies, booksellers, and political leaders.[41] The Great Famine

migration increased their numbers, and by 1860, 203,740 foreign-born Irish lived in New York.[42] In 1865 twenty-three of the thirty-two parishes (72 percent) in the city were English-speaking, and most of these were described as "Irish churches."[43] At mid-century the New York clergy were said to be "almost entirely Irish"[44]—of the 107 priests working in the Diocese of New York in 1845, 59 (55 percent) had been born in Ireland.[45] This predominance of Irish in city and church was rivaled by the Germans.

Like the Irish, German Catholics were early settlers in New York, and immigration increased their numbers during the first half of the century.[46] In 1860, 119,984 foreign-born Germans lived in New York, and in 1865 German was the language spoken in eight of the thirty-two parishes.[47] Between forty and fifty thousand Germans belonged to these national parishes.[48]

French Catholics were another immigrant group that had been present in the city since the early days of the church. Yet, unlike the Irish and the Germans, they were never very numerous, and in 1860 New York had only 8,074 French-born residents.[49] In the first decades of the century the French worshipped at St. Peter's Church, but in 1841 they organized their own parish, St. Vincent de Paul, on Canal Street in the lower city. Later, as the French Quarter moved uptown, the church moved to West Twenty-third Street, where services in French have continued to the present day.[50]

The Irish and Germans, and to a lesser degree the French, provided the variety of ethnic differences in New York Catholicism. Two other groups were also represented in the urban church: the Italians and the Negroes. Yet, they lived on the fringe of the Catholic community, and only in later years would their presence in the city substantially alter the ethnic profile of the church. The problems they encountered at mid-century, however, clearly foreshadowed the difficulties that each group would face in the later decades.

By 1860 contemporaries estimated that as many as five thousand Italian-born immigrants lived in New York.[51] The boundaries of Little Italy were already taking shape, and an Italian newspaper and at least one mutual aid society served the needs of the small community.[52] The first Italian parish opened for services in 1857, but by 1860 it had ceased functioning. During its brief life the Church of St. Anthony of Padua exhibited a moderate degree of vitality. Parishioners gathered together and sponsored a benefit concert to help pay the rent of the building they used for worship. Catechism classes had as many as fifty children in attendance.[53] After the church closed and the building was demolished in favor of commercial expansion, no fewer than 380 Italian families petitioned Pope Pius IX to provide them with a place of worship.[54] Nor did they neglect to plead their cause with Archbishop Hughes. Shortly after their pastor, Italian-born Antonio Sanguinetti, left for Rome to seek papal approval of their petition, the Italian community addressed a similar petition to the archbishop. They asked for a church "where they might all unite to pray and worship the Lord, and preserve incontaminated and intact the rites as transmitted to us by our ancestors. . . ."[55] Neither the pope nor the archbishop granted their request, and the Italians were without their own parish until 1866, when St. Anthony of Padua reopened its doors at a new location in Little Italy.

At the root of the demise of the Italian parish was the conflict between the Irish archbishop and the Italian pastor. Father Sanguinetti had fallen into disfavor because he had sought financial support for his parish from New York's Irish Catholics, a tactic which John Hughes did not approve. Nor did Hughes react favorably to the news that Sanguinetti had tried to discredit him in Rome on account of his lack of concern for the Italian community. Sanguinetti's behavior led Hughes to refuse him permission to return to the diocese, and this forced exile left the Italians with no priest to minister to their needs.[56] Without an available priest there was little hope that the parish would be reorganized.

Another reason for the failure of the parish was the archbishop's lack of enthusiasm for the Italian cause. The Italians desired their own parish, where, as they put it, "they could preserve intact the rites as transmitted to us by our ancestors." A committee from the community met with Hughes, but he did not evidence any desire to grant their petition, and his lack of support surprised them. Thus, said one member of the committee, "we are without a church."[57] Hughes's unhappy experience with Sanguinetti, the absence of any other Italian priest, and the lack of an available church building contributed to the archbishop's indifference. The Italian problem was one that could be delayed for the moment, given the comparatively small size of the community; in later decades, however, the problem would become more serious as the number of immigrants increased.

Like the Italians, Negro Catholics were also spiritual orphans. In the ante-bellum period few Negroes lived in New York. The census of 1855 found only 11,840, and fewer than 2,000 belonged to a church; all but a small number of these were Protestant.[58] Twelve years later it was estimated that 1,500 Negro Catholics lived in New York, and "not one hundred attend Catholic worship."[59] Despite their small number the Negroes posed a problem for the white church. The crux of the problem was racial discrimination.

Discrimination was especially evident in Catholic schools. When a group of Negro Catholics protested this, the answer given to them was that "white children was not willing to have colored taught with them."[60] If Negro children wanted to attend a Catholic school, the only alternative was to enroll at a small pay school sponsored by St. Vincent de Paul Church for "young colored girls and boys."[61] This pattern of segregation in education was also true for the public school system in New York. Another area of discrimination was in the organization of ethnic parishes. If the Irish, Germans, French, and Italians could have their own parishes, why prevent the Negroes from enjoying the same privilege? It was certainly not because Catholics favored integration in parish services. In fact, the opposite was the pattern encouraged at this time. Negro Catholics did desire their own parish, but they were unsuccessful in achieving this goal until 1883, when the first Negro parish was organized in New York.[62] Until then they were spiritual orphans in the church, and very few were practicing Catholics.

The situation in New York was not unique. In large northern cities the church was not very successful in its apostolate to the Negro community. Catholics in general looked down on the Negroes and considered them an inferior race. The leading spokesmen for the church did not condemn slavery and shunned any connection with the abolition movement.[63] In New York Negroes believed that Archbishop Hughes "does not consider the Black race to be part of his flock." In fact, one Catholic Negro observed that it was "well known by both white and black that the Most Rev. Archbishop do hate the black race so much that he cannot bear them to come near him."[64] The Irish community also manifested an open dislike for the Negro; and one historian has observed that the "antagonism between these two peoples was undoubtedly one of the harshest inter-group hatreds in American history."[65] This antagonism visibly erupted during the New York Draft Riots of 1863, and the scars of hatred were slow to heal. A few years later a Catholic journalist publicly admitted that "we will want as little as ever to have negroes in our houses or near us."[66] One highly respected spokesman of the Germans stated that Negroes would not attend their parishes since "they do not understand the language," and if they did attend, they would not "meet with a kind reception."[67]

An unfavorable opinion of the Negro and lack of sympathy for the anti-slavery crusade favored a climate of prejudice among Catholics. Competition for jobs in the northern city reinforced this attitude, but in manifesting their prejudice Catholics were only following the example set by Americans in general. However one seeks to explain it, the fact still remains that Catholics manifested an anti-Negro attitude both before and after the Civil War, and what efforts were made to minister to their needs produced only sporadic success. It was such prejudice that caused one historian of Negro Catholicism to admit that many Negroes rejected the church in the closing decades of the century.[68] The roots of this prejudice in New York and elsewhere can be traced back to the era of John Hughes, when the patterns of discrimination first emerged with a vengeance.

Despite their small number and their marginal participation in church life, Italians and Negroes added to the ethnic mixture of urban Catholicism. The church's inability to deal successfully with these groups illustrates one of the more serious problems of the church in a rapidly growing city. Faced with increasing numbers of immigrants and the pressing need for more parishes, it was not able to meet the needs of all Catholics. As one priest remarked, "the number of priests, churches and schools [were] entirely inadequate to the wants of the Catholic population."[69] Given this inadequacy of resources, the expedient choice for the church was to focus its attention on the Irish and the Germans. Indifference toward the Italian and prejudice against the Negro facilitated the decision, but in focusing on the larger communities the church willy-nilly neglected these more marginal groups. Thus, the diversity of urban life, while it contributed to the variety of Catholicism in New York, became the Achilles heel of the church. As new immigrants moved to the city in later decades this weakness became more noticeable.

At mid-century, then, New York Catholicism was predominantly Irish and German. These two groups provided the major strains of ethnic diversity. Fundamental to this heterogeneity was the environment in which the people lived. Suburban communities attracted one type of family, while the old city neighborhoods attracted other types of people. Elite parishes existed where native Americans congregated, while other churches served the shanty Irish of the Famine migration. As the city expanded its limits each decade, new parishes emerged, and such growth generally added a new ingredient of difference to the church. To understand this variety one must study the environment in which the parish existed. Like the people it serves, the church does not exist in the city; it stands in a particular neighborhood and ministers to a specific group of people. One neighborhood that shaped the future of urban Catholicism was the ethnic village.

TWO

The Ethnic Village

O N A WARM DAY in August 1858 a
large crowd gathered on the outskirts of the city to take part in the
groundbreaking ceremony for the new Catholic cathedral on Fifth
Avenue. Decorating the vacant lots were the flags of many nations.
The banners of Ireland, France, Austria, and the Papal States were
proudly displayed alongside the colors of England and the United
States. They represented the homeland and loyalties of New York
Catholics. Such variety, common to the city, was especially visible
that day in August. The two largest groups in the crowd were the
Irish and Germans.[1]

One of every four New Yorkers in 1860 had been born in Ireland.
The Famine migration had brought many of them to the port city,

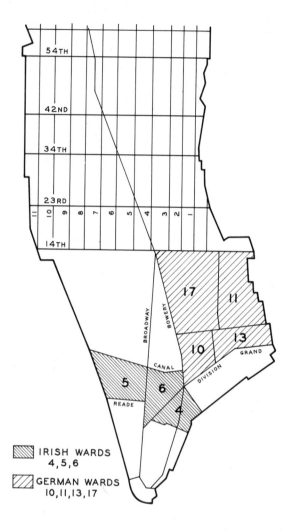

MAP 3
Irish and German Districts, 1865

and they scattered throughout the island. While every ward had its
Irish contingent, some neighborhoods were more Irish than others.[2]
One favorite section was located south of Canal Street in the
Fourth, Fifth, and Sixth Wards. In the 1830s the Sixth Ward was

reputed to be the largest Irish community in the nation. It was also the center of Tammany Hall and the Democratic party.[3] The two other wards were heavily Irish as well. In 1855 one of every three people in the area had been born in Ireland. Despite a decrease in population the same ratio prevailed in 1865. Add to this number the second-generation Irish, and their presence was even more pervasive.[4]

Like the Irish, the Germans were early settlers in New York, and after the War of 1812 immigration increased their numbers. German immigration peaked in the decade ending in 1855. During this period, 1846–55, more than one million Germans entered the United States; in one month alone, May 1854, 32,600 Germans arrived in New York. In 1860 at least one of every six New Yorkers was German.[5]

Even though every ward could claim some German residents, their concentration in certain neighborhoods was more pronounced than that of the Irish. The distinctively German district of the city was the Lower East Side; in 1865 more than half of the German-born New Yorkers lived in this area. Along the Bowery Road bakeries, grocery stores, and butcher shops displayed German signs. The area around the Tenth Ward was popularly known as Little Germany; it was so distinctive that one foreign visitor said that it had "very little in common with the other parts of New York."[6] Wards Eleven, Thirteen, and Seventeen were also heavily populated with German immigrants, and in 1865 the four wards of the Lower East Side had a total of 57,796 foreign-born Germans.[7]

The urban frontier was a common experience for both Irish and Germans. Whether they lived on the same street or in separate neighborhoods, they shared many features of city life. Despite its distinctive character Little Germany did not differ greatly from Little Ireland. Poverty and wealth were next-door neighbors in both communities. Broadway was the boundary line of the Irish Sixth Ward. It was the avenue of fashion and wealth. A few blocks away at the juncture of Worth, Baxter, and Park Streets was the notorious Five Points slum. Charles Dickens described it as the home of everything "loathesome, drooping and decayed."[8] Elegant trees and five homes marked the site of St. John's Park in the Fifth Ward. Hidden behind these first-class dwellings were factories and workshops.

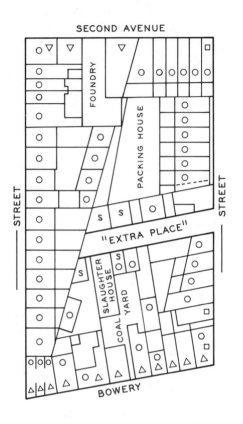

SECOND AVENUE

FOUNDRY

PACKING HOUSE

STREET

STREET

"EXTRA PLACE"

SLAUGHTER HOUSE

COAL YARD

BOWERY

O   TENEMENT HOUSE
△   RETAIL STORE
□   DRAM SHOP
S   STABLE

MAP 4
Tenement Block, Seventeenth Ward

West of the park coal and lumber yards dotted the streets, and people lived in wooden houses rather than stone mansions.[9] Such contrast was also visible in the German settlement. On the edge of the Seventeenth Ward stood Stuyvesant Square, the center of fine homes. Less than a block away were tenements infested with typhus. Second Avenue was described as "one of the choicest residence streets in town," while rows of tenements lined First Avenue, a street noted for decaying piles of garbage.[10]

Each neighborhood also exhibited the indiscriminate use of land common to the early-nineteenth-century city. Since strict zoning regulations were absent, tenements, factories, and slaughterhouses were promiscuously mingled together. One tenement block on the Seventeenth Ward illustrated this pattern.[11] Almost every available patch of land was occupied. Tenements leaned against one another for support; spread out behind them were small backyards that provided what little open space there was available on an otherwise crowded block. Behind these dwellings were a large packing house, a slaughterhouse, four horse stables, a coal yard, and a foundry. Extra Place was a dead-end alley lined with tenements and stables. The lane was well traveled by cattle and horses, and the odor of the stables and the slaughterhouses was nauseating. Samuel Gompers described what it was like to live next-door to an East Side slaughterhouse:

> Our house was just opposite a slaughter house. All day long we could see the animals being driven into the slaughter-pens and could hear the turmoil and the cries of the animals. The neighborhood was filled with the penetrating, sickening odor. The suffering of the animals and the nauseating odor made it physically impossible for me to eat meat for many months. . . .[12]

Along the Bowery Road and at each corner of the block were retail stores and shops; above the stores were apartments.

A trademark of the immigrant neighborhood was the grog shop. The grog shop, or saloon, was the poor man's club, and every block appeared to have one or more such establishments. There were only three in the Seventeenth Ward block; other blocks had many more. In the Tenth Ward 526 such establishments competed for the neighborhood trade—an average of more than ten shops on each block.[13] While the small grog shop attracted a daily clientele, the German spirit of *Gemütlichkeit* was especially noticeable in the large beer gardens. They recalled familiar scenes of the old country, and colored murals depicted landscapes of the Rhine or the Black Forest. German music filled the air, and thoughts drifted back to the fatherland; for a moment the streets of New York resembled village lanes along the Rhine. Such halls could accommodate two to three thousand people, and many stayed open "until a late hour at night."[14]

Although the Irish could not boast of any large beer halls, they supported numerous small establishments where beer and whiskey were readily available. The Sixth Ward had one grog shop for every six people in 1864.[15] In other districts they stood "on all corners, in the center of the squares, and frequently one after another in a row; they were all in a flourishing condition, and seemed to encourage each other."[16] The Irish saloon was a neighborhood club where people gathered to hear the latest news from abroad and to debate the issues of ward politics. The saloon keeper, who was often involved in local politics, performed many functions for his customers. Peter Barr Sweeney, for example, was a member of the Tweed Ring and ran a saloon in the Sixth Ward. The price of admission was ten cents, and whiskey sold for three cents a glass. "It was a place shunned by all decent citizens; but it was also a place to build a political following."[17]

Another common experience of the Irish and Germans was poverty. New York always had a contingent of deprived residents, and their numbers increased in the ante-bellum period. By the 1820s pauperism had increased to "an alarming extent," and the city fathers sought new approaches to combat the evils of poverty.[18] Depression struck in 1837, aggravating an already serious problem. Many businesses collapsed, and the numbers of poor increased.[19] In 1844 over fifty-three thousand people applied for public aid. Thirty to forty private societies also provided relief for the city's poor. Ten years later the number of people receiving public aid jumped to 121,217.[20] Close to three thousand people a year ended up in the poorhouse, while children roamed the streets "filthy and ragged, begging for morsels of bread."[21]

During the 1850s two more depressions gripped the city. The first hit hardest in the winter of 1855, at which time a city missionary remarked that "destitution had increased to an extent unknown in the city."[22] A second depression struck in 1857. One welfare organization reported that "multitudes of the laboring classes are cut off from the means of earning their daily bread";[23] and a New York patrician, George Templeton Strong, noted in his diary that "this is far the worst period of public calamity and distress that I've ever seen."[24]

Poverty did not discriminate between nationalities; all groups of people experienced its hardships. Yet, the Irish poor outnumbered all others. In 1852 the New York Association for Improving the Condition of the Poor stated that half of the people assisted that year were Irish; three out of every four aided were Catholic. In 1858 64 percent of the people admitted to the city's Alms House were Irish.[25] The prevalence of poverty among the Irish led Bishop Hughes to remark that they were "the poorest and most wretched population that can be found in the world—the scattered debris of the Irish nation." He believed that those who had the means and the desire passed through the city to the interior of the country, while "the destitute, the disabled, the broken-down, the very aged and the very young [remained] for want of means or through want of inclination to go further."[26]

Although the Irish have traditionally been portrayed as the chief victims of urban poverty, the Germans also experienced its hardships. German poor taxed the benevolence of New Yorkers in pre-revolutionary days, and the problem persisted in the early nineteenth century. In the 1840s and 1850s large numbers of poor left Germany, and many found homes in New York.[27] Journalists, priests, and ministers commented on the poverty of these newcomers. One visiting Catholic clergyman, Canon Josef Salzbacher of Vienna, particularly noticed the poverty of German Catholics and the difficulty they had in finding work.[28] The German Society of New York, founded in 1784 "to promote emigration from Germany and to assist immigrants in distress," operated two relief agencies on the Lower East Side. In 1858 more than twelve thousand Germans received aid from these two dispensaries.[29] The historian of the German parish of Most Holy Redeemer noted that some parishioners even returned to the old country rather than endure the hardships encountered on the urban frontier.[30]

One of the most visible indicators of poverty were the hovels the immigrants lived in. By the second decade of the nineteenth century major slums had developed in several sections of the city, and Irish and German squatters had already constructed "shanty towns" on the outskirts of the city.[31] As the city's population increased, housing

33

deteriorated further. A city inspector in 1834 described the housing situation of a large portion of New York's population as "crowded and filthy." In his report he said that "there are . . . so many mercenary landlords who only contrive in what manner they can stow the greatest number of human beings in the smallest place."[32] Concerned citizens urged reform, but it was not until 1853 that the first tenement-house report appeared. The committee concluded that "a decent and healthy home was an impossible luxury for multitudes."[33] As a result of this report the state legislature appointed a committee in 1856 to investigate living conditions in the city. What they found were tenements with "dim, undrained courts oozing with pollution, dark narrow stairways, decayed with age, reeking with filth, overrun with vermin, rotted floors, ceilings begrimmed . . . and windows stuffed with rags . . . [inhabited by] gaunt, shivering forms and wild ghastly faces."[34] These investigations did not bring about any substantial improvements; in 1863 the Association for Improving the Condition of the Poor reported that "it remains true as in years past that most of the dwellings of the poor were wretched hotbeds of disease, which are unfit for human habitation."[35] In 1864 a group of leading citizens formed the Citizens' Association of New York to investigate the city's housing. As a result of their work New York City passed its first tenement-house law in 1867.[36]

At mid-century a tenement was a house in which three or more families rented apartments for a month or less. Put more graphically, it was "a structure of rough brick, standing on a lot twenty-five by one hundred feet; it is from four to six stories high, and is so divided internally as to contain four families on each floor—each family eating, drinking, sleeping, cooking, washing and fighting in a room eight feet by ten, and a bedroom six feet by ten; unless, indeed—which very frequently happens—the family renting these two rooms takes in another family to board, or sublets one room to one or even two other families!"[37] People often christened the tenements with such names as "Sweeney's Shambles," "Folsom's Barracks," and the "Bagdad Hotel,"[38] epitaphs which left little to the imagination.

When an investigator wanted to visit the worst tenements in the city, he inevitably toured the Irish and German districts. Baxter, Park, and Mulberry Streets in the Sixth Ward were lined with such tenements. Father, mother, and children lived together with pigs in crowded quarters; one block housed 1,562 people in old, worn-out buildings. When cholera struck New York in 1849, it chose a Baxter Street tenement as its breeding ground and an Irish laborer as its first victim.[39]

On Park Street, near City Hall, fifty Irish families lived in a seven-story tenement. On the rear lot a smaller tenement housed seventeen Irish families.[40] There was space for 120 families in "Sweeney's Shambles," located in the Irish Fourth Ward, where living conditions were so bad that people rarely stayed beyond a period of two years. When a state committee visited the "Shambles" in 1857, they found four hundred Irish residents.[41]

Not far from the German Church of Most Holy Redeemer was "Folsom's Barracks." Cholera also claimed its victims here, and the corpses of a man and woman were found alongside a dead dog in the basement apartment. A housing committee said that it was "one of the worst places they had seen."[42] Many Germans worked as ragpickers and bone gatherers. Some lived in "Rag Pickers Paradise" in the Eleventh Ward, which in 1864 was a rambling row of tenements housing 120 people, fifty dogs, and thirty cats amidst piles of dirty rags and bones.[43] One Protestant missionary described the Germans in the Seventeenth Ward as "mostly of the shiftless, less desirable class [living in] wretched hovels that are unfit for human habitation . . . ill ventilated tenent houses, which are surrounded to excess by the reckless and uncleanly."[44]

Located on James Street in the Fourth Ward was a tenement described as "typical" of many in the city. A liquor store operated by the landlord occupied the first floor of the five-story building. Upon entering, one had to pass through a dark hallway; a staircase two and one-half feet wide led to the second floor. There were four two-room apartments on each floor. The front room measured fourteen by twelve with a ceiling eight feet high. Two windows in the room provided ventilation for the entire apartment. The front room served as kitchen, living room, and workshop; the back room, measuring nine by twelve, was the bedroom. It had space for two beds, and the floor provided room for four people. Six people lived in this two-room apartment, which, because of poor ventilation, gave off a "sickening and stifling odor."

On the back of the lot stood a smaller tenement, in worse condition than the front tenement; the rates were also cheaper. To get to the rear tenement one had to pass through a narrow alley that opened onto a small, shaded courtyard. The day's washing decorated the yard, and muddy turf provided poor footing. In the middle stood the common outhouses for residents of both front and rear tenements. One observer noted that the privies were "quite as perceptible to the smell as to the sight." The rear building had a basement apartment, in which a family of six lived in an area of eighteen square feet.[45]

The cost of rental of these homes varied. Some districts averaged four dollars a month for a two-room apartment. Other areas were more expensive, charging as much as nine dollars a month. Within a building the price fluctuated.[46] As a German rent collector put it, "I scharge in basement not so much as vay up high."[47] Rooms facing the street cost more than those overlooking the courtyard, and apartments in backyard tenements were cheaper than those on the street. Since tenements were a profit-making enterprise, high rents were not uncommon. The poor had to pay rent that was "much more, proportionately and in fact, than is paid by the rich who dwell sumptuously in their avenue palaces."[48]

Rents had to be paid in advance, by the month or sometimes by the week. If the tenants did not pay the rent, their next stop was the street. One witness testified before an investigating committee that "the poor must and do pay the rent. It is the first thing they think of, and many . . . deny themselves the necessaries of life . . . because they know they are liable, at any moment, to be turned into the street, perhaps with loss of their scanty effects. . . . The rent, sir, must be, and in nine cases out of ten, is met."[49]

In addition to paying high rents, tenants also had to pay high prices for poor food, prices that varied "from 20% to 60% higher than the rate charged at decent stores."[50] Generally the first floor of the tenement housed a grocery store and a liquor store owned by the landlord. Such an arrangement meant that the landlord not only collected the tenants' rent but provided them with food and drink. If they did not pay the rent, they went without food. If they could not pay for their food, they went out on the street. As a result the landlord or his agent held the tenants in a state of dependence that was described as "little short of absolute slavery."[51] Frequently, Irish or German immigrants who had advanced one rung up the ladder of success acted as agents of the landlord; they were described as "among the hardest and most unprincipled" of people in dealing with the tenants.[52]

The living conditions of immigrant city dwellers shocked native reformers. Yet, the newcomers did not have as high a level of expectation as their American neighbors. Life in New York did not differ greatly from life in the slums of Dublin or Cork; the peasant's lot in a famine-stricken countryside was not any better than life in the Sixth Ward. "It is but truth to say," John Hughes wrote, "that their abode in the cellars and garrets of New York is not more deplorable nor more squalid than the Irish hovels from which many of them had been 'exterminated.' "[53] Despite its blemishes the city attracted the immigrants; in the words of a Protestant missionary "[the Irish] cling to their own homes with a tenacity which is truly astonishing when we consider their wretchedness."[54]

A visitor to Little Germany noted that the Germans were "satisfied, happy and contented, and most significantly among their own people"; they enjoyed life in the city where they "could speak their own language and live according to their own customs." He added that "according to the standards of the German workingman one can live like a prince for ten to fourteen dollars a month." Despite their shabby apartments, he believed that "they would never willingly leave their beloved *Kleindeutschland*."[55]

There was a great degree of truth in what the German visitor said. The Germans, like the Irish, adapted themselves to the tenement-house culture. Poverty at home had prepared them for poverty in New York. Despite disappointments in the city, they were not quick to give up life in the New World for the sake of returning to the old.[56] Yet, he was wrong in assuming that the Germans never left "their beloved *Kleindeutschland*." They might not have booked passage back to Europe, but they did keep their bags packed, ready to move both within the city and beyond to other frontiers.

Recent studies have stressed the mobility of the urban population in the nineteenth century; such mobility was especially characteristic of the foreign-born.[57] Between 1830 and 1860 approximately 60 percent of the population of Boston left the city each decade. In

Philadelphia the rate of mobility out of the city was even higher, approaching 70 percent.[58] A study of the residential mobility of individual families confirms that New York was no exception to this pattern. To determine the degree of mobility among Irish and German families a random sample of the heads of families was selected from the 1850 baptismal registers of Transfiguration parish in the Sixth Ward and Most Holy Redeemer parish in the Seventeenth Ward. The two sample groups were traced through the city directories and parish registers for twenty years.[59] The results clearly indicated that Irish and Germans were on the move.

For many immigrants New York was not much more than a brief holding area before moving on to another destination. Among the Irish sample 19 percent lived in New York long enough to have their child baptized, but they left the city shortly afterwards. Samuel Young was typical. After arriving in New York, he settled on Water Street; a few months later he moved to upper New York State.[60] In addition, there was the family that remained in the city for a few years but left by the end of the decade. In the group studied 19 percent belonged to this category; their average length of residence was four years and two months. This meant that by 1859, 38 percent of the families had moved out of New York.

This pattern of movement was also present among Germans. German newspapers carried advertisements of hotels and boarding-houses that catered to recently-arrived immigrants who were stopping in New York for a short period of time before continuing on to the interior.[61] The German Society of New York also offered aid to this traveler.[62] When Bishop Hughes sought additional financial help from the Leopoldine Society in Vienna, a reason given for refusal of aid was that "most of the German Catholic Wanderers stay but a short time in New York."[63] In the sample group 26 percent were transient newcomers. Other families remained for a longer period of time but had left by the end of the decade. This category claimed 17 percent of the sample; their average length of residence was four and one-half years. By 1859 43 percent of the German families had left the city.

One factor that influenced the rate of persistence, that is, the percentage of those who remained in the city, was death. Living in city tenements was a hazardous existence, and fatal accidents or illness claimed many victims. In the Sixth Ward one of every seventeen persons died in 1854;[64] in "Sweeney's Shambles" one of five adults died in a period of thirty-two months.[65] Consumption was a special scourge of the Irish; John Hughes described it as "the natural death of the Irish emigrants."[66]

The sample group in Transfiguration parish reflected this high death rate. Between 1850 and 1859, 21 percent of the group died, many at an early age. Thomas Lawlor, a day laborer, died 6 November 1853 at the age of thirty-three. Daniel Cunningham lived on Mulberry Street in 1854; he died there a year later at the age of forty-one.[67] Taking into consideration the number of deaths in the Irish sample, the rate of persistence from 1850 to 1859 was 41 percent.

The mortality rate of the Germans was considerably lower. In 1854 the populations of the Sixth Ward and the German Tenth Ward were almost identical; yet, the Irish mortality rate was double that of the Germans.[68] The Irish also crowded the city's hospital, in striking contrast to the comparatively small number of German patients.[69] In the sample group of Most Holy Redeemer not one death occurred; this meant that their rate of persistence was 57 percent from 1850 to 1859.

In the following decade the rate of mobility out of the city among the Irish was 41 percent, and the rate of persistence was identical. Death claimed 18 percent of the group. Thus, in a twenty-year period 55 percent left the city, 17 percent remained, and 28 percent died. Between 1860 and 1869 27 percent of the Germans left the city, and the rate of persistence was 70 percent. Only one person, or 3 percent of the group, died. During the entire period 1850–69, 58 percent of the German sample left the city, 40 percent remained, and 2 percent died.

The destination of immigrants who left the city is difficult to determine. A recent study of Boston's population indicates that such a search is more feasible than previously imagined. This study also emphasized the point that the destination of many people was often nearby.[70] This was certainly possible for the mobile population of New York Catholics. Brooklyn was a favorite home of the Irish, and close by was the German settlement of Williamsburg. Yet, some undoubtedly migrated beyond the environs of New York.

TABLE 2. MOBILITY OF IRISH AND GERMAN CATHOLICS

Years	No. of families	Death rate (%)	Mobility rate (%)	Persistence rate (%)
Irish				
1850–59	53	21	38	41
1860–69	22	18	41	41
1850–69	53	28	55	17
German				
1850–59	53	—	43	57
1860–69	30	3	27	70
1850–69	53	2	58	40

Farming was a possibility, especially for the Germans. But it was difficult for immigrants to set up homesteads in rural America. Even though German immigrants generally brought more money with them than the Irish, such relatively small sums were inadequate.[71] An advertisement in the German press estimated that to settle in Nebraska in 1858 a person needed at least four to six hundred dollars;[72] recent studies have indicated that it took much more. At mid-century an aspiring farmer needed one thousand dollars to purchase transportation, equipment, livestock, and food.[73] Nor was the jump from city to farm as widespread as expected. Generally the transition was gradual, since prospective farmers had to acquire sufficient capital before they could make their move. Frequently their odyssey to the rural frontier involved several stages from town to country. The first step was always a move from the port of arrival in the United States; for some this took longer than it did for others.[74]

From a study of the mobility rate of Irish and German Catholics one conclusion is evident. Both groups left the city in large numbers. Close to three out of five persons in each sample, 55 percent of the Irish and 58 percent of the Germans, abandoned the city in a twenty-year period. This conclusion compares favorably with other mobility studies and underlines the transiency of immigrant city dwellers. Yet, there was a difference between the Irish and German rates of persistence, which suggests that not all immigrants moved with the same degree of frequency. This is especially evident when one considers the number of deaths among the Irish. Excluding those who had died, in the twenty-year period only 24 percent of the Irish families remained in the city. This suggests that the tendency to remain in the city was greater among Germans than among Irish.

A possible explanation for this difference is that in the case of the Germans the influence of the ethnic village was stronger; and the longer they remained there, the less inclined they were to leave. Among Catholics there was the added factor of the bond between language and faith. For many, language meant faith.[75] For a Catholic, to leave his neighborhood and church with no assurance of finding another German-speaking parish was tantamount to abandoning his religion. A New York German who had moved with his family to Kenosha, Wisconsin, described this sense of loss: "We met with sad experiences," he said. "Coming from New York we found in Wisconsin neither church, school nor priest. This pained me more than anything else, for knowledge of the duties of Christians surpasses all other things."[76] A transient Irishman, however, had a greater possibility of finding an English-speaking parish than his German-speaking counterpart. Even if the Germans had learned to speak English, their language was so interwoven with religion that not finding a German parish often meant not having a Catholic parish. In the case of the Germans, then, ethnic loyalties tended to strengthen their rate of persistence in the city.

For the Irish and Germans who remained in New York, living in the city was not necessarily a stable existence. In his study of the Americans Daniel Boorstin noted that the churning, casual, circular motion in the West was "as characteristic of the American experience as the movement in a single direction."[77] Such churning, circular motion was also commonplace on the urban frontier. New Yorkers changed their residence with little hesitation; one visitor remarked that "it is no uncommon circumstance to meet with individuals who have resided in a dozen different houses in as many years."[78]

The traditional moving day in New York was May 1. It was a day when the entire city "turned topsy-turvy, thousands of persons being in the act of removal, the streets filled with carts laden with furniture, porters, servants, children, all carrying their respective movables" to a new address.[79] Newspapers carried announcements of doctors, lawyers, priests, and tailors who changed their residence or place of business almost annually. John Dubois, bishop of New York from 1826 to 1842, said that every year "at the first of May half of the inhabitants of the city moved from one corner of the city to another."[80] This coming and going of New Yorkers on May 1 symbolized the transiency of the people; one reason for such movement was the neighborhood change generated by an expanding city.

In the lower districts of the city new industry and commerce forced the relocation of residents. The wealthy moved uptown, and their homes passed into the hands of boardinghouse keepers and real estate agents. The cost of renting such homes was reasonable at first, but "the rapid march of improvement speedily enhanced the value of property in the lower wards of the city . . . the rents rose, and accommodations decreased in the same proportion."[81] The better class of tenants gradually moved uptown; new commercial buildings replaced old homes; houses lingered on for a time and "were filled from cellar to garret with a class of tenantry living from hand to mouth."[82] Like waves repeatedly pushing against the shoreline, the expansion of the city moved the population farther uptown. Tenement houses filled vacant lots. Greenwich Village replaced Bowling Green and Barclay Street as the center of fashionable residences. In 1860 Fifth Avenue, from Washington Square to Central Park, was a favorite address of high society. Nearby, Lexington Avenue had become the breeding ground for New York's brownstones, inhabited by the well-to-do.[83] By the end of the Civil War the expansion of the city had pushed people off Manhattan Island, and they scattered to the suburbs "in all regions around New York."[84]

The poor were also caught up in this churning motion. Renting their apartments by the week or month left them free to search for better bargains. A New Yorker observed that because of short-term rentals "it is very common to find the poor tenants moving from place to place every few weeks."[85] A study of Irish and German families confirmed these observations about the city's floating population.[86]

When New Yorkers changed their address, they could have moved out of the neighborhood or within the same district; occasionally the same family made both moves. Among the Irish four out of five families moved at least once while they lived in New York; of these families two out of five moved more than once. These residential moves were of short distances; in fact, most parishioners in the sample group did not move beyond Fourteenth Street. This did not mean that they never left the neighborhood; on the contrary, three out of four families who never lived above Fourteenth Street did move out of one neighborhood into a different ward.

The Germans were also on the move. Three out of four families changed their residence at least once; of this group two out of three moved more than once. Like the Irish, they did not move very far. Only 16 percent of the group left the four wards of the Lower East Side, and almost half of them eventually returned to addresses in this area.

It was not unusual for a family to move several times in the same neighborhood. People would move around the block and often to a new address on the same street. Timothy Scannell was a stevedore living in the Seventh Ward near the East River wharves. While in New York, he changed his address three times, but he never moved out of the Seventh Ward. Matthew Reichart, a bookseller, lived on Avenue A near Most Holy Redeemer Church for more than twenty years. He moved three times, each time to a new address on Avenue A. Christian Ege, a carpenter, lived in Little Germany for twenty years. During this time he moved five times, but always to another location in the same neighborhood.

Such mobility within the city coupled with mobility out of the city illustrates the fluidity of the ethnic village. Based on the sample study, two of every five people who lived in the Irish and German parishes in 1850 had left by 1860. Sample studies for successive years would have to be made to reinforce this pattern; yet, the conclusion of this sampling, together with other mobility studies, illustrates the unstable nature of the immigrant population. The ethnic neighborhood maintained its stability as Irish and German newcomers replaced transient immigrants; but the people who lived in the neighborhood in 1860 were to a large degree not the same individuals who lived there in 1850.

The coming and going of immigrant Catholics betrays the image of a stable ethnic parish. The church was firmly rooted in the neighborhood, but people passed through the city and the parish with great frequency. Yet, as each wave of newcomers arrived, they encountered an environment similar to that experienced by their predecessors. The variety of nationalities living on the urban frontier was quite unlike the homogeneity of a German village or an Irish countryside. Living within eyesight of fashionable homes, they became accustomed to the tenement-house culture of the city. Poverty was a way of life for both Irish and Germans, and for many New York was only the intersection of a more ambitious journey in the New World.

One landmark that Catholics recognized on either the urban or rural frontier was the church. Transplanted from the old country, it was a nostalgic reminder of what had been. In New York Irish and German parishes were located within walking distance of one another, but they were as distinctive as German beer and Irish whiskey. They reinforced the ethnic differences of the people and enabled neighbors to build cultural barriers among themselves. As the center of their religious life the neighborhood parish exhibited the piety of the people, and the differences in piety proved to be more striking than the similarities of the urban environment.

THREE

The Irish Parish

THE CATHOLIC CHURCH in Ireland emerged from the darkness of the penal days during the nineteenth century. New churches appeared, and their conspicuous locations signaled the surfacing of an underground community. After the 1829 Act of Emancipation church building increased throughout the country; in the next one hundred years over three thousand new churches were built, and the Catholic Church became "the most grandiose builder in nineteenth century Ireland."[1] The Catholic revival also witnessed an increase in the number of priests, religious orders, and charitable and educational institutions. After the Great Famine Irish Catholicism underwent what Emmet Larkin has happily labeled a "devotional revolution," and religion evidenced a new vitality that contrasted dramatically with the moribund state of Catholicism in the early years of the century.[2]

Critical to this development was the renewal of parochial life. New buildings, increased devotions, and more responsible pastors signaled this reawakening, and the parish became the focal point of the revival. During the campaign for emancipation the parish church had served as a center of political as well as religious activity; in the rural countryside the small church, with its earthen floor and thatched roof, occupied a central position in the lives of the villagers.[3] As the church gradually emerged from the underground, diocesan synods sought to organize ecclesiastical affairs. In the summer of 1850 the first national church council since the penal days took place at Thurles. The bishops produced a body of laws that laid the foundation for all future councils, concentrating heavily on the reorganization of parochial life.[4]

When the Irish left their homeland, they brought with them a religious heritage that was fast becoming parish-oriented. Upon arrival in the United States they found a church that also was parish-centered. By the 1830s American Catholicism was beginning to consolidate the modest expansion that had taken place since the appointment of the first Catholic bishop in 1789. As in Ireland, diocesan synods and national councils sought to organize ecclesiastical affairs. The First Plenary Council of Baltimore convened in 1852, two years after the synod of Thurles, and a central concern of the bishops was the strengthening of parochial life.[5] Thus, when the Irish arrived in the New World the parish church was a familiar landmark; it provided a link with the old country, and even the architecture resembled the Gothic style of new churches in Ireland.[6] As the center of Catholic life the neighborhood church occupied a position of significance not unlike that of its counterpart in Ireland.

One parish that became the spiritual center for Irish immigrants was Transfiguration Church in New York City, which served the needs of the Sixth Ward Irish. The baptismal and marriage records reflect the hegemony of the Irish, and the list of parish officers resembles a roll call of the Ancient Order of Hibernians; hence, it is ironic that the founding pastor, Felix Varela, was a Cuban refugee.[7]

Father Varela arrived in New York in December 1823 in search of political asylum. As a leading exponent of democratic principles in

Cuba he could no longer live in his native land, which was then under the rule of King Ferdinand VII of Spain. Varela's work in Cuba had established him as one of Cuba's foremost spokesmen for independence, and in later years he emerged as a national hero. One twentieth-century biographer called him "the forger of the Cuban conscience"; another gave him the title of "Precursor of the Cuban independence revolution."[8] The irony of history is that this man, who spent the major part of his adult life in New York City, has, until recently, been almost entirely forgotten in New York, while at the same time he has become a folk hero in Cuba.

Varela began his pastoral ministry among the Irish in St. Peter's Church on Barclay Street. After a brief period of time he purchased an old Episcopal church on Ann Street with funds provided by some of his friends. In 1833 a weakened structure closed the building. After a brief period in temporary quarters, the congregation was divided into the two parishes of St. James and Transfiguration. Father Varela remained as pastor of the latter, and in 1836 he moved with his people to a Presbyterian church on Chambers Street.[9]

For the next seventeen years the parish on Chambers Street suffered through a period of financial chaos. This struggle against impending bankruptcy was not an uncommon experience for many parishes in New York City: the poverty of Catholics and the depression in the nation's economy made it almost inevitable. In 1840 St. Peter's Church had a debt of $135,000, on which it paid a 7 percent annual interest on money loaned to the church. The annual income was so low that the parish had an annual deficit of $6,450.[10] The parish established a society to help liquidate the debt, one of the priests journeyed to Ireland to collect funds, and the trustees looked for new ways to raise money. Yet, the situation deteriorated, and the church eventually was sold at auction. The buyer was an agent for Bishop Hughes, who, through this action, prevented the loss of the property to the Catholic church in New York.[11]

St. James on James Street had a debt of $42,798 in 1836 and, like St. Peter's, had an annual deficit and could not even pay the interest on money loaned to the church.[12] Other parishes in the city were not in any better financial condition, and in 1841 Hughes decided to organize a Church Debt Association to relieve the financial burden of the urban parishes. In a speech to the members of the association

John Hughes summed up the problem of a church struggling to meet the needs of a rapidly expanding membership. "Our situation," he said, "has been that of a people unprovided with churches, and who in providing them, have contracted a heavy debt, the interest of which alone from year to year, if it be paid only tends to impoverish us the more."[13] After one year of labor and with constant encouragement from the bishop at monthly rallies, the Church Debt Association was able to raise only seventeen thousand dollars. Such meager returns forced Hughes to admit that "this result, together with difficulties of the times, exercises disheartening influence on the people."[14] It suspended operations after one year.

The depressed state of the national economy, the prevailing high interest rates (7 percent), and a three-hundred-thousand-dollar debt persuaded Bishop Hughes to seek financial help in Europe. He sailed in July of 1843, hoping to obtain a low-interest loan in Belgium. But his trip was financially unsuccessful, and he was back in the city by September, as bankrupt as ever.[15] In the meantime Transfiguration Church still struggled with its financial problems.

Like most parishes at this time, Transfiguration Church was incorporated in the name of a board of trustees. They were laymen, elected annually by the parish community, and their task was to manage the temporal affairs of the parish. For the trustees of Transfiguration this was no easy task. When the parish had decided to relocate in 1836, it had had to pay fifty-five thousand dollars for the vacated Presbyterian church. To raise this money the trustees, together with Father Varela, established a fund, similar to a savings bank, in the name of the church corporation. The people of the parish, along with friends of Varela, loaned money to the corporation at 7 percent interest, payable semiannually. It was the legal responsibility of the trustees to see that the interest was paid and, if necessary, to pay back the entire loan within ten days.[16] In this unique manner the trustees raised the money to buy the church. Yet, they put the corporation in a dangerous position, since they were not able to meet the high interest payments or to pay back the loans.

There was little additional money flowing into the church treasury, and when the depression took hold in New York in 1837, people began "to besiege the door of the trustees' room, on evenings when they are in session, demanding from them the whole or parts of money they so generously and confidingly lent" to the church.[17] Those who could afford it hired a lawyer to plead their case and threatened the church corporation with legal action. The poor who had loaned small sums of money besieged the trustees for a portion of their "just dues."[18] They told of how their few pieces of furniture were being seized as payment for rent and how they had been out of work for months and "in the utmost distress." Others sent messages "from their bed of sickness begging a small portion of their money to procure necessary food and care."[19] The situation deteriorated, and the church was in danger of being sold at public auction. In October 1843 the city's sheriff advertised the church for sale, but a last-minute agreement was reached with the claimants, and the sale was postponed.[20]

According to a 1784 state law, the lay trustees of Transfiguration held legal title to the church property and building.[21] They paid the salaries of the priests and the other employees and managed the temporal affairs of the parish. Despite the advantages of having lay trustees who were "in the daily habit of transacting business, buying and selling and . . . more competent than the priests to perform the ungratuitous task of making hard bargains, and economizing small sums,"[22] the trustee system failed in the case of Transfiguration Church. One of the principal reasons was that the trustees were not able to deliver in the area where they claimed to be competent— "making hard bargains and economizing on small sums." Given the poverty of the parishioners and the economy's depressed state, the trustees could not raise enough money to pay the loans. The same situation prevailed in other New York churches, and this financial failure on the part of the trustees during the 1837 depression was a contributing factor to the demise of the trustee system.

During the eight years of financial chaos (1836–44) the trustees, together with Father Varela, unsuccessfully tried several different ways to raise money. They rented pews at bargain prices for advance payment and took up collections throughout the city. They formed a church debt society to raise money, sponsored an oratorio in the church, and organized annual fairs to help reduce the debt. But the crisis continued. Father Varela did not receive his salary one year; the organist was not paid; even the organ was mortgaged to meet the claims of a creditor.[23] Collections at Sunday Mass, pew rent payments, and donations from friends of the parish helped to meet a significant amount of the debt, but the people continued to besiege the trustees for promised payment.

In April of 1844 the trustees finally decided to turn the entire problem over to Father Varela. At a general meeting of the congregation, the trustees, with the consent of the congregation, gave Varela the deed to the church and real estate.[24] This marked the end of an effective lay trustee system in Transfiguration Church, and it remained for Varela to pay off the debts. He had no more success than the trustees. In 1849 the church was again in danger of being sold at public auction in payment of an overdue mortgage note.[25]

In 1853 the sale of the Chambers Street church for seventy-five thousand dollars eased the financial crisis. The parish bought an old Episcopal church on Mott Street for thirty thousand dollars, and the balance paid off the debts and finally put Transfiguration parish on sound financial grounds.[26]

The financial problems of New York City's churches were not unique. Other urban churches struggled with the same dilemma— that of a young church striving to meet the needs of a rapidly expanding membership. Bishops wrote letters to European missionary societies begging for financial relief; priests traveled to foreign countries seeking help; parishes sponsored fairs, concerts, lectures, and special collections. The depression of 1837 and those in the 1850s dulled their efforts, even though the flow of immigrants increased demands on the church. During these years of fiscal crisis Transfiguration parishioners emerged from behind the veil of anonymity. The parish records reveal a community struggling to meet personal as well as parochial needs, and this period of crisis provides a window through which to view the social stratification of a parish community.

The lay trustees were men who had time and leisure to spend on church affairs; their reputation among the parishioners was well enough known to assure them victory in the annual trustee election. Only men who rented pews could vote in these parish elections.[27] This constituency, however, represented no more than one quarter of the community.[28] Even this educated estimate appears high when one considers the small size of churches in the city. Based on a sacramental index, Transfiguration was the largest parish in New York in 1840. Even if its population in 1840 is conservatively fixed at 10,000, this would mean that 2,500 people rented pews. Since the church building, only fifty feet by seventy feet, could not have provided seating facilities for that number at any one time,[29] this scarcely seems possible.

An indication of the proportion of the parishioners who could afford to rent pews was given in a meeting of pew holders in St. Patrick's Church on Mott Street, just north of the Sixth Ward. The meeting was an important one. Scheduled for Sunday afternoon, Bishop John Hughes was to speak to the assembled crowd. Thus, the conditions to encourage good attendance were present—an important issue, a well-known speaker, and a convenient hour for most people. At that time St. Patrick's had at least ten thousand parishioners, mainly Irish; yet only five to seven hundred people attended the meeting.[30] This incident would indicate that less than 10 percent of the parishioners rented pews. Bishop Dubois, however, believed that 25 percent was an accurate estimate, and he blamed such small participation on the poverty of the parishioners. The poor in the parish could not afford the price of renting a seat, and the city dwellers were so mobile that many could no more afford a permanent seat in church than they could manage a permanent address in the city.[31] Furthermore, the renting of pews was not a custom familiar to Irish immigrants. Though it existed in England, it was not native to Ireland, and this also may explain the small number of pew holders.[32]

The pew rent system has generally been associated with Protestant churches, but it was also a widespread custom in the American Catholic church. During the ante-bellum period in New York, pews were normally rented once a year at public auction, but in some cases financial conditions were so precarious that collectors frequently stood in the aisles of the church before and after Sunday services urging people to rent pews.[33] In some parishes the income from pew rents was the principal source of revenue, but in others the ordinary Sunday collections equaled the pew rents. From 1836 to 1842 the pew rents in Transfiguration Church almost equaled the Sunday collections ($15,454 from pew rents and $16,126 from collections).[34] The front pews were auctioned off at prices higher than those in the rear. Some parishes sought to auction off front seats at rentals as high as $100 and $150 a year, and it was said that they met "no opposition."[35] The system of pew rents seldom became a divisive issue in the community, but the high cost of enjoying a reserved seat in church was symptomatic of the class distinctions in the city parish.

In Transfiguration Church the men whom the pew holders elected as trustees reflected this distinction. The trustees were not day laborers or stage drivers; they represented the upper levels of the occupational hierarchy—professional men, proprietors of small neighborhood businesses, and skilled artisans.[36] Thomas Scanlon, president of the board of trustees in 1840, was a merchant who lived in the First Ward. Daniel Hogan, a doctor living in the Sixth Ward, served on the board from 1841 to 1844. Six of the trustees were neighborhood grocers. The best known was Felix O'Neil, an immigrant from County Sligo, who lived in the Sixth Ward and served as its alderman during the late 1830s.[37] One of the outstanding members of the board was John Delmonico, a Swiss immigrant and one of the founders of the famous New York restaurant.[38] He contributed substantially to the parish and was instrumental in purchasing the church on Chambers Street in 1836.[39] The financial reports of the church list his contribution in 1836 as thirty thousand dollars, at least half of which was in the form of a loan.[40] Mr. Delmonico served as a trustee from 1836 to 1840, and he died suddenly in November 1842 while deer hunting on Long Island.[41]

Although a large number of the people in the parish were poor, the occupational status of the trustees indicates that by 1840 Irish Catholics in New York were represented at all levels of society. The poor loaned the widow's mite to the church, the middle class of people contributed sums of fifty and one hundred dollars, and the well-to-do loaned one thousand, twelve thousand, and as much as thirty thousand dollars.[42] A random sample of heads of families listed in the baptismal register of 1845 further illustrates this diversity of people and occupations within Transfiguration Church.[43] Within the group 18 percent were unskilled laborers and 25 percent did nonmanual work, but the large bulk fell in the middle categories of skilled and semiskilled occupations.

The occupational distribution of the 1850 random sample group, previously used in the analysis of residential mobility, also demonstrates this pattern of class diversity.[44] At the bottom of the occupational hierarchy was the unskilled laborer, representing 21 percent of the group, and at the top were the nonmanual occupations, totaling 19 percent. But as the sample of 1845 demonstrated, the large bulk of men occupied the middle group of skilled and semiskilled trades. In both samples there were no professional men listed, and within the nonmanual class most were engaged in small neighborhood trades, such as groceries, liquor, and oysters. The Irish of Transfiguration Church were not prominent in the upper levels of the occupational hierarchy, nor did the bulk fall into the class of the unskilled laborer. Rather, the skilled and semiskilled trades, such as the building trades, tailoring, and shoemaking, claimed the majority of the people.

This predominance of workers in the skilled and semiskilled trades is not surprising for mid-nineteenth-century New York. Immigrants swelled the city population, and skilled hands were necessary to build homes for the newcomers.[45] The transportation revolution provided jobs for the Irish driver, who became a familiar sight along the avenue, sitting atop the stage with his derby hat and Irish brogue.[46] Irish tailors and shoemakers were also numerous,[47] working in their own apartments or in a second- or third-story shop; their countrymen regarded them as a "respectable and generous" class of people.[48] The immigrant grocer was another familiar neighborhood institution. Among the sample group this entrepreneur stood out. He relied on the patronage of his newly-arrived countrymen, who sought out a familiar face and a recognizable accent to serve them. For some, the grocery store became a stepping stone to an active political career.

This large representation of Catholic Irish in the middle ranges of the occupational hierarchy, together with their smaller representation at both ends of the scale, reflected the social distinctions present within the community. Despite such occupational differences, the local Catholic community was united by its common bond of faith. The culture of poverty might have separated the laborer and the craftsman from the lawyer and the politician, but a shared faith and nationality were able to bridge this gap in the neighborhood parish.

When the immigrant Irish came to the United States, they

brought their religion with them. In fact, among the Catholic Irish it was difficult to distinguish between nationality and religion. In the early nineteenth century, Ireland was struggling with Protestant England for political and religious freedom, and the two issues became inextricably interwoven. The passing away of the old Gaelic culture in the late eighteenth century had given rise to an intensified Catholicism, and, as one historian has put it, the Irish "found their securities in the Church and their leadership in the priesthood."[49] The church in Ireland became a fighting church enjoying no vested privileges, and during the struggle on behalf of Catholic emancipation, religion and nationalism were united in a common cause. An Irishman in America observed that the St. Patrick's Day festival "represents the two prominent traits of the Irish people, fidelity to their faith and loyalty to their country . . . religion and patriotism so closely interwoven, so thoroughly identified. The English Government, by banning both, made religion dearer and patriotism more noble; by placing the love of God and the love of country in the same category, it made martyr and patriot synonymous terms."[50] This union between God and country was strengthened in the United States by the prevalence of the Protestant culture with its anti-Catholic tendencies. Bishop Hughes believed that the anti-Catholic and anti-Irish attitudes "tended powerfully to unite Catholics."[51] The Irish-American press reflected this sense of group consciousness; by emphasizing the religious and ethnic distinctiveness of its readers it reinforced their self-identity at a time when they were under severe criticism in the United States.[52] For the post-Famine immigrants the link between religion and nationality appeared even stronger. The devotional revolution forged this bond, so that "Irish and Catholic have become almost interchangeable terms in Ireland."[53] This was the cultural heritage they transplanted to America.

The Irish considered religion "as the most important of all topics."[54] They preserved it at great personal sacrifice, and whether they practiced it or not, religion was ingrained in their life. "Beliefs maintained at great personal sacrifice were not lightly held," Oscar Handlin correctly judged, "and among those Irish who came to America the Church gained particular prestige, for it was one of the few familiar institutions that followed them across the Atlantic."[55] When they arrived in New York City, they followed the paths of earlier immigrants to Irish settlements. In these ethnic villages the local church enjoyed a conspicuous position, and as a house of worship it provided a familiar experience for the newly-arrived Irish. The parish was the center of their devotional life, and if religion was not visible there, then it scarcely existed anywhere.

At the council of Thurles certain basic norms shaped the direction of the decrees. One cornerstone of the legislation was fidelity to Tridentine Catholicism. The sixteenth-century Council of Trent reformed Catholic life, and its legislation commanded the landscape of Catholicism until the twentieth century. Faithfulness to the Tridentine decrees was a sign of orthodoxy, and nineteenth-century Catholicism in both Ireland and the United States sought to reproduce the spirit of Trent. Centuries of persecution in Ireland had necessarily forced the Irish to adapt their devotional life to a hostile environment; in the United States a young church spread out across a vast countryside also had to modify itself. Yet, the sources that both churches returned to as persecution ceased and consolidation took place were those of Tridentine Catholicism. During the pontificate of Pius IX (1846–78) this trend became clearer, as the church underwent a period of Romanization.[56]

For Catholics the principal act of worship was the Mass. A popular manual described it as a "means of sanctification," and the sacrament of holy communion was "beyond all expression and all conception, not only the most powerful stimulative to faith, hope, love and contrition; but also the most efficacious means of obtaining these and all other graces from the divine bounty."[57] In the middle of the nineteenth century frequent communion was not customary for Catholics in the United States, and the same was true in Ireland. Yet, practicing Catholics received communion at least once a year, generally at Easter time. In a letter to Rome recounting his twenty years experience in New York, John Hughes said that a "great body" of people received communion "once or twice a year; and very many, once a month, and even once a week."[58] Even if the worshippers did not receive communion, they still were present at the drama in which, according to their belief, Jesus Christ became truly present and was offered in sacrifice to God. For Catholics the Mass was "the most sacred, and the very essential part" of the church's liturgy.[59]

Worship took place daily in the parish, but Sunday services were the principal events of the week. Church law required Catholics to attend Mass on Sunday and other special feast days. To hear Mass on these occasions was "a necessary duty," and Catholics were reminded that "to be absent without a strong reason is a mortal sin."[60] In spite of such admonitions, not all Catholics attended Mass regularly. Bishop Hughes believed that even though many did not have the means of attending Mass on Sunday, for want of decent clothing or through want of inclination, the great body of Catholics did comply with the law, and churches were always crowded.[61] Hughes's optimism was not entirely accurate. The pre-Famine Irish were not avid churchgoers. Many reasons account for this; one is obvious—the dearth of priests and churches, which resulted in the absence of a regular churchgoing tradition for many years. A recent study concludes that about 40 percent of the Catholic population in pre-Famine Ireland regularly attended church.[62] Only in later years did regular Mass attendance reach extraordinary proportions. In New York the inadequate supply of priests and churches also prevented many people from attending Sunday services. A rapidly increasing population aggravated the problem: "the insufficient number of churches has been, and is now," wrote John Hughes in 1858, "an immense drawback on the progress of religion."[63] How great a drawback is difficult to determine, but a study of the Catholic population, the seating capacity of New York churches, and the number of Sunday Masses indicates that not more than 60 percent and closer to 40 percent of the people attended Sunday services in the 1860s.[64] Given the seriousness of this obligation for Catholics, this was not a sign of extraordinary religious practice, but it does mirror the culture from which the immigrants came.

The lack of personnel and facilities helps to explain the low level of church attendance, but such an analysis might naturally lead one to conclude that all that was necessary to increase church attendance was to multiply the number of clergy and churches. This does not logically follow, however, and an examination of church attendance figures in recent years when there was an abundance of clergy and churches illustrates this point.[65] Thus, one has to look for other reasons as well to account for the religious indifference of the Irish immigrants. One persuasive explanation was the high level of religious ignorance among the newcomers.

A study of London's Irish clearly indicates that many pre-Famine immigrants were strikingly ignorant of basic Catholic beliefs and practices.[66] A similar pattern can be found in the United States in the ante-bellum period. Missionaries frequently bemoaned the low level of religious understanding among Catholics. People did not know if there was one God or three, and one priest recorded that "many young men were exceedingly ignorant with regard to religion, some of them not knowing the principal mysteries."[67] Even such a simple ritual as the sign of the cross had to be taught to people for the first time. Many young adults and "not a few quite advanced in life" had never received communion and appeared to be Catholic in name and little more.[68] As one New York priest described the situation, "half of our Irish population here is Catholic merely because Catholicity was the religion of the land of their birth."[69] The reason he gave was that their instruction in religion had been neglected. Many Catholic immigrants simply "had no clear explicit knowledge of Catholic doctrines."[70]

It is clear that all Catholics did not come to the United States in sound spiritual condition. Many had not regularly attended worship services in Ireland, and others had not received the sacraments of confession or communion for years. In their adopted homeland such habits were not quickly discarded, a fact priests giving parish missions noted time and again. It was not unusual to find people "who for years, some even 30 or 40 years,"[71] had not been to confession or communion. Add to this the degree of religious ignorance found among Catholics, and the end result was hardly widespread religious fervor in ante-bellum Catholicism. The task of the church was not only to preserve the faith of the immigrants; in many instances it was to change nominal Catholics into practicing believers. Such a spiritual climate among Irish immigrants goes a long way toward explaining why church attendance figures were so low.

The custom of attaching a financial obligation to Sunday Mass also seems to have influenced the pattern of church attendance. All New York parishes favored the system of pew rents, since it was a major source of revenue, but the poor could not always afford the price. The custom did come in for criticism precisely because it excluded those "who are too poor to have pews."[72] "Free churches" were encouraged so that the indigent and floating population would feel at home, but only one parish in the city inaugurated the practice and for only a brief period of time.[73] Pew rentals became the norm, and some parishes even locked the benches vacant at Solemn Mass "to prevent the poor from occupying them."[74] At the early Masses, however, the pews were "open to every comer." In addition to renting out the seats in church, some parishes went a step further by charging an entry fee to Mass. Commenting on this, a priest acknowledged that "it is very hard to ask money when the people go to mass, but the necessity of the church seems to require that those who are willing to pay are admitted in preference to those who are unwilling; we have not enough church room for all."[75] The price of admission at some Masses was only ten cents, but it appeared sufficient enough to dissuade the unwilling. Such practices not only would have discriminated against the poor, but they also would have discouraged the lukewarm and the indifferent from attending Sunday services.

The distinction between churchgoers and nonchurchgoers illustrates the division within the Irish immigrant community. Some newcomers, Catholic by birth and heritage but not in practice, lived on the fringe of parish life. They were the anonymous Catholics, and we know very little about them except that they did exist and in mid-century New York comprised approximately fifty percent of the immigrant community. Since they did not care very much about their religion, they have remained silent on this aspect of their lives, and few traces of them can be found in parish records. In itself, however, the presence of such a large number of Irish immigrants is a significant fact. It shows that the urban parish was not coterminous with the immigrant community. It was only one institution in the neighborhood, and in the ante-bellum period it attracted a limited percentage of newcomers. In the final analysis it can be said that the immigrants reproduced in the United States the type of religion with which they were familiar in the old country. For some it was an active spiritual life centered in the parish; for others it was an indifferent attitude toward religion, and the immigrant parish was hard-pressed to change these patterns of tradition.

Despite the limited success of the city parish and the corresponding low level of Mass attendance, churches were always crowded on Sunday. The crowds were made up of the immigrants who were concerned with their religion, and they filled the pews and over-flowed into the galleries that were open to all comers. In Trans-figuration Church men had to be appointed to keep order. People crowded into the aisles, and those gathered on the street outside were almost as numerous as those inside. The important point, how-ever, is not that the churches were always crowded but that they were inadequate to the needs of a large Catholic population.

The church buildings reflected the initial poverty of the Catholic community. Like many new pastors, Father Varela began his minis-try in a church basement; once funds were available he bought an old Protestant church and converted it to use for Catholic services. This was a common practice in New York at the time. Protestant congregations were moving out of the old city below Fourteenth Street, and Catholics, eager for more houses of worship, purchased these abandoned churches. One of four New York Catholic parishes in 1865 began this way.[76] The churches that Catholics built or purchased in the early decades were very plain stone structures.[77] By the 1860s, however, old churches were renovated, and new ones appeared exhibiting an architectural extravagance that illustrated the accumulated financial resources of many city parishes. Trans-figuration underwent such a renovation at the expense of fifty thou-sand dollars; this capacity to spend large sums of money was a far cry from the hard days of fiscal crisis in the 1840s.[78]

The neighborhood church came alive on Sunday morning. At Transfiguration the first Mass began at seven o'clock, followed by another service one hour later. The early Masses took place in an atmosphere of solemn stillness. The only sounds were those of peo-ple rising and kneeling as they followed the actions of the priest. The most solemn acts of the Mass were announced by a stroke of a bell; an intense stillness followed the gonglike noise, and "a low, eager whisper of prayer could occasionally be heard" as people be-came lost in devotion.[79] The priest rarely uttered an audible word, and the people followed his movement and gestures in prayer books in which the Latin ritual was translated into their mother tongue. The service lasted about thirty minutes, and after a few brief an-nouncements in English the priest left the altar accompanied by two young altar boys who had assisted him at Mass. It was a simple but solemn ritual, carried out in the same manner as in the old country.

At ten thirty the grand Solemn Mass took place. Music and song enlivened the service, and a further attraction was the principal sermon of the day. People who rented pews generally attended this Mass, and the church was crowded with numerous worshippers. Like most city parishes, Transfiguration had a choir and an organist, who performed at this Mass.[80] "Good music," wrote one priest, "was a powerful motive" for people to attend church.[81] Some parishes in the city gained renown for their excellent song and music; others were criticized because their services resembled music concerts, and people allegedly came only to listen and not to pray.[82]

In addition to morning Mass, the parish also had afternoon and evening services (this pattern was also the custom in Ireland).[83] Afternoon services, called Vespers, featured the recitation or singing of psalms and other prayers, while evening services often featured lectures on Christian doctrine.

The language of the Mass was Latin, but some priests favored having Mass in the vernacular.[84] A young New York priest, Richard L. Burtsell, frequently bemoaned the fact that the liturgy was in Latin: he believed that English "would be so much more effective of good."[85] Despite the use of a foreign language, the Mass did provide the local neighborhood with a liturgy of solemnity and grandeur. Special events, such as the consecration of bishops or the dedication of churches, also provided the opportunity for a public manifestation of faith. On such occasions prominent civic and religious figures appeared, and accomplished preachers and colorful ceremonies highlighted the day.[86] Commenting on the Transfiguration community one observer noted that "they have little that is pleasant to the eye or cheering to the sentiment in the internal order," and the splendor of the liturgy, he believed, was good for the people and expressed the soul of their religion.[87] In a neighborhood distinguished for its miserable poverty, such ceremony provided a distraction from the cares of the earthly kingdom.

In addition to their Sunday obligations, parish priests were busy every day of the week performing marriages and baptizing newborn members of the community. Among Catholics, baptism was "in point of order and necessity" the first sacrament of the church, and parents had their children baptized shortly after birth.[88] Death frequented the neighborhood, and funerals among the Irish were

60

unique events. Mourning and merrymaking highlighted wakes in Ireland for many decades, against which strange custom bishops and priests spoke out.[89] This tradition was brought to the United States, where it again evoked criticism from the clergy. In the early years the custom of a funeral Mass was not widespread, and tradition favored a wake at home followed by a procession to the cemetery.[90] The number of carriages in the procession measured the status of the family, and benevolent societies often provided the funds. In the 1840s John Dillon and his brother Christopher had a large part of the funeral trade, and they advertised for rental everything needed for a successful funeral—scarves, crepe, and gloves together with carriages and hearses.[91] Bishop Dubois and others spoke out against the high cost of dying, and Dubois alluded to the fact that the funerals were more like festivals with "frequent drinking instead of holy water, distasteful conversation instead of prayers."[92] Despite the displeasure of the hierarchy, festive funerals continued. In 1861 the New York Provincial Council of Bishops again spoke out against funerals that had "degraded into an exhibition of ostentatious and unseemly display, sometimes even into an occasion of revelry and rioting," urging that the deceased be brought "without pomp or parade" to the church, where Mass would be offered.[93]

The controversy over the Irish wake did not center only on its festival spirit. A more important reason for the controversy was that the custom challenged the central position of the parish church in the religious life of the people. Bishops legislated that the ceremonies of baptism, marriage, and death must take place in the church, where the names of the faithful could be officially recorded in the parish registers.[94] The pioneer conditions of early American Catholicism often did not allow this, but as parishes multiplied, the possibility of meeting these directives increased, and baptisms and marriages became regular church events. Such ceremonies enhanced the authority of the priest and underlined the importance of the parish church. It was the official place of worship; and the faithful Catholic was to receive the sacraments from the hands of the parish priest, who would baptize him, marry him, and bury him. The Irish went along with baptism and marriage, but the custom of the wake was not readily abandoned. To bury an Irishman was as much a social event as a religious one, and the parish church did not enter into the ceremony. A wake at home followed by an elaborate procession to the cemetery and burial was the order of events. The bishops wanted to change this tradition and make it less social by abolishing the wake and more spiritual by requiring a Mass at the local church. The Irish eventually accepted the latter and in doing so accepted the role of the parish church in the burial of the dead. But the wake was slow to disappear. In fact it never disappeared. The church, unable to abolish it, simply incorporated the wake into its prolonged ceremony of death, and the parish priest became a regular figure at the Irish wake, where holiness and hilarity were combined in a strange mixture of events.

The practice of confession enjoyed a popular tradition in Ireland; crowds of people waited long hours to confess their sins to the priest.[95] While traveling in Ireland, Alexis De Tocqueville noted that in a village of ten thousand people, only one person allegedly failed to make his annual confession.[96] Frequent confession was not common, but the people generally confessed once or twice a year. After the Famine more frequent confession and communion developed. The increase in religious confraternities encouraged this practice, since members were urged to frequent the sacraments.[97] In the United States a similar pattern developed; by mid-century a priest could write that crowds of people lined the churches on Saturday afternoon and evening as well as on other days of the week.[98] The large population and the relatively small number of priests explained such crowds. Hearing confession was one of the "more serious obligations" of priests, and they remained in the confessional until they could listen no more and the task became burdensome.[99] Long hours in the confessional were considered unique to the city parish, and to hear for "only four and a half hours" in one day was a luxury.[100] This penitential tradition reflected a profound awareness of sin. One very popular manual of piety vividly described the misery of the sinner. By serious sin, it claimed that you have

given the death-blow to your immortal soul; you have drawn down upon yourself the anger and punishment of the living God, a God who in his just vengeance is awful and terrible; that he it is who cast forever into hell the holy angels when they first rebelled against him; that, alas! many of the damned who are now groaning in the eternal pains of hell, have not committed so great and so many sins as you.[101]

Sin "like a mountain lie heavy upon" the souls of sinners, and the sacrament of penance absolved these sins; without such cleansing personal salvation appeared unattainable.

In addition to the Mass and sacraments, the local parish also had special devotions during Lent in preparation for the feast of Easter. According to church tradition, this was a time of fasting and a special period of preparation to receive the sacraments of penance and communion at Easter.[102] Special services were held on weekday evenings with sermons preached to "crowded congregations."[103] By 1840 a public evening service was held every night in a different city parish, consisting of a performance by the choir followed by prayers and an instruction appropriate to the season.[104] The season of Lent culminated in the holy week preceding Easter, and the church went all out to impress upon the faithful the mystery of Christ's death. "Every suffering of Christ," a priest wrote, "was portrayed so as to render the ceremonies as sorrowful and as beautiful as possible."[105]

Other seasons of the year also sought to nourish the piety of the people. The month of May was a special time of devotion in the parish. Evening services honored the Blessed Virgin; and the press commented on the large crowds.[106] The feast of Corpus Christi, honoring the sacrament of the Eucharist, was another occasion of extraordinary prayer, and Father Varela would extend the celebration for one week to encourage this devotion. In addition to extraordinary liturgical services, the parish sponsored several religious confraternities.[107] A rosary society encouraged prayer to Mary; the Confraternity of the Immaculate Heart of Mary urged prayer for the conversion of sinners; the Confraternity of the Sacred Heart increased devotion to the suffering Christ. Such confraternities had their counterparts in Ireland, and on both sides of the Atlantic they sought to foster the piety of the people.[108] The confraternity was not unique to the nineteenth century, but it did take on renewed importance during the devotional revival of the pontificate of Pius IX.

The key person in the spiritual life of the parish was the priest. He held the keys to the kingdom. He alone was able to forgive sins, baptize children, bury the dead, and preach the gospel. Without the priest the Catholic community was without the Mass, "the center of . . . [their] religion," and without the sacraments, "the means of their sanctification."[109] In Ireland the priests were not only spiritual functionaries: they were also the "trusted leaders of the people," and the people looked upon them as their friends.[110] A contemporary Irishman remarked that between priests and people there were "very kindly feelings . . . : they [the priests] visit them when they are sick, and speak of religious subjects with them and advise them on all affairs; they are continually among them. If a poor man wants a favor asked of some great man, he gets the priest to ask that favor of him; if he is in distress or difficulties, he goes to his priest, and looks upon him as his friend and protector."[111] This bond between priest and people was also apparent in the United States. Despite his Cuban nationality, Felix Varela was beloved by the Irish of Transfiguration Church. He served as chaplain to the Hibernian Universal Benevolent Society and was vicar general for the New York Irish. Even after Varela's death, his picture occupied a prominent position in some Irish homes.[112]

In the middle of the century the image of the priest was a stereotype. Not all priests in New York lived up to the image, and the people did not hesitate to rebuke an irresponsible clergyman. But the ideal was there for priests to follow and people to extol.[113] The priest was the one who labored with the poor and visited the sick "at all hours of the day and night."[114] Such descriptions reflected the heroic dimension of the priest, and there was no greater way to meet death than by contracting a fatal illness while visiting the sick at home or in quarantined ships.[115] In the mind of the people, the priest was to reclaim "those who were careless or intemperant" and to assist them "most generously in their hour of need."[116] He was not to fear death and was expected to be present "in every pesthouse and focus of contagion."[117] The priests viewed their responsibilities in a similar light. For them the Mass was "the support and consolation of [their] daily work," and the most essential pastoral duties of the priest were confession and the visitation of the sick.[118] Both priests and parishioners stressed these two responsibilities as

the principal duties of the priest. And when Father Alexander Mup-
piatti of Transfiguration Church died, the editor of the Catholic
paper summed up the popular feeling by praising the willingness of
this priest "at any hour of day or night, in any weather, to hasten to
any part of the city at the call of the sick or the dying"; in the
opinion of the editor his zeal in the confessional was "unwearying,"
and he was kind to all there.[119]

With the passage of time the image of the parish priest changed.
A new ingredient appeared in the ante-bellum period: the brick-and-
mortar priest. In 1853 a papal visitor to the United States, Archbishop Gaetano Bedini, observed that the "most outstanding priest is
the one that has built the most churches and begun the most institutions."[120] Bedini believed that this emphasis could be traced to the
American desire for demonstrative success. Large churches, like private mansions, were prestigious symbols. For an immigrant church
in an alien culture, such monuments enhanced the image of the
community as well as the reputation of the priest-builder.[121]

Bishop Hughes attributed this secularization of the priest to the
collapse of the trustee system. He observed that "as the Bishop was
to be the owner of the ground on which the church was built, he
had necessarily to take his rank, unwillingly, among men devoted to
secular business . . . so it was necessary that the Bishop should be a
lawyer and merchant, a contractor, a money-payer, a borrower."[122]

The ascetic appearance of Varela and his devotion to the poor and
sick overshadowed any traces of business acumen. Yet, when history
recorded the pastorate of Varela's Irish-born successor, Father
Thomas Treanor, the qualities of the brick-and-mortar priest were
emphasized. His most memorable achievements were the renovation
and expansion of the church and the construction of a belfry.[123]
When the priest of the brick-and-mortar tradition died, the eulogy
focused on his building accomplishments, and he was remembered
not only as a good, zealous, and faithful priest but also as a man of
excellent business habits.[124]

The income of the priest supported this emphasis on material
success. The salary of a pastor at mid-century was six hundred dollars a year, and an assistant pastor received a salary of four hundred
dollars.[125] Added to this were stipends offered for Masses, weddings, and funerals, which averaged as much as one thousand

dollars a year for each priest.[126] For an unmarried man receiving his room and board, this was a relatively high income. It certainly placed the priest in an income bracket higher than that of most of his parishioners, and, as one priest remarked, many were able "to live luxuriantly."[127]

Despite his economic status, the parish priest was not necessarily divorced from the poor. Father Varela was born into an aristocratic milieu and counted among his friends men of modest wealth. Yet, his work with the poor was the most memorable feature of his life. In later years Father Edward McGlynn, raised in a middle-class home in New York, gained renown as the poor people's priest.[128] The American gospel of success, however, altered the image of the priest, and men like Varela and McGlynn were hard-pressed to find kindred spirits in the priesthood.

Respect for the priesthood was only one tradition that the Irish carried to the United States. Their devotional life, the confraternities they formed, and the churches they built all exhibited the stamp of Irish Catholicism. So pervasive was this influence that the Irish parish was a recognized institution in New York City and elsewhere by the middle of the nineteenth century.

As a religious institution the Irish parish exhibited the spiritual fervor of the people. At first this did not appear extraordinary. In the 1820s Bishop Dubois bemoaned the spiritual neglect of several hundred Irish living on the outskirts of the city;[129] a continual refrain of New York Catholics was the inadequate number of priests and churches. In 1840 the average population of a Catholic parish was 8,500; by 1865 this increased to almost 11,000. The ratio of priest to people remained fairly constant during this period, averaging about one priest for every 4,500 Catholics.[130] Yet, even this figure surpassed the average ratio in the United States and Ireland.[131] In some parishes the ratio even reached the level of one priest for 7,000 Catholics. Such statistics, together with the incessant plea for more priests and parishes and the relatively low level of regular church attendance, do not indicate extraordinary religious fervor. The spiritual activity of the parish, however, indicates that many immigrants had scarcely lost the faith. Crowded devotions during various seasons of the year, well-attended parish missions, long-lasting parish confraternities, hundreds of children baptized each year, hundreds more making their first communion, the financial resources of the parish in the 1860s, the renovation of the church, and the building of a schoolhouse all point to a degree of religious fervor. How extraordinary this was is difficult to measure, but every indication is given that such fervor was increasing by the 1860s and would continue to accelerate in later years as the number of parishes and clergy increased, confraternities multiplied, and regular church attendance improved. One thing appears certain, however: emigration did not cause a radical loss of faith among the Irish, and for the immigrants who carried their religion with them, the neighborhood parish was the institution that helped to preserve this faith.

In 1854 Philip Schaff commented on the Catholic church in America: "The doctrine, constitution and worship," he said, "are the same in the New World as in the Old."[132] While it is true that an Irish parish in New York could have easily passed for a church in Dublin, there was no mistaking the difference between an Irish parish and a German one. They were as diverse as Munich and Dublin. Though they both inherited the spirit of Tridentine Catholicism, their distinct cultures fashioned different versions of this tradition. It was natural then that the German immigrants organized their own churches in the city. Both groups could live in adjoining streets, but when Sunday morning dawned they passed each other by to attend the church where they felt most at home. For many New York Germans the parish of their choice was Most Holy Redeemer Church.

FOUR

The German Parish

T HE RELIGIOUS SITUATION in Germany differed considerably from that in Ireland. Religious wars had divided the country after the Protestant Reformation, and church and state were bound together in the person of the ruling prince. The age of Napoleon brought an end to these last vestiges of the Holy Roman Empire, and the act of secularization in 1803 deprived the church of its privileged position and ushered in "a profound revolution in the life" of the Catholic church.[1] Ecclesiastical property passed into the hands of civil authorities, Catholic universities closed, and the church became subject to the state. Even though the effects of secularization varied from region to region, all of Catholic Germany was entering a new age after 1803. Napoleon had altered the map of Germany, and in the process church life changed.

Subsequent decades witnessed a political and religious meta-morphosis in Germany. The quest for national unity slowly developed until under Bismarck it reached its zenith. At the same time the church struggled to find its place in the new Germany. Although political questions remained in the forefront of ecclesiastical concerns, the renewal of piety formed the foundation for the restoration of Catholicism. The romantic revival at the beginning of the century had enlivened the spiritual life of Catholics, and an intellectual renaissance challenged accepted traditions of Roman Catholicism. Political and theological questions divided Catholics, but in city and town the piety of the people remained visibly present. With the passage of time Catholic life exhibited the signs of renewal as parish missions increased, religious confraternities multiplied, and Catholic culture developed. An important ingredient in this revival was the parish church.[2] For centuries the parish had been the center of church life, and the nineteenth-century renewal emphasized its significance. In 1848 the German hierarchy assembled at Wurzburg to chart the course of Catholic Germany. They recognized the importance of the parish in the lives of the people, and to renew their fervor they urged the revival of parochial life.[3]

The German Catholics who emigrated to the United States brought these concerns with them. In a land noted for its diversity of nationalities German immigrants sought to establish their own brand of religion. This link with the fatherland was especially strong, and from the very beginning it presented serious problems of adjustment for the church in the United States. The revival of church life in Germany and an increasing sense of nationalism reinforced the distinctiveness of German Catholicism, and later immigrants reflected this loyalty to a specific religious heritage.

The issue of religious nationalism emerged in New York City in 1808. Prior to that German Catholics had worshipped together with the Irish and French, but it was not a happy arrangement. Finally the German community petitioned Archbishop John Carroll of Baltimore to send them a priest "who is capable of undertaking the Spiritual Care of our souls in the German language, which is our Mother Tongue." They were optimistic enough to inform the archbishop that they would soon organize their own church, since they had "no doubt that their number will soon increase."[4] The desired priest never arrived, and the parish did not open.

The goal of a German parish was finally realized in 1833 with the organization of St. Nicholas Church. At that time three thousand Catholic Germans lived in New York. Immigration increased their numbers: an estimate given in 1842 counted fifteen to eighteen thousand German Catholics. By the end of the Civil War there were as many as forty to fifty thousand Catholics divided among eight German parishes in the city.[5]

As the number of people and churches increased, German Catholicism inevitably made its mark in the urban church. Their numerical strength—about one seventh of the total Catholic population —reinforced the bond between religion and nationality. The expanding community required more priests and parishes, and the distinctive needs of the Germans demanded priests who were "capable of undertaking the Spiritual Care of their souls in the German language." Gathered together in the urban village, they desired to recreate the familiar religious customs of the fatherland. They wanted separate churches "in which their traditional religious observances and customs could be carried out, where they could hear sermons in their mother tongue, go to confession as they had learned to confess from early childhood, and take an active part in parish life through their beloved societies."[6] Such fondness for the customs of the fatherland was not quick to disappear. As Mack Walker pointed out in his study of German emigration, the emigrants were people who "went to America less to build something new than to regain and conserve something old."[7] The same may be said of their religion. They sought to transplant it to the New World. Years of struggle for religious freedom in Germany and Austria enhanced its value, and a transatlantic voyage was not sufficient to wipe away their cherished customs.[8]

Intense devotion to religion and nationality, exhibited among Germans in general, was especially evident among priests. They campaigned to preserve the German language and customs, and their slogan was "language saves faith."[9] As many judged the situation, the problem was "for Germans to preserve German," and in encouraging this the priests themselves became increasingly nationalistic.[10] Archbishop Bedini, a papal visitor, noticed this tendency among the clergy. He believed that they were "too zealously nationalistic. [They try,] unfortunately, to develop this national feeling as much as possible in a land where there are more Irishmen than Germans." Bedini also pointed out that the priests found support for such enthusiasm among the people, who wanted "everything in German, and if they are ever obliged to have Irish or American priests, they complain loudly about this insult."[11] During the 1880s German priests spearheaded the campaign to procure equal rights for Germans in the American church, forming local and national organizations to advance their cause. Before the decade was over they went so far as to petition authorities in Rome to vindicate their claim that "religion and nationality go hand in hand."[12]

In the United States the principal solution to the issue of religious nationalism was the formation of national parishes. New York City adopted this approach in 1833 with the organization of St. Nicholas Church; nine years later diocesan law formally approved it.[13] The national parish eventually became the trademark of German American Catholicism; as a church within a church it satisfied their unique religious needs and reinforced their group-consciousness. In New York this was particularly evident. For the Germans it was a question, not only of preserving their identity in an American city, but also of protecting their traditions in an Irish-dominated church. The national parish was one way in which they could achieve these goals: it strengthened their sense of ethnicity and fenced them off from the Americans and Irish around them. An indication of the success of this tendency was exhibited in the rate of intermarriage between the Germans and Irish: at mid-century Germans rarely married outside of their own ethnic community. This low level of intermarriage pointed to the strong social bonds that cemented the community together; the national parish was one institution that reinforced this cohesion.[14]

As a solution to the problem of religion and nationality the national parish emerged wherever German Catholics settled. Since people, rather than the environment, created the need, farmlands and cities faced the same problem. In the metropolis of New York the issue was as critical as it was in Ferdinand, Indiana. The solution of both communities was identical: the national parish.[15] As religious nationalism declined among the Germans, the ethnic parish gradually disappeared. At mid-century, however, it was an integral part of the German experience.

When Bishop Dubois approved the formation of St. Nicholas, he told the people that their church would "never be used but for Germans and their descendants."[16] John Hughes accepted the decision of his predecessor, and even though he was never a driving force in the organization of German parishes, he did authorize the building of seven additional churches during his episcopacy.

The indifferent attitude of Hughes toward the organization of German parishes reflected his general policy of seldom interfering in the religious affairs of Germans. In his opinion, they exhibited a "narrow national feeling," and he found it "particularly difficult" to satisfy their demands; he was content to delegate this responsibility to his German vicar general, John Raffeiner.[17] Hughes dedicated new churches and confirmed German children, but as an Irishman he never bridged the gap separating him from German Catholics. After Father Raffeiner died in 1861, the position of vicar general remained vacant. The apparent lack of concern in not appointing a successor caused some people to remark that church authorities "almost ignored the existence" of Germans.[18] German priests deplored this neglect, but they seldom complained of episcopal interference in their religious affairs.

The organization of new German churches also illustrated the indifference of the bishop. The initial impulse to establish German parishes, in contrast with the case of Irish parishes, frequently originated among the laity. According to Catholic tradition in the nineteenth century, the bishop had complete authority in his diocese. Yet, this authority was frequently activated only through pressure from the laity, who occupied the lowest place in the pyramid of church government. An example of such grass-roots initiative was the first petition for a national church in 1808. Later, as the need for churches increased, community leaders would organize their countrymen, purchase some land, and build a small church. Only then did they seek the bishop's approval by asking him to appoint a priest to the parish. This was the pattern followed in the organization of St. John the Baptist Church in 1840.[19] When the need arose for another parish on the West Side, once again the laity took the initiative. They canvassed the city seeking financial support from their countrymen. With their donations they were able to build a small church; then they waited for the bishop to send them a priest.[20] The

Germans followed the same procedure in the formation of St. Boniface on the East Side.[21]

This pattern of lay initiative not only illustrates the lack of episcopal direction but also shows the group-consciousness of the immigrants. As Catholics they exhibited a concern for their religion, but as Germans they expressed this concern in a specific manner. They wanted their own parish, with a German-speaking priest, where they could follow the traditions of the old country. Membership in an Irish parish was accepted only as a temporary arrangement, and the Germans were not satisfied until they had their own church. For them it was as much a cultural, national trademark as it was a center of religion. As Catholics they wanted the bishop's blessing on their work, and Hughes never refused it; as Germans, however, they would not wait for him to act. When they finished their work, he had little alternative but to approve their decision.

The showplace of German Catholicism in New York was Most Holy Redeemer Church, located on Third Street on the Lower East Side. The formation of the parish grew out of a dispute between the parishioners and the pastor of St. Nicholas Church. After two years of conflict, the pastor, Gabriel Rumpler, received permission from Bishop Hughes to organize another parish just two blocks from the scene of his trials.[22] The organization of the new parish did not halt the feuding, which would continue for several years and divide the loyalties of Catholics on the Lower East Side.[23]

The members of Most Holy Redeemer parish came from all parts of Germany. A large number, however, emigrated from Southern Germany and the Rhineland provinces: the 1850 sample group clearly indicated this pattern and reflected the general flow of Catholic immigrants to the United States. Although no one province dominated the parish community, Catholic Bavaria was the birthplace of 16 percent of the sample group.[24] The relatively large number of Bavarians in the parish reflected the distribution of foreign-born Germans in New York. Austrian-born Germans were not very numerous in Most Holy Redeemer, and this too was mirrored in the small number of Austrians in the city.[25] The wide variety of birthplaces among the parishioners, evident in the church records each year, clearly indicates that the German Catholic parish was a mixed community of people. No single province claimed a widespread loyalty, and there was no indication of any group migration in the parish. The one bond that united the diverse peoples was their common Catholic heritage and the sense of *das Deutschtum* that they developed in a strange new world.

The variety of birthplaces present in the German parish was not the only indication of diversity in the ethnic community. As was true with the Irish, a significant degree of social stratification was also present. Since the trustee system was not operative in Most Holy Redeemer, it cannot serve as an indicator of class distinctions; yet, the parish records reveal such social diversity. Certain individuals emerged as prominent members of the parochial community, and like their counterparts in Transfiguration Church, many of them operated small neighborhood businesses. Henry Pfaff was a good friend of the parish and was involved in its organization; he also owned a grocery store. Henry Graf operated a grocery store on Fourth Street near the church; his affluence enabled him to contribute six thousand dollars toward the church debt. The founder of the parish militia society was George Schmitt, a tailor; and his successor as presiding officer was George Schlichter, another neighborhood grocer.[26]

Also indicative of social differentiation was the pew rent system. As in most city churches, parishioners rented pews in Most Holy Redeemer. The price of rental was relatively substantial, and pews in the front of church, a priest noted, claimed a "sufficiently high price."[27] Not all parishioners could afford the annual pew rent, and the mobility of the immigrants further discouraged such permanent obligations. Among pew renters the location of one's seat in church revealed his status and affluence: to occupy the front seats was as high as one could rise. A sample study of the parishioners' occupations more clearly illustrates this variety of classes in the community.[28]

As with the Irish, the large bulk of German parishioners (55 percent) belonged to the skilled and semiskilled classes. Cabinetmakers and tailors were especially prominent and outnumbered all other tradesmen. The ship industry along the East River waterfront also attracted many workers. As one New Yorker put it, the area had a "greater number of artisans, workers in wood and metal, than among the other districts in the city";[29] the sample group included a

74

number of such artisans. Unskilled laborers had an unusually large representation (25 percent). Five years later only 5 percent of the entire German work force in the city were laborers.[30] One reason for this discrepancy could have been the location of the parish near the shipyards, where there was a special demand for laborers; a study of the neighborhood reported that the shipyards employed "many thousand hands to whom a residence near is a great necessity."[31]

The third major classification represented nonmanual trades. This group constituted 20 percent of the sample, a proportion similar to that of the Irish. The variety of trades mirrored the German predilection for certain occupations, such as butcher, baker, and grocer. Unlike his Irish counterpart, the German businessman generally did not speak English upon his arrival in America, and he depended heavily on the trade of his countrymen. After one or two years he usually was able to speak a "tolerable English" and to make his way more easily in the business community.[32]

A comparison of this sampling with the Irish reveals the absence of substantial differences in their occupational distribution. They chose trades characteristic of their nationalities, but the general distribution of both groups was remarkably similar. Unskilled, semiskilled, and skilled occupations claimed 80 percent of the Germans; the corresponding figure for the Irish was 81 percent. Neither group included professionals, and the percentage of nonmanual occupations was almost identical—20 percent of the Germans and 19 percent of the Irish. Yet, each sample had a built-in bias, which helps to explain the similarity: the individuals studied were married men with at least one child.

In the middle of the nineteenth century the workingman's religious life was centered around the parish church. It was the setting for the liturgical reenactment of the Christian life, and the immigrants fostered the same devotions that their ancestors had practiced in Germany. As the religious revival gained momentum in the old country its effects were felt in the United States, and devotional life took on the characteristics of nineteenth-century Catholicism. An important characteristic of Catholic piety at this time was devotion to Jesus Christ.[33] Jesus had always been a central figure in the piety of Catholics, but with the passage of time this devotion acquired an endless variety of expressions, all of which were visibly present in Most Holy Redeemer.

Christmas was an important feast for Catholics, and the parish proudly displayed a nativity scene carved from wood and imported from Germany.[34] The death of Christ was visibly dramatized during Holy Week by an elaborately decorated tomb, and the priests were told to spare no expense in its decoration.[35] Honoring the presence of Christ in the Eucharist was another manifestation of the people's piety. Eucharistic processions were commonplace in Germany, and the tradition continued in America.[36] Forty hours of continual devotion to Christ in the Eucharist preceded the opening of the Lenten season, and the closing ceremony featured an elaborate procession. Thousands of people jammed the church to witness the pageantry. One hundred men in military dress led the march; the American and papal flags along with the banners of the parish confraternities spotlighted the loyalties of the people; parishioners carried candles; and "young virgins in white dresses with tapers in their hands" diligently followed the line of march.[37] The same scene was reenacted on the feast of Corpus Christi. In addition, benediction of the blessed sacrament took place every week of the year; this devotion, also honoring the presence of Christ in the Eucharist, was often repeated many times a week.[38] The cross, the symbol of Jesus' suffering and death, occupied a special place in the piety of the people.[39] Field crosses decorated the countryside of Germany, and in the urban village the cross was also prominently displayed. Set above the church at a height of 250 feet, it was as distinctly visible on the Lower East Side as it was in the Bavarian countryside.

Another dimension of popular piety was devotion to Mary. Even though this tradition intensified in the nineteenth century, it was centuries old, especially present in Germany during the Baroque period of the eighteenth century.[40] Parish celebrations of Mary's Assumption and her Immaculate Conception were special events; and a sister in the school commented on the large crowds at church on the feast of the Assumption.[41] The Redemptorist priests who worked in the parish encouraged this Marian devotion, and their own spiritual life emphasized it to an extraordinary degree. Mary was their special patron; each day they recited the rosary and a litany of prayers to Mary, and every priest had her picture in his room.[42] The founding father of the order, St. Alphonsus Liguori, had encouraged this devotion. One of his more popular writings at the time was *The Glories of Mary*, the first American edition of which appeared in 1852: it offered in voluminous theological detail ready-made talks on the glories of Mary, expounding her virtues and suffering.[43] "After Jesus," Alphonsus wrote, "I have placed my entire hope of salvation in [Mary]."[44] The priests communicated this mentality to the people, which reinforced the inherited tradition.

A shrine to Mary, highlighted by her picture and a statue imported from Munich, occupied a prominent place in the church. Every Saturday of the year parishioners gathered to honor Mary in prayer and song.[45] At one such service a newly-arrived immigrant happily remarked, "O so we find ourselves again in a new, holy Germany."[46] The ceremonies, prayers, and songs recalled a familiar scene, and she was pleased to find herself in such surroundings again. Several confraternities, each with a specific purpose, encouraged this Marian devotion. Such confraternities, long popular in Germany, found support in the American parish.[47] One of the oldest was the Archconfraternity of the Holy Rosary, whose specific purpose was to foster the praying of the rosary. Another society was the Archconfraternity of the Immaculate Heart of Mary for the conversion of sinners.[48] Both societies were also active in the Irish parish, since devotion to Mary was a common feature of Catholics everywhere. The confraternities met regularly, and they had a specific program of devotions that nourished the piety of their members; one German church in New York claimed that as many as four thousand people belonged to the parish confraternity of the Immaculate Heart of Mary.[49]

Another favorite society was the Archconfraternity of the Holy Family. The Redemptorist order fostered the spread of this society throughout the Catholic world, and it naturally occupied an important place in the galaxy of parish societies. Membership was open to men and women, married or single; married men met together each month; single men met at other times; and the division of women was similar. Each group had its own program of spirituality, and the aim of each was to encourage more frequent communion in the parish.[50]

Particular saints also received special attention in the parish. A statue of St. Joseph, made in Germany, occupied a prominent position in the church. German piety singled out Saints Teresa, Joachim, and Anne, whose statues and shrines decorated the church. St. Alphonsus was another popular saint on Third Street. The celebration of the feast days of all these saints enhanced their position in the spiritual life of the parish.[51]

The setting for the reenactment of the Christian life was the church. The original wooden structure, built in 1844, became too small for the rapidly growing community, and a new church replaced it in 1851. Its grandeur was such that the New York Germans referred to it as their cathedral.[52] A visitor to New York reported that they took "great pride in their church,"[53] and on the occasion of its consecration the preacher, Bishop John McCloskey of Albany, also noted this theme of ethnic pride:

> A good work has been successfully accomplished. A labor of love has been happily achieved. Here on this spot, by the side of that rude and simple temple in which but yesterday you worshiped together, there arises in beauteous and striking contrast with it, an evidence not only of your increasing numbers, but also of your increasing generosity and zeal—a grand and glorious temple. . . . This is the temple of God, to be bequeathed as a precious legacy to your children and your children's children who in ages to come, shall gather around this same altar and offer up their fervent praise and prayers and bless the names and the memories of their fathers.[54]

The preacher did not fail to link the church to the cherished faith of the old country, where German Catholics had also built "glorious and majestic piles in honor of their faith." In building such a house of worship the New York Germans proved that they had "the same faith . . . the same generosity . . . the same zeal [as] their pious fathers."[55]

This link with the faith of the fatherland was visible in many other aspects of German parochial life. As Catholics they shared the beliefs and devotions popular with Catholics throughout the world, but as Germans they added their own native touch. As one German priest said, they "love the beauty of the church edifice, and the pomp of ceremonies, belfries and bells, organs and sacred music, processions, feast days, sodalities, and the most solemn celebration of First Communion and weddings. These, and other like things, foster piety and are so dear and sacred to the faithful that not without great danger could they be taken away from them."[56] On Third Street both the old and new churches boasted of bells made in Germany. They enlivened the liturgy, and the bell ringers were important enough to be memorialized in the parish history.[57] The organ was also a necessary fixture. It was said that even the smallest churches in Germany had organs, and the church on Third Street was no exception. Some parishioners boasted that it was the best in the city.[58]

Music played a prominent role in the liturgy of the Germans. Solemn occasions, such as the first Mass of a newly ordained priest and the first solemn communion of the parish youth, brought forth a variety of musical splendor. Orchestras performed, and accomplished vocalists sang different parts of the Mass.[59] Elaborate processions were the order of the day; bands and choirs of various societies, each distinguished by colorful banners, enlivened the celebration. In Most Holy Redeemer the parish militia society, the *Jägercompagnie*, added a degree of color as they paraded in their military uniforms.[60] It was inconceivable for German Catholics to celebrate a religious festival without a colorful procession, a tradition to which the Catholics on Third Street remained faithful.[61]

In both German and Irish parishes music enhanced the Solemn Sunday Mass, but unlike the custom in English-speaking parishes, Germans also featured music at other Sunday Masses. A parish choir, the *Cazilien Verein*, which often sang at the Solemn Mass, elicited a favorable response in the German press.[62] On occasion the children's choir would sing English hymns; at other times the sisters of the parish school would lead the congregation in German hymns. The people followed the Mass in books printed in German and Latin, and they used similar booklets at afternoon Vesper services.[63]

According to Catholic theology the Mass celebrated in Irish and German parishes was identical. Priests recited the words of the liturgy in Latin, and their movements about the altar were the same. The difference, however, was the style of worship. Among Germans the sense of pageantry and the pomp of ceremony were more evident. They took obvious pride in elaborate ceremonies, which they expressed enthusiastically in frequent letters to the editor of the German paper. The Irish also took pride in their liturgy, but it was less noted and more low-keyed. Solemn simplicity characterized their attitude; only on special occasions did they feature liturgical extravaganzas. A common religion would naturally exhibit similarities of expression, but in those customs "not essential to Catholic faith and life" there was a noticeable degree of difference between the Irish and the Germans.

Spiritual confraternities were common among German Catholics in the nineteenth century. In addition to these societies, the parish also fostered the growth of associations organized around more secular concerns. In the last half of the century there was a multiplication of these vereins in Germany and the United States, and a motivating force was the separatist mentality of nineteenth-century Catholicism.[64] For New York Catholics the alternative to a parish society was a non-Catholic organization. Since the church frowned on such fraternization, parishioners were urged to join Catholic vereins because "they contribute to one's spiritual end and the good of the church."[65] This confessional mentality colored the attitude of Catholics towards the *Turn-Verein*.

The *Turn-Verein* was one of the more popular German organizations. Since it was not Catholic, it was "not good for young Catholic blood. . . . The right spirit does not prevail there."[66] Some feared that if a Catholic joined the *Turn-Verein*, this association would "turn him out of the church."[67] Such a mentality encouraged the organization of an elaborate array of societies which reinforced the sense of community in the parish by separating its members from their non-Catholic countrymen.

The most popular parish verein was the *Unterstützung-Verein*, which had as its main purpose the raising of money for the relief of the sick, the poor, and families of deceased members. It functioned as a savings bank, and in time of need it provided insurance money for its members.[68] The *Unterstützung-Verein* was common in the United States, but it was not very widespread in Germany. German vereins were more centered around political, social, or cultural aims, and even though some did provide relief for their members, the insurance verein was peculiar to the immigrant experience in the New World.[69] The oldest relief society in the parish was the St.

Joseph Verein, founded by Father Rumpler in 1843. During the next twenty years four more vereins appeared, and their number continued to multiply in later years.[70] Generally the founder of such a society was a priest, and the members adopted a Catholic saint as their patron. Different age groups joined different societies. Young people belonged to the St. Aloysius Society, which in 1857 had more than five hundred members.[71] Some societies were for men only; others included both men and women.

In addition to their relief work, these associations contributed to the liturgical and social life of the parish. They participated prominently in religious celebrations and paraded in processions with their distinctive banners; some even had bands to provide music on such occasions. They also sponsored frequent outings for their members and friends.[72]

One of the more colorful parish societies was the *Jägercompagnie*. The Jaegers, as they were commonly called, were initially a parish militia society organized to protect church property during the disorders of the Know-Nothing era; eventually they became a mutual relief society.[73] They were always present at liturgical ceremonies in their colorful uniforms; and like other associations, they sponsored parish outings, on which occasions the parish school closed so the children could join in the festivities.[74]

Militia societies were very popular in Little Germany. Following the separatist attitude of the day, a few of these were for Catholics only. One such group was the Henry Henning Guards. Like their non-Catholic counterparts, they wore attractive uniforms, held sharpshooting contests, marched in parades, and sponsored outings for their coreligionists.[75]

A central figure in the spiritual and social life of the parish was the priest. Even though many complaints were heard about the lack of German-speaking priests in America, Most Holy Redeemer parish never faced this problem, since the Redemptorist order of priests staffed the parish. St. Alphonsus Liguori had founded the Congregation of Redemptorists in Italy in 1732; their apostolate eventually spread to Austria and other German-speaking countries.[76] In 1832 they sent their first missionaries to the United States to work with the increasing number of German immigrants, and by the end of the Civil War they were located in many major cities across the country;

their first permanent mission in New York was Most Holy Redeemer Church.[77] The priests and brothers who worked in the parish at mid-century generally came from the German-speaking countries of Europe. Six different pastors administered the parish between 1844 and 1865, all of them born in different German states. Like their parishioners, the priests came from various regions in Germany; Bavaria was the birthplace of three of these pastors.[78]

In 1851 the Redemptorists opened their own seminary in the United States, which further assured the order of American educated priests to staff their parochial missions. Seven priests and six religious brothers were assigned to Most Holy Redeemer in 1850; fifteen years later, at a time when three priests in a parish would have been considered a luxury, there were still seven priests and seven brothers in the parish.[79] Even though some of them worked in outlying mission areas as well as in the parish, the comparatively large number of priests was a decided advantage for the parochial apostolate on the Lower East Side.

The familial relationship between priest and people among the Irish is well-known. Such close bonds between German priests and people are not so well-known, but they did exist. While it is true that anti-clericalism, imported from the German principalities, did surface in the United States, German priests generally gained the respect of the people.[80] In New York the Redemptorists especially won such esteem, which was enhanced by the prestige of the order in Germany.[81] People came to the priest, one German said, "bringing their children and asking for all kinds of advice."[82] When the laity were organizing a society, religious or secular, the editor of the Catholic newspaper reminded them that if the society was to be Catholic, a priest must approve; he further remarked that "nothing should be discussed and described which pertains to church affairs without priests present."[83] Such prominence given to the priest was also evident on the occasion of a young priest's first Mass. The day was given over to celebration in the parish: every available society took part in the festivities, and the press proudly reported the event.[84] Several Redemptorists died from diseases contracted while visiting the sick, and such unselfish service also enhanced the heroic image of the priest.[85]

The respect rendered the priest did not necessarily arise from close personal relations with the laity; in fact, the rule of the order prohibited such familiarity. When lay people visited the home of the priests, they had to remain in certain rooms, and most of the house was off-limits to them. Priests were not to visit the homes of parishioners alone, and when they did visit, it was only to comfort the sick or dying.[86] They were not allowed to attend parish picnics or excursions "under whatever pretext, ever, without the written permission of their superior."[87] The rule was more strict regarding their contacts with women than it was regarding their contacts with men. It provided for exceptions, with the permission of the superior, but its general tenor was clear: a priest in New York could smoke, but "never in those places where one can be seen by lay people."[88]

Since they took the vow of poverty, individual Redemptorists evidenced little concern for the gospel of wealth. They were to live a spartan life, and their rule carefully described the use of food and money.[89] In administering the parish, however, they did become involved in financial affairs. One pastor, Joseph Mueller, was especially zealous in collecting pew rents. Parishioners delinquent in their payments lost their seats in church. Hard-pressed by the debts of the church, Father Mueller constantly pleaded for money. The parish chronicler stated that Mueller's frequent pleas disturbed the other priests, and he did not agree with the pastor's "insistence on money and contributions from the faithful."[90] Some people did accuse the priests of "cupidity for money,"[91] but despite such complaints the parishioners paid off the debt. In later years their contributions enabled the priests to decorate the church in elaborate style, and eventually the parish was able to loan money to churches in less fortunate circumstances.[92] Thus, despite their vow of poverty, the Redemptorists proved to be adept financiers.

The principal work of the priests focused on the spiritual development of the people, an apostolate which proved to be more difficult than is generally assumed. The roots of this problem had their origins in the old country. The influence of the Enlightenment and the state control of the church had weakened the fervor of many Catholics.[93] After the act of secularization in 1803 a revival did take place, but religious fervor never appeared extraordinary. The number of priests declined in some dioceses,[94] and in other areas many priests, "touched by the spirit of the enlightenment, were devoid of piety and zeal."[95] The faith of the people endured, but their religious practice was mediocre: after visiting Munich, a French priest noted that "Catholics have gained in fervor and zeal; but, as in France, they have lost in number."[96] Another observer remarked that upper-class Catholics were "religious only in appearance, [and among] the low classes one can hardly find true religion anymore . . . above all one has become indifferent."[97] The German hierarchy was aware of the situation and sought to remedy it through an increase in religious confraternities and parish missions.[98]

Immigrants coming to the United States reflected this lack of concern for religion. Since many settled in the cities, it was especially noted there. New York, a principal port of arrival, became the home of many Germans who had been away from the sacraments for years. Baltimore and New Orleans experienced the same phenomenon.[99] The clergy were well aware of the situation. They knew that many people arrived in poor spiritual condition and that if they were to reach these immigrants and preserve the religion of the faithful as well they needed more priests and churches. "More than 60,000 German immigrants live in the Diocese of New York," Father Raffeiner wrote to a bishop in Germany, "and wherever I go I find them without priests and without churches, deprived of Christian instruction and the sacraments. What else can be expected under such conditions than that the priceless heritage these people brought from the Fatherland gradually disappears."[100] For Raffeiner it appeared that all Germans shared this "priceless heritage" in the same degree, but such was not the case. Many were Catholic in name only.

The chronicler of Most Holy Redeemer parish acknowledged that "many people had given up the Catholic faith; others were Catholics in name only."[101] A priest writing about Germans in another section of the city said that they "seemed, in great part, to have lost all sense of religion. Very few of them come to church . . . and they never filled the church at divine services."[102] A visible sign of this neglect was the relatively small number of marriages in the parish. Catholics were subject to civil marriage laws in Germany, which forced them to marry in a civil ceremony; many never bothered to have the church bless their marriage, which often led to further neglect of religion.[103] Even though the United States did not have this law, many immigrants followed the practice of the old country, which in the opinion of the parish chronicler inevitably led to religious neglect.[104]

Thus, as was true among the Irish, not all German immigrants were practicing Catholics. Because of the lack of priests in some areas children were baptized in Protestant churches, where their parents were attending services. Neglect of Sunday Mass was not unusual, and reception of the sacraments took place at intervals of twenty, thirty, or forty years.[105] This distinction between faithful and indifferent German Catholics was also evident in the pattern of regular church attendance.

Most Holy Redeemer Church was able to accommodate about 3,500 people, but such an overflow crowd was customary only for the Solemn Mass.[106] The size of the parish community in 1865 was approximately fifteen thousand, and the church, if filled to capacity at every Mass, was able to accommodate the entire parish.[107] But the church was not always full. A more reasonable estimate would be that as few as 6,500 or as many as 9,500 attended Sunday Mass. In other words, between 43 and 63 percent of the parishioners regularly attended Sunday services. This was not a sign of unusual religious practice: it paralleled the level of fervor throughout the city.

In spite of its limitations in reaching the entire immigrant community, the German parish was a beehive of activity. The number of religious confraternities, thousands of Easter communions, hundreds of annual baptisms, and the large number of confessions all reveal a noticeable degree of spiritual vitality. Parish missions were enthusiastically received, and the closing pageantry of the forty-hour devotion would attract an overflow crowd of 6,500 people.[108] The financial contributions of the faithful were another sign of their commitment to the church. In less than ten years they were able to build a new church, and within another decade they could boast of an elaborately decorated church; by 1870 the treasury was large enough to enable the parish to loan forty thousand dollars to a new church in Boston.[109] Although many immigrants may have neglected their religion, large numbers of them practiced it with vigor, and the ethnic parish was the setting where they reenacted the faith of their ancestors. Without it, the loss of faith would have been much greater.

The cultural and spiritual heritage of the Germans, like that of the Irish, naturally found its expression in the national parish. Each group formed a religious oasis in the city, and through the parish they were able to build cultural barriers that separated them from each other. They desired such independence in their religious life, and the ethnic parish was the solution of both groups. It satisfied their religious needs, continued the tradition to which they had grown accustomed in the old country, and preserved the peace in the multi-ethnic community of Catholic New York. When this harmony was disturbed, an inevitable cause of the trouble was the failure of church authorities to recognize the unique demands of a particular ethnic group. One example of such conflict was the intermingling of Irish and German Catholics in the same parish. Despite their common religious heritage, each group desired its own particular brand of religion, and if the needs of one group were neglected in favor of the other, then bitter conflict erupted. Such conflict clearly illustrated the peculiar religious customs of each group and emphasized the difficulty of preserving unity in the nationally diverse urban church.

FIVE

Conflict in the Church

THE URBAN FRONTIER was the crossroads of the world. Immigrants from all nations settled in the city and stamped it with a cosmopolitan quality that has remained synonymous with urban life. As the principal port of arrival for thousands of newcomers New York City evidenced this diversity from its very beginning. A Jesuit missionary in 1643 wrote that "on the island of Manhate there were men of eighteen different languages"; two hundred years later Walt Whitman described New York as a city of the world where all nations were gathered together.[1] Every ward in the city mirrored this diversity; each avenue was an intersection of races, and the sounds of different nations echoed throughout tenement halls. In the midst of this gathering each ethnic group sought to form its own community, to set itself off socially and culturally from the foreigners around it. In building their ethnic enclaves and establishing their particular identity these groups could not prevent the intrusion of strangers; the city was too open, streets were too numerous, and tenements were too large to permit the total dominance of a neighborhood by any one group. A heavy concentration of a single ethnic group in one area certainly marked the neighborhood with a specific flavor, and foreigners knew that east of the Bowery was Little Germany and north of City Hall was the home of the Irish. But even these ethnic villages could not prevent the intrusion of foreigners. Irishmen lived in Little Germany, Germans lived in the Irish quarter, and native Americans were found in both places.

Such ethnic diversity, compounded by class antagonisms and racial prejudice, furnished the raw material for urban violence. The conflicts took many forms, and New York had them all. Bread riots pitted the hungry poor against affluent merchants; race riots scarred the city during the summer of 1863; anti-Catholic nativists harassed Catholic foreigners.[2] All conflict, however, was not so violent, and the lines of battle were seldom so severely drawn; this was particularly true in the Catholic community.

American Catholicism experienced exceptionally few instances of schism. Indeed, conflict often erupted in the church, and Catholics argued openly over control of church property, the appointment of pastors, and recognition of national religious traditions. The hierarchy did not encourage such strife and tried to cover it up as much as possible. The conflict did not cease, however, nor did it breed widespread schism. One principal reason why such severe schism did not occur was that the disagreements were seldom centered on the theological foundations of the Catholic religion. The major reason for conflict was the presence of various immigrant subcultures under the aegis of a single church. Various national traditions confronted one another, and conflict was often the result. But these disagreements were not centered on the core of religious beliefs; cultural and not theological issues were at stake. As an institution the church possessed a degree of elasticity and was able to tolerate such disagreement, since beneath the strife existed a fundamental consensus based on a common faith that was strong enough and sufficiently widespread to sustain such differences. Given the variety of ethnic groups in the church, such conflict appeared inevitable and was an essential element in the formation and persistence of group life. Given the measure of flexibility in the church, this conflict did not tear the institution apart.[3]

Concentrated in the city, Catholicism was necessarily vulnerable to the social conflict latent in a multi-ethnic community. In the early decades of the nineteenth century French and Irish openly argued over the control of St. Peter's Church in New York. Ostensibly the issue centered around the authority of parish trustees, but national prejudices were so intermingled with the trustee debate that it was difficult to separate the two. Frenchmen described the Irish as "an ignorant and savage lot," and the Irish feared a French takeover of the parish.[4] When the Frenchman John Dubois became bishop of New York in 1826, the Irish fear of a French coup increased. "I wish to gratify the Irish as much as possible," Dubois wrote to an episcopal colleague, but his efforts were not very successful;[5] two years later one bishop feared that "the germs of a most formidable schism [were] fixing their roots" in New York.[6] The schism never erupted, but conflict continued until the French founded their own parish in 1841, by which time the Irish had gained control of New York Catholicism by the sheer strength of their numbers.

The Germans were the next group to challenge the hegemony of the Irish. Their general complaint was that the Irish exercised an "undue influence" in church affairs.[7] In a letter to his former spiritual director, a young German-born priest, John Neumann, expressed the fear that if Dubois's successor was an Irishman, German Catholics would not fare well.[8] Parishioners in St. Nicholas Church shared a similar apprehension. They were afraid that after building their own church, some later bishop, unsympathetic to Germans, might deprive them of it. When the Irishman, John Hughes, was appointed as Dubois's successor, the fears of the Germans became more real, and conflict inevitably emerged.

There was little doubt that Hughes found the needs of the Germans particularly difficult to satisfy, and on occasion he challenged their independence in church affairs. One such incident was a controversy over a separate cemetery for German Catholics. Parishioners of Most Holy Redeemer claimed that they suffered insults from the Irish when they buried their dead in the Catholic cemetery. Rather than tolerate such insults, they bought land in Williamsburg, established their own cemetery, and began to bury the deceased there rather than in the official Catholic cemetery. Bishop Hughes, however, did not approve of their action. In a letter to the priests and people of the parish he announced that there would be "only one Catholic cemetery for Catholics of all nations [and] if any insults should be offered it shall not be unpunished or repeated."[9] Despite Hughes's warning, some Germans continued to use the Williamsburg cemetery; hearing of this, the bishop then threatened to interdict the church and lock its doors. The pastor of the parish advised his superior that the bishop would use all means possible to assert his authority, and he believed that Hughes was serious in his threat to close the church.[10] The conflict ended when the Germans accepted their bishop's decision and sold the land. One year later a similar controversy erupted in the German Church of St. Francis. The people wanted to use the land adjacent to the church as a graveyard. Hughes would not allow this and threatened to close the church if the people opposed him. The conflict subsided with the Irish bishop again victorious.[11]

German Catholics did not spend all their energies quarreling with their Irish bishop. In fact, conflict inside the German community was more frequent and more intense. Hughes's experience led him to believe that they were "exceedingly prone to divisions and strife among themselves."[12] German priests acknowledged this tendency: in a letter to a friend one wrote that "for no other intention is there more need for prayer than for unity among the Germans—not only in the German fatherland but also here in America."[13]

The first sign of conflict among New York Germans appeared shortly after the organization of St. Nicholas Church in 1833. Many parishioners disliked the founding pastor, John Raffeiner, and in 1840, after a few years of dissension, he finally left the parish. During the next two years pastors came and went. The root of the problem centered on control over parish affairs. The trustees wanted to run the parish their way and to put the priest in a position of subordinate authority. The priests would not yield to these demands and challenged the trustees' position. The priests had their supporters, while other parishioners rallied around the trustees, who appeared to hold the balance of power in the struggle. Successive pastors, rather than submit to the control of the trustees, moved on to other, less threatening assignments. It appeared that no priest could successfully exercise the pastoral ministry in St. Nicholas, and Bishop Hughes despaired of the situation.[14] Finally, he turned the entire problem over to the Redemptorists, who appointed a young priest, Gabriel Rumpler, as pastor in 1842. In his opening sermon Rumpler told the people that he desired "subjection, obedience and a spirit of peace and not dissension";[15] but his words fell on deaf ears. The trustees treated him like a hired hand, telling him how many candles he could light for Mass and even threatening him with bodily harm. Like his predecessors, Rumpler was not able to gain control over the affairs of the church and was continually at odds with the trustees. After two years of struggle he left the parish and founded a new church, Most Holy Redeemer, two blocks from St. Nicholas.[16] Those who supported him in his struggles joined the new parish, and this division in the neighborhood led to bitter feelings between the two communities for many years; the Redemptorist priests were even afraid to walk the streets of the neighborhood.[17] A similar struggle took place in the German community on the West Side, which led to the founding of a new parish, St. Francis, only a few blocks from the original church of St. John. But the organization of the new parish did not halt the feuding in St. John's Church. In 1851 the church closed for a brief time "on account of the obstinacy of the parishioners"; after several years of peace conflict erupted again, and the archbishop finally had to close the church in 1869.[18] Such dissension, leading to the division and multiplication of parishes was not unique to New York and convincingly verified the impression of Hughes that the Germans were "exceedingly prone to division and strife among themselves."

Another source of conflict in the German community arose with the arrival of the liberal-minded refugees of the abortive 1848 revolution. The priests described them as "liberal in their thinking"; and though they did not reject all religion, they challenged the wisdom of the parish priests.[19] Many of them "did not see the necessity of parochial schools supported by the people when you had free public schools";[20] others opposed the priests in their attempts to raise money among the parishioners; and the parish historian pointed out that the liberal forty-eighters were especially delinquent in their pew rent payments.[21]

Such incidents of conflict did not tear apart the church in the German community. Dissent and even division took place, but no permanent schisms erupted. Because of the close relationship of the opposing groups the conflict was often bitter and long, but the structure of the church was sufficiently resilient to tolerate such dissent and endure in spite of it.

When German Catholics were not arguing among themselves they often opposed a common enemy, their non-Catholic countrymen. At mid-century German immigrants manifested a sectarian loyalty based on either religious or political ideologies, and when these loyalties intersected, tempers flared. Catholic Germans opposed Lutheran countrymen; club Germans, especially the supporters of the *Turn-Verein*, antagonized Catholics because of their liberal ideology. Such conflict served to solify the Catholic community by reinforcing their group loyalty and giving them an identity that was important for their survival in the city, where religious and ethnic diversity was commonplace.[22]

The Irish were also prone to conflict and division. Shortly after the founding of St. Peter's Church in 1785, open dissension surfaced in the parish; at this time the debate centered around the pastor and his preaching skill. The community divided its allegiance between two Irish-born priests, and the struggle lasted for several months.[23] During the school controversy of 1840 Catholic Irish again divided into factions supporting or opposing the organization of a separate school system. The custom of the Irish wake was another incident of division; in this case the people challenged the authority and advice of the clergy. Political controversies were frequent; one of the more celebrated issues involved the nationalist Fenians. The well-to-do Irish disliked the movement, and the Catholic archbishop of New York, John McCloskey, supported their opposition. In 1866 the Fenian Brotherhood planned an outdoor rally, which McCloskey forbade Catholics to attend. Despite the archbishop's disapproval, over one hundred thousand Irish showed up to cheer the speakers.[24] New York was also the scene of bitter conflict between Catholic and Protestant Irishmen during the summers of 1870 and 1871. Irish Catholics hurled paving blocks at parading Orangemen, and only the firepower of the Eighty-fourth Regiment drove the Catholics off. As one historian put it, the Irish were "prisoners of history," and conflict was a legacy of their past.[25]

In the old country the course of history had nurtured the seed of conflict among the Irish and the Germans. The intermingling of the two groups in the New World, however, sowed new seeds of controversy, especially in the sensitive area of religion. The ethnic parish provided a safety valve by separating Irish and German Catholics from one another and fulfilling the particular religious needs of each group. As long as Germans could worship as their forefathers did and practice those devotions learned in childhood, they were content; when this security was threatened by the intrusion of foreigners, a battle for survival ensued. Since the Irish were much more numerous than the Germans in New York, their invasion of a German parish not only disturbed the religious peace but also threatened the continuance of the German community. As long as the parish was ethnically homogeneous, the church was able to serve as a link with the old country by fostering the religious traditions of the fatherland and passing these customs on to American-born immigrants. If the continuation of the process was threatened, the link with the old country and its religious heritage was in danger of being broken; in the case of an Irish intrusion, the danger was not merely of weakening the ties with the fatherland but of having an entirely new and foreign religious tradition replace their cherished German heritage. In New York City most German parishes did not have to confront this delicate dilemma, but St. Alphonsus Church did, and conflict between German parishioners and Irish intruders inevitably developed.

St. Alphonsus was located in the Eighth Ward on the Lower West Side of the city. No one immigrant group dominated the neighborhood; in fact, native-born Americans outnumbered the foreign-born residents.[26] This district also had the largest concentration of Negroes in the city: 2,918 in 1860.[27] When compared with the adjacent Sixth Ward, the diversity of the neighborhood becomes more apparent. In 1855 70 percent of the Sixth Ward was foreign-born, the Irish alone made up 42 percent of the district's population. The Eighth Ward population was only 44 percent foreign-born; the Irish were 21 percent of the total population, and the Germans made up 11 percent.[28] The Sixth Ward was commonly known as the home of the Irish, whereas the Eighth Ward was recognized as a polyglot community. The tenements in the area also reflected this diversity: one tenement housed nine familes—four Irish, four German, and one French; another had twenty-one families, with Irish, Italian, French, and Americans living side by side.[29]

Until 1847 there was no Catholic church in the area. English-speaking Catholics attended St. Peter's parish downtown or St. Joseph's in nearby Greenwich Village. German Catholics, however, had to travel across town to Most Holy Redeemer or St. Nicholas or uptown to St. John or St. Francis. The inadequate care provided for German Catholics persuaded the pastor of Most Holy Redeemer to organize a parish in the Eighth Ward. Land was purchased, and a small brick church was built within a few months; in November 1847 the parish opened. Officially it was a national parish for German-speaking Catholics, but the mixed population of the neighborhood and the absence of churches in the area meant that other ethnic groups would attend the church. Thus, from the very beginning the German parishioners had to contend with foreign intruders.[30]

There was little evidence of tension in the parish for the first few years, but in 1852 a Belgian-born priest, Edward Van Campenhout, began giving sermons in English, which marked the beginning of a prolonged and intermittent controversy between the German parishioners and Irish intruders.[31] In addition to giving English sermons, the priests cared for the spiritual needs of the Irish as well as of the Germans. This division of labor irked the Germans, who "complained that too much was being done for the Irish and English was usurping the place of German in too many instances."[32] The crux of the issue focused on the question of language used in sermons and in catechetical instruction.[33] As English sermons and instructions gradually appeared together with German sermons and instructions, the people feared the erosion of their religious heritage. Their language was intimately bound up with their religion, and the use of English threatened the continuance of their native tongue and ultimately the preservation of their religious customs. The complaints of the Germans persisted, and there was "much bitterness against the Irish who were looked upon as intruders by the Germans."[34] The antagonism between the two groups increased to the extent that the Redemptorists even considered leaving the parish. However, the priests remained; but the pressure applied by the parishioners did succeed in bringing about the discontinuance of English sermons and instructions by 1857. A relative peace prevailed for the next four years, as the priests concentrated on the German-speaking community. In 1861, however, the new pastor, Bavarian-born Eugene Grimm, reintroduced the English-speaking apostolate, and conflict surfaced again.[35]

The reasons behind Grimm's decision were not hard to discover. Irish outnumbered Germans in the area, and past experience had shown that if they were welcomed, the Irish would attend services at St. Alphonsus. In addition, the Irish, more than the Germans, were judged to be good contributors to the church, and a new parish required continued financial support. Germans "were poor in this world's goods," observed one priest, "and they never filled the church at divine services. But with the accession of the Irish the Little Church was always packed."[36] The attendance of the Irish at the German parish also disturbed Irish pastors in the surrounding areas, since what was St. Alphonsus's gain was their loss. The financial records of the parish verified the concerns of the neighboring pastors: there was a marked increase in revenue once the Irish were welcomed back into the church.[37] The pastors raised the question of the legitimacy of an English-speaking apostolate in a German parish at the diocesan synod in 1868; despite their protest, however, St. Alphonsus remained a mixed parish with divided loyalties.[38]

The manner in which Father Grimm resumed the practice of English sermons reflects his desire not to rouse the ire of the Germans. Rather than deliver lengthy sermons in English, the priests would only make a few announcements in English and then offer "a few comments about going to Mass, keeping holy days, etc."[39] Since the address was so brief, the people remained standing; but gradually the brief comments expanded into a twenty-minute sermon, and the people sat down.[40] The Lenten season featured English devotions and sermons on Wednesday evenings, when many confessions were heard. In the following year English sermons increased. They first appeared at the Sunday eight o'clock Mass; then Sunday evenings in Lent featured English instructions and devotions. Such

Sunday devotions also took place during the month of October.[41] With the passage of time English services increased, with the result that the parish was offering almost identical services for both Germans and Irish. There were separate Masses and sermons, separate devotions, and German missions as well as Irish; during Lent two courses of sermons were given, one in English and another in German; the parish also sponsored religious confraternities for each group.[42] By 1866 the archbishop had formally approved this arrangement, but it still remained a source of contention among the Germans.[43] The priests' cupidity for Irish money annoyed them; indeed, one priest claimed that this kept some Germans away from church.[44] When it came time to build a new church, a proposal was made to build a double church with upper and lower chapels. The priests favored this arrangement, and the plans were drawn. "But protest ensued and the Germans let it be known that they would not go down stairs and have the Irish over their heads";[45] they knew they would get the worst of the arrangement because of their inferior numbers. A compromise plan was agreed upon, and one church with one altar was built, where both Germans and Irish worshipped, but at separate times.[46] The new church opened in 1872, and the order of events on the day of dedication indicated which way the parish was moving: the main sermon was given in English, and it was followed by a shorter address in German. During the next ten years events followed a similar pattern as the English-speaking parishioners continued to outnumber the Germans. In 1881 the first communion class numbered 225 English-speaking children and only 59 German candidates. The following year the archbishop officially recognized what had been taking place for two decades: the parish legally ceased to be a German national parish, and full parochial rights were given for all Catholics living in the area, regardless of nationality.[47]

The pastoral care of the Germans did not cease, but they no longer enjoyed the luxury of having their own national parish. Unlike Most Holy Redeemer, St. Alphonsus became a multi-ethnic parish, and when the people celebrated the feast of their parish patron in 1883, both the Irish and German flags decorated the main entrance of the church.[48] Such a scene would have been hard to envision in either Most Holy Redeemer or Transfiguration.

A principal reason for the transformation of St. Alphonsus from a national parish into a territorial or multi-ethnic parish was the population of the surrounding neighborhood. When the church was organized in 1847, the thinking was that the neighborhood would become another Little Germany. This did not happen, and as a result there were never enough Germans to ensure the continuation of an independent national parish. They never constituted more than 17 percent of the neighborhood population, and each census indicated that the Irish outnumbered them.[49] Moreover, the church did offer Catholic services, so Irish could attend and fulfill their religious obligations even though church law said that they should worship in English-language parishes. But no such churches existed in this area west of Broadway, and the closest possible choices, either St. Peter's or St. Joseph's, were each about one mile from St. Alphonsus. To attend these churches meant walking a long way, which presumably some people did before St. Alphonsus appeared on the scene. But after 1847 why suffer such inconvenience if there was a Catholic church down the street? The problem of course was that the new church was a German parish, and the Irish did not belong there. But in time the atmosphere changed, and the priests of the parish encouraged them to attend, and they accepted the invitation. The parish records indicated this clearly. During the years they were welcomed they frequented the parish, and the priest baptized them, married them, and buried them. When the welcome mat was withdrawn, there was almost a total absence of the Irish in this aspect of parochial life. Once the welcome was extended again in 1861, it was never retracted. Eventually St. Alphonsus became an Irish parish as well as a German parish, serving the needs of both groups.

In theory St. Alphonsus was to be only a German parish, but the ethnic composition of the neighborhood simply did not allow this legal stipulation to be actualized, since the population was changing in favor of the Irish and not the Germans. There was no Irish parish in the neighborhood to act as a safety valve to prevent the intermingling of the two groups. Nor did the Irish need another church, since they had found a home where the priests not only welcomed them but catered to them. For the German parishioners, however, the Irish presence was a problem; the church was founded specifically for them, and the intrusion of the Irish and the welcome they received threatened the continuance of the parish as an uniquely German institution. The persistence of the Germans in this struggle indicated their attachment to the national parish as a link with the old country. Eventually, with a decrease in their number and the passage of time, the Germans lost out to the Irish, but equally significant was the fact that it took so long for the Germans to succumb.

The national parish did not succeed in the Eighth Ward, and instead of reducing tension it caused dissension. But the concept did succeed in parts of the city where the concentration of specific immigrant groups was sufficiently large to support such ethnic institutions. At mid-century a mixed parish was more the exception than the norm, but it illustrated what problems an ethnically diverse urban population posed for the church. In later years, as new immigrants arrived in the city, the problem would surface again as neighborhoods changed; and mixed parishes would increase with each new wave of Catholic ethnics. In the case of St. Alphonsus the ethnic conflict did not destroy the parish. The church was able to tolerate such differences; beneath the unrest was a fundamental consensus centered around a common faith shared by both Irish and Germans. It was the Irish and not the church that the Germans resented, and to identify the Irish with Catholicism and eventually to despise both was a step that few Germans would take.

SIX

Handing on the Faith

$\mathbf{I}$N FUNCTIONING as a social institution the parish provided a center around which immigrants could gather. Parish societies gathered them together and enabled them to recapture and relive the spirit of the old country. As a religious institution the parish recreated the devotional life familiar to foreign Catholics. Popular saints, hymns, and devotions reinforced the link with the fatherland, and statues, paintings, and shrines turned the interiors of American churches into replicas of old-world churches. A German beer hall could evoke memories of the past with its colorful murals and nostalgic songs; a Catholic church was able to elicit the same sensible feelings through music and art. As both a place of worship and a center of social life the church was neces-

99

J.D.R.H.S.

sarily an educative institution. It sought to transmit the truths of Catholicism in a myriad of popular and informal ways. As an educative institution the church had also developed more formal methods of instruction: manuals of prayer, catechisms, and devotional literature explicitly sought to educate Catholics in the eternal truths; cheap editions of these works were widely available, and their popularity fostered the growth of many Catholic publishing houses.[1] But the most educative means that the church developed in the United States was the parochial school. It has become, for better of worse, the hallmark of American Catholicism and until recently was the principal institution for handing on the faith.

Throughout Catholic Europe education was a primary concern in the nineteenth century. As nations became more secularized Catholics struggled to protect their past investment in education and to insure their future educational freedom. During the pontificate of Pius IX the struggle intensified, as the pope waged a relentless campaign against the secularization of society.[2] James McMaster, a vocal crusader for Catholic schools, wrote that "this question of education now rings and vibrates throughout the whole Christian world. Everywhere it is the same cry. In France, in Germany, in Ireland, in America, it is the turning point of Catholic liberty."[3] In a society no longer Catholic, education remained one of the principal and time-honored means of transmitting the culture of Catholicism to the young. The separation of church and state jeopardized the educational enterprise, and its future looked bleak. The situation in the United States was substantially different from that in Europe, where altar and throne had been united for centuries in many countries. Despite its unique historical tradition the struggle for Catholic education in America became as critical as it was in Europe. The issue was so central to the life of the church that John Hughes could state that "in our age the question of education is the question of the Church."[4]

In searching for the reason why Catholic schools began when they did most authors point to the anti-Catholic bias present in public schools. Recent studies have not altered this general conclusion, but they have put it in better perspective, so that such a simple answer needs some qualifying explanations to be historically adequate.[5] Other influences, less tangible but no less real, also account for the origin of Catholic schools in the United States. One obvious element was the greater attention given to formal education in the early nineteenth century, a change having little to do with religion and more influenced by the changing role of the family in the sphere of education. In the colonial period the family played a major part in the education of children, but in the beginning of the nineteenth century the school assumed increasing importance, as it acted more and more *in loco parentis.*[6]

Education was not only an intellectual enterprise; it offered moral training as well. In his Twelfth Annual Report Horace Mann spoke for nineteenth-century educators in acknowledging that "our system earnestly inculcates all Christian morals; it founds its morals on the basis of religion."[7] Catholic spokesmen recognized the same dimension in education. "The spiritual concerns" of children were paramount, and teachers were selected not merely for their educational attributes but for their moral character as well.[8] "Religion," Father McClellan, pastor of Transfiguration Church, told a school assembly, "is the most important element in their [children's] education"; and the school affords them "the advantages of a solid secular education resting on a firm religious basis."[9] In an immigrant community, where the family frequently could not give this intellectual and moral training, and in a society that generally accepted this twofold aspect of education, the school naturally assumed greater importance. A child growing up in nineteenth-century America was to be intellectually and morally educated, and the school increasingly became the institution that provided this training.

The rise of the common school served to strengthen the importance of formal education in society, but at the same time it presented Catholics with a dilemma. Prior to the 1830s and 1840s Catholics were not confronted with a widespread system of public education, and formal education was often a denominational enterprise. But the emergence of the common school expanded the options available to Catholic parents. The problem, however, was that public schools transmitted a clearly Protestant culture.[10] As formal education became more ingrained in the national culture and Protestantism shaped the moral content of this education, Catholics confronted the dilemma of supporting the value of formal education if they were to be in step with the priorities of their adopted homeland

and avoiding the unorthodoxy of public schools if they were to be faithful Catholics.

Another reason for the origin of Catholic schools was the ethnic consciousness of the immigrant community. To assure their cultural survival in a new and hostile environment Catholic immigrants built up a community school system. Because the neighborhood school system often ignored their ethnic as well as their religious heritage, many newcomers turned away from public schools and organized their own institutions.[11] While it may be true that ethnicity was a factor in the organization of Catholic schools for some immigrant groups, this was certainly less true for the Irish. The cultural divergence between them and the Americans was not so great as with other groups: for one thing, they spoke the same language, which alone was an important bridge between the two cultures; furthermore, the Protestant Irish integrated into American society, and many Catholic Irish felt at home in public schools. For the Irish the more critical issue was not ethnicity but religion and the anti-Catholic bias of nativist America. For the Germans, however, ethnicity played a more important role in education because of the language barrier confronted in public schools. Coupled with religion, it helped to keep many of them out of public schools.[12]

The importance of formal education, the rise of the common school, and ethnic consciousness all helped to prepare the way for Catholic schools, but the alliance of public education and Protestantism became the decisive point on which the issue turned and ultimately forced Catholics to organize their own separate educational system. This conclusion is the central point that emerges from a study of the school controversy in New York City.

Catholics founded their first elementary school in New York in 1800. Periodically St. Peter's School received financial aid from the state, but this assistance ended in 1824.[13] In subsequent years more schools appeared, but they could scarcely accommodate the needs of the community. Almost all of them were located in damp church basements; the children were "so closely packed together that they hardly had room to move."[14] Since the schools no longer received aid from the state, and since many churches were in debt, adequate resources were absent, and parishes "were unable to provide fit school-rooms, nor in many cases could they afford to pay for competent teachers."[15] In addition to these free schools there were several private tuition academies patronized by the upper-class Catholics.[16] The situation was not promising: Catholics admitted that without financial relief many of the schools would have to close.[17]

Hope came to New York Catholics in 1840, when Governor William H. Seward in his annual address to the state legislature urged public financial support for Catholic schools.[18] Catholics reacted quickly to Seward's suggestion: they planned their strategy and petitioned the city government in February for a share of the common school fund. The main reason given in this petition was financial need, but as the debate intensified and positions hardened, the more fundamental issue of religion became the center of controversy.[19] The vicar general of the diocese, John Power, clearly stated the case in a lengthy letter published in the Catholic newspaper. After attacking the Protestant sectarianism of the city's public schools, he posed the question that would remain paramount throughout the century: "How can we think of sending our children to those schools in which every artifice is resorted to in order to reduce them from their religion?"[20] In a pamphlet distributed throughout the city the Catholic position was again clearly put forth:

A brief experience of the Public School system in the City of New York convinced us that we could not discharge our conscientious duty to our offspring, if we allowed them to be brought up under the influence of the irreligious principles on which these schools are conducted. . . .[21]

In September the Catholic community, now under the aggressive leadership of John Hughes, sent a second petition to the Common Council asking for financial aid and in detailed fashion continued to attack the Protestant sectarianism of the public schools.[22]

Few people could challenge the accuracy of the Catholic charges. The city's schools were under the direction of the Public School Society, and they provided a Protestant education. But the spirit of nativism was in the air, and the Protestant outcry against the Catholic petition was too strong to overcome. Defeated in the city, Catholics shifted their campaign to the state legislature, where they sought to break the monopoly that the Public School Society held on the city's schools. With the passage of the Maclay Bill in 1842 the control of the Public School Society was broken, and a new school system was established in New York City. But "Catholics were really no better off than they had been in 1840. Hughes had sought public funds for Catholic schools and he received instead public schools allegedly devoid of sectarianism."[23]

The struggle in New York had its precedents in Europe, where the same religious fervor was also evident. German Catholics were debating Protestant governments over freedom of education, and "the important issues concerning nineteenth century Irish education were defined by nineteenth century Irishmen as religious problems."[24] Catholics came to the United States conditioned by these experiences, and when the battle lines were drawn in New York, the emotional issue of religion served to intensify the educational controversy. John Hughes shrewdly exploited this link with the past and told an Irish gathering that "we are in the same situation as they were in Ireland from the Kildare Street Society, where for years they tried the fidelity of that people who never were recreant to their faith. The case is identically the same. . . ."[25] To preserve their religious heritage and remain loyal to their past, Catholic immigrants were forced to challenge the Protestant sectarianism of American schools. Their challenge defeated and the hope of public aid denied, they saw no other choice but to build their own school system; and with John Hughes at the helm, New York eventually became "the center of the parish school movement."[26]

The decision to organize a separate school system was a decisive break with the past. Prior to 1840 Catholic schools had operated in the city, but they were more the result of a particular parish's endeavors, not part of an organized plan. Catholics in New York and elsewhere had still not made the choice of a parochial school system. But the two-year debate changed the course of events in New York: under Hughes's leadership the church now began to wage an organized crusade to develop a separate system of education for Catholics. Any possible compromise with sectarian public schools had disappeared, and Catholics emerged from the controversy convinced "that the benefits of public education are not for us."[27] John Hughes, who had foreseen this development early in the struggle, wrote to the bishop of New Orleans: "Whether we shall succeed or not in getting our proportion of the public money, at all events the effort will cause an entire separation of our children from these schools,—and excite greater zeal on the part of our people for Catholic education."[28] In subsequent years the number of parochial schools multiplied, and the commitment to a separate school system gathered increasing support: by 1858 New York Catholics had built an educational system valued at more than two million dollars.[29]

The decision to organize a separate educational system, however, did not change the basic problem of supply and demand that the church had confronted for many years in New York. In fact the problem was to become more aggravated than ever with the sudden increase in immigration during the 1840s and 1850s. As a result, what at first glance appears as impressive gains in parochial education in the final analysis emerges as a prolonged struggle merely to keep pace with the record of the past.

In 1840 on the eve of the controversy an estimated five thousand children attended parochial schools; this represented 20 percent of the total school population. In succeeding years the church pushed its campaign for parochial schools, and within ten years after passage of the Maclay Bill some ten thousand students were enrolled in parochial schools; by 1865 the number swelled to sixteen thousand. Yet, the 1865 figure represented only 16 percent of the school population in New York, a decrease of 4 percent after twenty-five years of expansion.[30] During the 1850s the school system had expanded, adding eleven new schools and reaching a total of twelve thousand students by 1860. For the next five years expansion slowed considerably as the Civil War diverted people's energies to other concerns and a lingering illness forced John Hughes to abandon his leadership in church affairs.[31] After Hughes's death in 1864 and the end of the war a year later, the church resumed the educational campaign with a renewed spirit under new leadership. By 1870, 22,215 children were under instruction, and three new schools were in operation. The parochial school population had increased to a level of 19 percent of the city's school population, an increase of 1 percent over 1860 but a 1 percent decline since 1840. Thus, despite thirty years of vigorous campaigning, Catholic education could not keep up with the increase in population.[32]

TABLE 3. GROWTH OF CATHOLIC SCHOOLS

Year	Total school population[a]	Catholic school population	Percentage of total school population	Common school population	Percentage of parishes with schools
1840	24,673	5,000	20	19,673	—[b]
1842	28,671	4,000	14	24,671	54
1853	54,061	10,000	18	44,061	46
1860	67,050	12,000	18	55,050	74
1865	102,674	16,000	16	86,674	75
1870	116,884	22,215	19	94,669	68

Sources: William Bourne, History of the Public School Society of the City of New York (New York, 1870), pp. 171 and 528; Thomas Boese, Public Education in the City of New York (New York, 1869), pp. 129 and 221; William's N.Y. Annual Register, 1840, p. 336; Freeman's Journal, 2 July 1842 and 4 August 1853; Metropolitan Record, 28 July 1860; Catholic Directory, 1870, pp. 86–87; and Annual Report of the Board of Education of New York City, 1870, pp. 93 and 165.

[a] The figures represent average attendance.

[b] In 1840 all parishes had some type of basement school or academy.

In the final analysis, then, the decision to organize a separate school system did not greatly change the record of the past. Progress had been made—schoolhouses instead of cellar classrooms, better trained teachers, more numerous teaching religious orders—but substantial improvement was also evident in public schools. The problem was that the Catholic community was expanding too rapidly for the church to keep pace, and it was hard-pressed to match the achievements of 1840. In 1865 three out of four parishes had schools, but even such a high percentage of support for parochial education could not alter the basic problem of too many children to educate. Parish populations were very large, and one schoolhouse was no more able to serve the needs of a parochial community than a single church. Estimates of the percentage of Catholic children who attended their parish schools vary from 17 percent in 1858 to 33 percent in 1867.[33] One reason for such low participation was that the demand far outdistanced the supply in the neighborhood community. There were just too many children to be educated and too few schools to undertake the task. The church had made a decision in 1842 that it found difficult to implement, and despite the protestations of the clergy, public education remained a viable alternative for many Catholics.

Insufficient facilities, however, do not entirely explain the relatively low percentage of Catholics in the parochial school system. Another reason was that, with the emergence of the ward school in 1843, Catholics were able to attend a public school that no longer threatened their religious beliefs. The editor of the Catholic newspaper wrote in 1845 that "many of our common schools are filled with Catholic children."[34] Four years later he estimated that "more than one-half, and if we are not misinformed, more than three-fourths of all the children attending them [ward schools] are of Catholic parents."[35] Why so many Catholics chose this option was clearly illustrated in the Sixth Ward, the home of Transfiguration parish.

Father Varela was an ardent supporter of Catholic education. He had come to New York with a background of considerable educational experience in Cuba, where he had written articles on education as well as a textbook for Cuban schools.[36] As an educator it was natural for Varela to focus his concerns around his immigrant parish. By 1828 he had opened a school in the parish, which, following the custom of the day, was a private school that charged tuition for various services. Spelling and reading cost $1.50 a quarter; spelling, reading, and writing cost $2; and the full course of instruction, including arithmetic, grammar, and geography was $2.50 a quarter. The boys and girls, who came from the level of society that was able to afford the cost of private education, were instructed separately by lay men and women. The profits of the school were to go to the poor children of the parish and helped to finance the Sunday School. Little else is known about the school, and no record of its existence remains after 1830.[37]

When the parish moved to Chambers Street in 1836 a school opened in the church basement. Like its predecessor, it was a private pay school. It was also short-lived, and by 1851 a parishioner was able to remark that there was "not the ghost of a day school—free or not free—about Transfiguration Church."[38]

The reasons for Varela's lack of enduring success were not hard to find. The lack of religious teaching orders necessitated the employment of lay teachers, and competent teachers were not readily available. When the ward school opened in 1843, many new teaching positions were created, and competition for good teachers was especially keen. Catholics were not adverse to teaching in the ward schools, and it was quite common for talented lay people "to begin teaching in the parochial school and then transfer to the public school because of the prospect of advancement and financial security."[39] Coupled with the short supply of teachers was the attraction that the local ward school had for Catholics. These schools were supervised by a committee elected by the people, and the list of board members in the Sixth Ward read like a roll call for the Hibernian society and included two trustees of the parish.[40] Many teachers were also Catholic, and the Protestant Bible was not read in school.[41] Thus, the religious sensibilities of Catholics were protected in the neighborhood public school, and parents could send their children off to school and not worry about them becoming Protestants. Many parents did just that, and in 1843 the ward school was already reported to be "filled with Catholic children."[42] Similar situations existed in other neighborhoods, and there was no denying the fact that many Catholic children attended public schools; in some instances parochial schools shut down because the competition from public schools was too great.[43]

In 1856 the educational scene changed in Transfiguration. Financially solvent for the first time in many years, the parish could afford to build a schoolhouse. The Sisters of Charity took charge of educating the young girls, and in 1857 the Christian Brothers arrived to take charge of the boys. The total enrollment that year was five hundred. For the first few years the school charged tuition, but by 1862 the school was free, and the enrollment had increased to twelve hundred.[44] But the school was still not able to meet the needs of all Catholics in the neighborhood, and many continued to attend the local ward schools, where fear of losing one's faith was not a major concern.

The question of finances also posed a problem for the parochial school. One obvious reason for the demise of Transfiguration school prior to 1856 was the financial indebtedness of the parish. It simply could not afford the cost of operating a school. Many parochial schools charged tuition, and "poverty prevented [some children] from receiving the benefits of education" in these schools.[45] Redeemer parish supported a school from 1844. Classes were held in the church for two years, and then a schoolhouse was built. By 1850 enrollment had reached five hundred; nine years later a new school was built, and attendance increased to fifteen hundred and fifty in 1864.[46] From the very beginning the school had charged tuition, ranging from twenty-five cents to fifty cents a month. Many families were not able to pay this fee, and the School Sisters of Notre Dame, who had been operating the school since 1853, complained about the delinquency of parents. Eventually they had to insist on the payment of money owed, with the result that some families were forced to remove their children from school.[47] The tuition was nominal, but it was still more than some families could afford, and thus the free public school obviously attracted German Catholic children.

A further explanation for the lack of Catholic participation in parochial schools was that not all Catholics supported the idea of a separate school system. Even in 1852 the Catholic hierarchy still disagreed on the wisdom of establishing and supporting a separate school system: some hoped for a share of public funds, and others wanted to modify the public school to make it acceptable to Catholics.[48] There was little doubt where John Hughes stood on the issue, but not all the clergy and laity in New York were as adamant in their position as Hughes. The noted convert to Catholicism, Orestes Brownson, spoke for some Catholics: he favored the public school system, for he believed that the parochial school only tended to reinforce the separatist mentality of Catholics.[49] Some priests supported this position and added that churches, not schools, were the most pressing need in New York.[50] Financially the parish school was a drain on the church; one priest, exasperated with his debts, closed the school and marched the children to the local public school, where he arranged for their admission.[51] Moreover, some people, Catholic in name only, would not have been that concerned over the necessity of a Catholic school and would have had little inhibition in sending their children to public schools. That there was division in the community was clear, given the debate that ensued in New York in later years. Catholic novelists also entered the debate and pushed the necessity of a Catholic education with great fervor.[52] It would be difficult to explain such vigorous defense of the system if all Catholics supported it with equal enthusiasm.

The more numerous Irish had spearheaded the educational campaign in New York, and the German press supported these efforts. German Catholics also had signed the petition for public funds in 1840, but their participation in the ensuing debate was marginal.[53] On the parish level, six of the eight German churches in 1865 were supporting parochial schools housed in separate school buildings; the other two parishes, Assumption and St. Boniface, offered religious education classes in the church basement, more a Sunday School type of operation than a full-fledged elementary education. Unlike the Irish, the Germans faced the problem of language. The resolution of this problem in Most Holy Redeemer parish pointed to the dilemma.

The German language represented the old culture and brought to life the memories of the past. This was evident in the parish devotional life, and the school was one institution that transmitted the cultural heritage to the children of immigrants. The problem, however, was the necessity of knowing English in the United States. Parents were eager for the social and economic advancement of their children and recognized the importance of language in the process; as a result many families in the neighborhood sent their children to the public school to learn English, despite the clergy's warning of the danger to faith and morals in such a choice.[54] To counteract this tendency, English-language instruction was introduced in the parish school a few years after it opened. By 1853 classes were taught in both German and English, and bilingual instruction became the pattern of education in most German parochial schools.[55] Those Catholics who attended public schools also had the opportunity to preserve the German language in the course of their education, since the ward schools included German-language instructors.[56] Such an arrangement satisfied the bulk of German immigrants; for Catholics in Most Holy Redeemer parish it was especially congenial, since the German instructor in the neighborhood schools was Peter Lux, a distinguished member of the parish. He had previously taught in the parochial school, and while he taught classes in the Eleventh Ward schools, he continued to act as a substitute teacher in Redeemer school.[57] The bilingual approach to the problem of preserving the German language resolved the dilemma, and thus the issue of language did not become a major problem for New York Germans. In later decades and in other sections of the country it did become a problem when state legislatures sought to curtail the use of German in schools; predictably, Germans rose up in protest, and the issue became entangled in partisan politics.[58] But in the 1850s what New York Germans wanted most was for their children to learn English as well as German, and the schools responded to their desires.

Lack of facilities, the appeal of religiously neutral public schools, insufficient finances, and a degree of opposition to the idea all limited the success of the parochial school. Yet, it did continue as an important part of the church's work in the city. Its objective was clear: to transmit the values of the Catholic culture to younger generations and to reinforce the more informal education offered in the church and the home. As an ethnic institution it also aimed at preserving a national heritage which was in danger of being lost in a new environment. It strengthened the cohesion of the group and was another barrier separating Catholics from surrounding society. In time the ethnicity of the school began to diminish, and it became an increasingly American institution. The transformation was already underway in the ante-bellum period and became so evident in the closing decades of the century that some Catholics criticized the schools for being too similar to public schools.[59]

While the elementary school movement was gaining momentum, a similar revival was taking place in the area of secondary education. In 1850 thirty Catholic secondary schools for men were in operation; sixteen years later the number had doubled. A similar expansion was taking place among schools for females; in a single decade, 1840–50, fifty-six new Catholic secondary schools for girls opened their doors. These institutions were concentrated in the cities, and unlike the parish school, they were not organized according to ethnic allegiance.[60] They appealed to a citywide population and were supported by the rising Catholic middle class. It was unquestionably an upper-class educational system and tended to separate Catholic adolescents along class lines. Like the parish school, the private secondary school represented the church's response to the heterogeneous character of the city. It illustrated the cultural pluralism of urban Catholicism and reinforced the separation of Catholics from Protestant society, as well as drawing lines of division within the Catholic community.

As in the parochial school movement, John Hughes was the central figure in the rise of Catholic secondary education in New York. In 1840 only two select academies for girls were in operation. In 1864 New York Catholics were supporting three men's colleges chartered to grant degrees, three boarding schools for girls, a boys' academy, and numerous day academies for females. Each of these institutions was under the supervision of religious orders, and except in the case of the Sisters of Charity, Hughes was instrumental in obtaining their services and establishing their schools.[61]

The first men's college in New York was St. John's College, located about twelve miles from the city in the village of Fordham on a 106-acre tract of land purchased by Hughes in 1839. Modeled on the college seminary of Mount St. Mary's, in Emmitsburg, Maryland, the college was founded to train men for the priesthood and other professions. It opened in September 1841, and within a few months forty students were boarding at the college; four years later Hughes transferred control of the college to the Jesuits, and the first commencement took place on 15 July 1845.[62] In 1847 the Jesuits founded a second men's college, St. Francis Xavier, a day school located in the city on West Sixteenth Street. By 1864 St. John's was educating 250 men, and St. Francis Xavier had an enrollment of 450.[63]

Hughes described the students who attended St. John's as "young men of the wealthier families"; the annual fee of two hundred dollars for board and tuition confirmed his judgment. At the same time he stated the main principle operative in nineteenth-century Catholic education. In his opinion the school was necessary lest these young men be "exposed to lose their faith by being educated in dangerous intercourse with Protestantism."[64] The cost of education at St. Francis Xavier was considerably less than at St. John's—fifty dollars a year—and the school attracted students living in the city and its environs, though some did come from out of state.[65] Both schools sought to prepare men for professional careers; an observation about St. Francis College echoed this desire: "may we see its alumni sprinkling every land, the flowers of the bar, the first in the medical professions and the pride of the priesthood."[66] This same goal was written into the charter of Manhattan College, the third men's school founded during the episcopacy of Hughes. Established in 1849 under the direction of the Christian Brothers, Manhattan sought "to give young men who possess the proper qualifications the opportunity to broaden their intellectual horizons by increased culture, a refinement of morals, mind and taste and in this way to prepare them in a suitable manner for the various professions."[67]

One school representative of the upper class of female students was the Academy of the Sacred Heart founded by the Society of the Sacred Heart. Through the initiative of Hughes the society had settled in New York and opened the academy in the city in 1841. Six years later the school moved to the spacious grounds of the Jacob Lorillard estate in Manhattanville. The Madames, as they were commonly known, had a tradition of educating women "of the higher class"; the prospectus of the school confirmed that "the education of young ladies of the higher class [was] the special object of this institute."[68] The annual board and tuition was $250, and despite this high fee, 264 girls were under instruction in 1864.[69]

Catholic support for separate elementary and secondary schools developed at a time of transition in American education. Rather than back the popular movement for public education, Catholics were forced to make a choice for their own denominational schools, and in implementing this decision, they established a program of education very similar to that of the public schools. This similarity was especially evident in the curriculum offered in Catholic institutions.

Colleges for men pursued a classical education, and young ladies were instructed in the "habits of politeness, industry, neatness and order."[70] Parochial schools were also very similar to their public school rivals. In fact the spirit of competition seemed to demand that the Catholic school should not suffer in comparison with public schools, and the tendency to imitate public education eventually led to the Americanization of the parochial school.[71]

The similarity in Catholic and public education was most noticeable in the use of textbooks. Parochial schools used textbooks popular at the time; and Noah Webster's *Spelling Book* and Lindley Murray's *English Grammar* were standard items in both Catholic and public schools.[72] But the Protestant nature of public education nurtured textbooks that were anti-Catholic, and the hierarchy urged the publication of Catholic texts. Little was done to meet their request, and it was only after the parochial school movement was underway in the 1840s that Catholic textbooks began to appear in significant numbers.[73]

Textbooks designed for Catholics focused on areas of study that involved religious issues or interpretations. To offset the use of Protestant-inspired history texts, Catholic authors published histories that presented a Catholic interpretation of events. European authors wrote many of these texts, and they gave a favorable Catholic interpretation to such debated issues as the Reformation, the Inquisition, and the early Christian centuries. A popular text compiled by an American, Martin J. Kearney, was entitled *A Compendium of Ancient and Modern History*. Published in 1845, it went through thirty editions in twenty-two years.[74] It began with the biblical creation of the world and traced the history of man down to the nineteenth century, emphasizing the ancient and modern periods. Included in the text was a brief history of the United States, as well as an appendix containing the Declaration of Independence and the Constitution. Bible histories written by European authors were also popular and counteracted the Protestant interpretation of biblical history.

The most popular textbook was the catechism, the keystone for religious education in elementary and secondary schools. Of an estimated 374 Catholic textbooks published between 1764 and 1865, ninety-nine (27 percent) were catechisms; from 1866 to 1900 the catechism continued to be the most popular text, with 134 more editions published.[75] The catechisms, which presented the truths of Catholicism in concise fashion, were strikingly similar in content. Many were of European origin and were translated and published in the United States. Others compiled by American clergy were based on European catechisms that flourished after the Council of Trent. The most popular catechisms in the ante-bellum period included the text of Bishop Richard Challoner of London, *The Catholic Christian Instructed*. Written in 1737 and first published in the United States in 1786, it went through twelve editions by 1865.[76] Challoner's catechism was an apologetic defense of Catholicism, and though its style would have hardly recommended it to elementary school children, it became a useful handbook for clergy and teachers in answering standard objections against the dogmas of the church. The catechism of Bishop James Butler, of Cashel, Ireland, written in

1775, was another favorite text; its popularity can be measured by its substantial influence as late as 1884, when the hierarchy was composing an official American catechism.[77] Butler's catechism followed the brief question-and-answer format and was very suitable for young children. Individual dioceses also published their own catechisms; one adopted in many places was a catechism approved by Bishop John Carroll of Baltimore, *A Short Abridgement of Christian Doctrine*. The Catechism of the Council of Trent was also in circulation, and it went through seven American editions by 1865.[78] German-language catechisms were in demand; eleven editions were in circulation by the end of the Civil War. The sixteenth-century catechism of the Jesuit reformer Peter Canisius was popular and provided the framework for the German-American catechism of Bishop John Neumann of Philadelphia. Neumann edited two catechisms, the *Kleiner Katechismus*, a small thirty-two-page manual, and *Katolischer Katechismus*, a larger version in 180 pages. They were widely used in German parishes, and by 1889 the small pocket-size catechism had gone through thirty-eight editions.[79] The catechism that eventually commanded the widest popularity in German parishes was *Deharbe's Catechism*. Written by a German Jesuit, Joseph Deharbe, in 1847, it was used throughout Germany and was imported to the United States; both English and German versions were in use in dioceses across the country.[80]

The catechism was the most widely circulated Catholic book. The dogmas of Catholicism were drilled into parochial school students for thirty minutes each day, and public school children memorized the catechism in Sunday School classes. Catechisms with a more thorough presentation of the faith were aimed at adult readers and teachers, while smaller ones that sold for as little as two cents appealed to younger children. Manuals to aid teachers and parents in catechetical instruction also appeared, and anecdotal storybooks were available to enliven the presentation of the catechism's dry doctrinal material.[81]

The content of the catechisms scarcely varied. They contained the basic truths of Roman Catholicism and reflected the popular uniformity of Catholic dogma after the Council of Trent. They transmitted to children the faith of their fathers and were a strong link with the old country. Irish parents grew up with Butler's catechism in Ireland, and their American-born children learned the faith from the same book. Deharbe's catechism was a standard work in Germany, and the children of immigrants memorized the same questions and answers. Each catechism generally included prayers and devotions, and children learned the same prayers at home and at school that their parents cherished. The catechism was an institution in itself, a means of handing on the faith, and more than any other text it illustrated the connection of American Catholicism with the church in Europe. The European origin of the catechism naturally excluded any particular American style, and scarcely any reference was made to American society. The faith was the same on both sides of the Atlantic. A letter to the editor of a Catholic newspaper emphasized this point: "Can we attribute to children in America those sentiments with which we were want to be filled in good old Catholic Ireland?" the correspondent asked. And his answer was: "I say we can. They have the same faith that their fathers bled and died for in days of yore. We have changed the clime, but not the faith, and as long as our children are well instructed in their religion, we can attribute to them the same sentiments in America."[82] Though the catechism evidenced little influence of American culture on Roman Catholicism, it did present an interpretation of human life that is worth noting.

God made man to love and serve Him in this world so that he might be happy with Him in heaven. This was a basic principle in Catholic faith and often the first theme treated in the catechism. The salvation of one's soul was the highest law, and one learned the truths of religion so that he might achieve this eternal goal. The Catholic church was represented as the one true church—it offered the only path to heaven, since outside of the church there was no salvation. The church thus acquired an aura of importance in man's life that is difficult for twentieth-century man to imagine. Its laws appeared as important as the ten commandments, and it was to rule man's life from the cradle to the grave. Man lived in this world with an eye fixed on another kingdom, and he was instructed to remember frequently death, judgment, heaven, and hell.[83] Children were told: "Look up to Heaven! if you are firm and true; in serving God its joys are all for you."[84] This was the ideal presented to Catholics and the goal they were to strive for. As a religious institution, the church sought to achieve this end in everything it did, and as an educative institution, it sought to hand on this piety from generation to generation. Catholic histories reinforced this mentality, and readers used in schools extolled the uniqueness of the church and the necessary salvation of one's soul.

One aspect of Catholicism that appeared in some catechisms was an anti-Protestant tone. This was very minimal and was not always present in the manuals, but it was visible in some catechisms used in the United States, and the Protestant environment of the country naturally fostered it.[85] A standard presentation argued that the Roman Catholic church was the one true church and had never ceased to exist; Protestantism, however, was less than three hundred years old and thus was not the true church of Christ.[86] When they were taught the sacrament of matrimony, Catholics were told to avoid marriage with non-Catholics; the reasons given for this were the danger of losing the faith or of becoming indifferent and the difficulty of educating the children as Catholics.[87] This bias appeared more frequently in fictional stories, especially in Catholic novels written in the United States.[88] In emphasizing the divine nature of the church, the catechism treated the inadequacies of Protestantism only in passing, if at all. But the conclusion was evident: the one true church was the Roman Catholic church.

Another key to understanding the Catholic mentality fostered in the nineteenth century was the school reader. The first Catholic reader published in the United States appeared in 1837, and the number multiplied in later years. The impulse behind these texts was to offset the anti-Catholic tone of readers used in American schools. The readers did not attack Protestant beliefs but sought to present "the facts of religion as the best refutation of its adversaries."[89] For this reason they included brief sections on the history of the church; in addition to history they included selections on science and geography, as well as poetry and moral lessons. The readers sought to increase the student's vocabulary and to introduce him to "correct and elegant speaking."[90] Moral and religious lessons celebrated the virtues that students were to develop and offered heroic Catholic saints as models to imitate. The authors of the selections were most often European Catholics and included such personages as Fenelon, Massillon, and Chateaubriand. Readings from

Milton, Dante, and Shakespeare were also included, as well as the writings of Byron and Manzoni.[91]

The Christian Brothers of Ireland edited one series of readers used in American schools, and the Irish flavor of these books was pervasive. They featured selections on Irish history, Irish saints, and Irish virtues; one of the most popular selections was an essay entitled "Character of the Irish Peasantry." The portrait of the Irish peasant as sharp of wit, shrewd, hospitable, heroic, just, and cheerful, however romantic it might have been, could not have failed to instill a sense of pride in impressionable children.[92] Other readers were less ethnically oriented and placed more emphasis on religious essays.

One novel feature of these early readers was the obvious goal of instilling in the students loyalty and pride in America. Despite the discrimination directed against Catholics, the parochial school appeared intent in fostering a sense of patriotism. The Christian Brothers' reader offered speeches by Patrick Henry, Daniel Webster, and George Washington that emphasized the glory of the American Revolution. The wise sayings of Poor Richard were also featured, as well as selections narrating the early history of American Catholicism. One reader had an essay by Daniel Webster on the "Duties of the American citizen," in which the author said of Webster that "as an orator and statesman, the New World has as yet produced no man greater than he."[93] History texts reinforced this sense of national pride, and Catholic songbooks did not fail to include patriotic hymns in their repertoire.[94] Like most schools, Transfiguration held an annual exhibition to demonstrate to parents the skills of their children. These assemblies were decidedly Irish and American. Students recited Irish poetry, and *Columbia The Gem of the Ocean* and *Yankee Doodle* were perennial favorites. The American flag decorated the platform and visibly emphasized the recently-acquired loyalty of immigrant Catholics.[95]

A sense of patriotism and fidelity to Catholic tradition were two principal features of Catholic education. For many years Catholics had defended their loyalty to American democracy, and when nativist attacks increased, they argued their case more vigorously. But the Protestant heritage of the United States was too pervasive to be ignored, which fact inevitably compelled Catholics to withdraw from the mainstream of society and form their own educational system. The keystone of this enterprise was religion. It sought to transmit the culture of Catholicism to a new generation and to prevent the loss of faith in a hostile Protestant society. This was not a new experience for Irish immigrants, who had battled the Orangemen for centuries; and German newcomers came from a tradition that still bore the scars of religious wars. In the United States the truths of Catholicism were handed down to the children of these immigrants, and they grew up in a church that sought to influence every moment of their existence.

In educating and forming the children the church instructed them in the dangers of Protestantism. Every type of literature dwelled upon this theme, some more explicitly than others, and Catholics built up a wall of separation between themselves and Protestant society. They were armed with an arsenal of truths to defend their faith; and the worst calamity that could befall a family was that believing parents would be left with unbelieving children. An obituary notice in the Catholic press on the long life of an Irish Catholic mother underlined the importance of handing on the faith: Mrs. Manahan had raised ten children, and it was obviously to her credit that "not one to this day has ever died, or now lives out of the belief and practice of their mother and grandmother's faith."[96]

Coupled with this intense religious commitment was an ethnic allegiance nourished in national parish schools. Irish children learned the glories of Ireland's saints and scholars, and German children were urged to cherish the religious traditions of the old country. The German language was passed on to succeeding generations, and children prayed in the same way and with the same words as their parents. Like religion, with which it was so intimately connected, ethnicity tended to divide Catholic immigrants from the world around them. Though the distance of time would weaken the ethnic consciousness of the group, religion remained as a wall of separation in Protestant America.

Despite its obvious separatist tendencies and its limited success, the educational system developed in New York and elsewhere was an outstanding accomplishment for an immigrant community. In less than a generation Catholics had established an enduring institution that served the needs of the poor, as well as those of the rising middle class. But education was only one aspect of the church's apostolate; other needs had also to be met. The poverty of Catholics and the disruption of urban life called for a benevolent apostolate that would make poverty more comfortable and urban living more humane for immigrant newcomers. The church's achievements in this area were no less striking than its achievements in the area of education.

SEVEN

Social Catholicism

I N THE ANTE-BELLUM PERIOD the spirit of reform was in the air. Americans were challenging traditional institutions of society; and such issues as abolition, prison reform, the role of women, public education, and evangelical theology made up the galaxy of reforms that absorbed people's energies. At mid-century Catholics were alienated from these movements of reform and looked upon them with a great deal of suspicion. They appeared to be only American versions of Red republicanism, communism, or socialism, and the strong Protestant tone of many reform movements only made them more suspect. The nativist crusade reinforced these suspicions, and the church remained aloof from the arena of reform; in adopting this position it demonstrated how alienated it was from the rest of American society. This did not mean that Catholics ignored social problems, but it did indicate that the problems and their solutions would be defined in terms of the Catholic tradition, not in terms of the American reform movement.[1]

Catholics defined social reform in a very traditional and conservative manner: it was basically carrying out the corporal works of mercy and was directed toward the poor, the hungry, and the homeless. It was a crusade of charity and not one of social change. The emphasis was on bettering the lot of the individual, with the guiding principle always being the salvation of one's soul. The goal was to make the situation of the oppressed more humane—a stepping stone to salvation, not a stumbling block.

This view of social reform was rooted in Catholic theology and was judged by Catholics to be antithetical to reform movements abroad in America. "Social evils which afflict mankind are the result of Adam's sin," one priest wrote, and "all reform, properly understood, begins with a return to religion and the Church."[2] Orestes Brownson further developed the Catholic position:

> The Church teaches us to rely on moral power, the grace of God, and individual conscience. She demands the intervention of government only in the material order, for the maintenance or vindication of justice; what lies entirely in the moral or spiritual order, she regards as no proper object of governmental suppression. So of great moral and philanthropic objects. She does not call upon the government to enact them, and make it a legal offense to neglect them. Hence, she leaves the care of the poor, the provision for orphans, emancipation of slaves and similar good works, to the charity of the faithful, without calling upon the government to exact them as a matter of justice.[3]

In his opinion the American reform movement led to either despotism or anarchy; charity on the individual level was the only true avenue of reform. Society was a static, stratified social system, and man could not alter it. The charity of Catholics thus was able to adapt itself to capitalism as readily as it had to feudalism. This conservative view of society and social reform was the tradition that immigrants brought with them to the United States.

Irish immigrants came from a land where poverty, unemployment, and hunger were every day occurrences; the peasant was idealized and not disparaged. Confronted with such widespread suffering, the response of the church was, in the words of one priest to his hungry flock, "to have confidence in God."[4] A priest could comfort a dying man with the assurance that "when one has had as little happiness as you have had in this world, and when one has known how to profit by its miseries, one has nothing to fear in the next."[5] The Irish peasant was sustained by a religion that was little concerned with social reform, and by keeping his sights on the world beyond, he could find solace in the hardships of the earthly kingdom. Poverty, self-denial, and resignation to God's will were Christian ideals aptly suited for a peasant society, and Irish clergy were trained to reinforce this world view.[6]

German immigrants brought with them a similar tradition. During the first half of the century Catholics in Germany evidenced little concern for social questions. As in Ireland, the principal task of the church was to renew Catholic life in a changing social order. Political questions were paramount. Social problems were accepted as part of the divine plan, and no one could change the law of God. Unlike in Ireland, Catholicism in Germany eventually acquired a social awareness through the reform movement spearheaded by the bishop of Mainz, Emmanuel von Ketteler. But as late as 1869 von Ketteler was able to describe the German clergy as having little interest in the fate of the working classes "because they are ignorant of the existence and the impact of the dangers which lurk in these threatening social conditions, because they have failed to size up the character and the breadth of the social question, finally because they have no conception of possible remedies."[7] This was the prevailing tradition that clergy and laity brought with them to the United States, and it influenced the social thought of American Catholics until late in the nineteenth century.

The church's opposition to American reform movements underlined the foreignness of Catholics. Nativist attacks emphasized this aspect of Catholicism, and Catholics were forced to counterattack such charges by demonstrating their compatibility with the American system. This was the principal social issue confronting Catholics in the ante-bellum period, and the debate against Protestants and nativists left little time to examine the church's attitude toward the presence of human suffering in the New World.[8] In fact, why should one question the hallowed tradition of Christian charity that had worked so well in the past? American Protestants were moving along the same traditional path, and Catholics had little time or little reason to question its validity. What worked in the old country was sure to work in America, since it was God's plan to have rich and poor live together so that one could practice almsgiving and the other patience and resignation.

Few people dared to question this divine order. Archbishop Hughes emphasized this perception of society to a Baltimore audience:

> To every class and condition [the church] assigned its own peculiar range of Christian obligations: To sovereigns and legislators, those of justice and mercy in the enactment and execution of laws. To the rich, moderation in enjoyment and liberality toward the poor. To the poor, patience under their trials and affection toward their wealthier brethren. Toward all, the common obligation of loving one another, not in work, but in deed.[9]

God had permitted poverty, and the church was the protector of the poor; they were representatives of Christ, and Catholics were reminded that "to extend a generous and charitable hand to a fellow creature in distress is one of the most exalting and noble acts of man."[10]

This interpretation of society was echoed in the pulpit, the lecture hall, and the press. The salvation of one's soul was the highest law, and "as for the rest, though you should be reduced to the lowest condition; though you should be stripped of all your worldly possessions, all this is nothing if you arrive at length at the happy term of salvation."[11] For Father Jeremiah Cummings, a distinguished New York priest, who lectured on the topic of social reform, social reform was synonymous with spiritual reform, and only the Catholic church could achieve the necessary social reform, since it gave men supernatural powers and a supernatural motive.[12] The press also reinforced this attitude. The *Catholic World* was a progressive publication, alert to the social problems of urban life, but its outlook was very traditional: Christianity was the foundation of society;

without religion, society was doomed to failure. The journal urged Catholics to give more attention to the city's poor through "practical benevolence" (in this context "practical benevolence" meant alms-giving and establishing institutions for the sick and the poor).[13] The practice of good works, long a Christian tradition, still remained the fundamental approach to human suffering for nineteenth-century Catholics. If they exercised such charity, poverty, in the words of John Hughes, "would never have existed at all."[14]

Catholic fiction also idealized poverty and faithful resignation to God's will. Anna Dorsey wrote *The Oriental Pearl* in 1848 to prove that "confidence in the mercy and wisdom of God is the best preservative from temptation and despair." Following the fortunes of three German Catholic immigrants in the United States, the author emphasized the benevolent providence of God and the need to accept His holy will. "There are troubles our Good Lord permits to follow us," the father told his daughter, "so that our faith may be tried," and as long as the poor immigrant has his religion, nothing else matters because "a poor man's religion is a mine of inestimable wealth."[15] One of the more popular Catholic novels was *Willy Burke; or, The Irish Orphan in America,* written by Mary Sadlier in 1850.[16] Like most Catholic fiction at that time, it was a moralistic exhortation written to support the Catholic religion in Protestant America. Willy Burke gained success by keeping his mind fixed on God and remaining faithful to his religion. As long as he had trials to bear, he could not forget God; and trusting in Him was the way to sustain the sufferings of this world.

Catholics could emerge from poverty through hard work and fidelity to God. Such attitudes merited their reward in heaven as well as on earth. Because he remained faithful to his religion, Willy Burke inherited five thousand dollars from his employer, who was converted to Catholicism through Willy's example.[17] Other Catholic novelists, writing for both German and Irish readers, reiterated this theme of a moral life meriting material rewards. The main characters in these novels were often poor Catholics, but poverty was scarcely a hindrance to leading a good moral life. It was a way of life imitative of Jesus, who had "led a most holy life, in poverty and suffering";[18] his followers could expect no less, and they were continually reminded of how difficult it was for a rich man to enter heaven. For the poor the key to success was to persevere in one's state in life, trust in God, and possibly reap a tangible reward for living a good life.

Readers used in Catholic schools further reinforced the ideal of resigning oneself to God's will and to one's position in society. Tales depicted the heroic resignation of early Christian martyrs and other saints. Additional stories repeated this theme to the degree that acceptance of God's will became the singular trademark of the faithful Christian. Children were exhorted to be "completely resigned to God's will in all things."[19] A songbook summed up this theme in the following manner: "The blessing sent to win my love, O Lord, I freely take;/the trial sent my faith to prove, I bear for thy dear sake."[20]

Such were the ideals presented to Catholic immigrants. They reiterated the tradition of the old country and never sought to challenge the economic system. A faithful Catholic was told to accept his condition in life as part of God's will, and his focus was to be a world different from the one in which he lived. Such an attitude fostered a brand of religion that was socially complacent and unquestioning, but such a conceptualization of man's place in society did not remain isolated in the realm of ideas. What Catholics did reflected what the church taught, and the parish was the principal location where such ideals were put into practice.

A central figure in the social apostolate of the parish was the priest. Father Varela, pastor of Transfiguration, came to New York with the reputation of one "exclusively dedicated to the good of others."[21] While in New York, he lived up to this reputation. He visited the sick and poor at all hours of the day. His labors took him to quarantined ships; and during the cholera epidemic of 1832 it was said that he "lived in the hospitals."[22] Soon stories began to circulate about his unselfish work with the poor and sick. Tales recounted how he gave his clothes, his watch, and even his bedding to the poor who often gathered outside his window to receive such gifts. His friends gave him a watch to replace one that he had given away, but in a few days it was gone; later it was found in the hands of a poor parishioner ready to pawn it. While visiting the sick he often gave away the clothes on his back. When he ran out of clothes, he would call upon his friends to replenish his supply. People claimed that he gave away everything he owned.[23]

Another priest in the parish gained a similar reputation. Father Alexander Mupiatti worked at Transfiguration for only five years, but when he died in 1846, large crowds followed his body to the cemetery, and in later years people remembered him as a saint. An historical epitaph noted that "his day was divided between the confessional and the bedside of the sick . . . and all flocked to him for advice and direction."[24]

The Redemptorist priests carried on the charitable apostolate in the German neighborhood. They visited the sick and administered the sacraments to the dying; in addition to their parochial responsibilities, they also cared for German Catholics housed in the city's public asylums on Blackwell's Island. For a time they also ministered to the needs of German children in the asylum located on Randall's Island.[25] Unlike Varela, however, no priest in Redeemer parish gained exceptional notoriety for working with the poor. Several of them died from illnesses contracted while visiting the sick, but such unselfish service appeared to be commonplace among the Redemptorists.[26]

The individual efforts of the clergy illustrated the traditional approach of Catholic benevolence. Religion was the one avenue of reform in society, and charity was the key to such reform. Accepting poverty as a given condition of human existence, they desired to reduce the level of suffering by visiting the sick, comforting the dying, and clothing the naked. This concern for one's neighbor was also organized and channeled into parish societies, which provided an outlet for the charity of parishioners, in the hope of improving the lot of the poor.

Transfiguration Church had charitable organizations for both men and women. The Ladies Society of Charity was the principal female organization, and as the name suggests, they sought to realize the gospel ideal by performing good works. Their main task was to buy clothing for the poor and provide work for the unemployed in the making of clothes. In one year they distributed over 350 garments to poor parishioners. Women in the parish also organized annual fairs for the benefit of the poor.[27]

The principal organization for men was the St. Vincent de Paul Society, whose goal was "the exercise of charity in many ways, but chiefly, to visit poor families, to minister to their physical wants as far as means will admit and to give such counsel for their spiritual good as circumstances may require and to look after male orphans when they shall have left the asylum."[28] It was first introduced into New York in 1846, and by 1864 twenty parishes, including Transfiguration, had Vincent de Paul societies. Even though active membership in each parish numbered less than fifty men, many more supported the society's work. The principal boast of their annual reports was the number of visitations made to relieve the financial and spiritual distress of the poor.[29] Founded in France and imported to the United States, the St. Vincent de Paul Society was the principal Catholic benevolent organization. The press praised its work, and the hierarchy urged its formation in every parish. As an outlet for charity, it enabled laymen to practice the works of mercy; as a conservative expression of social Catholicism, it sought to alleviate the suffering of the poor rather than to prevent it.

Most Holy Redeemer did not have a Vincent de Paul conference until later in the century, but the parish did have its own version of social Catholicism. The most widespread form of this apostolate was the parochial relief verein. These vereins were parish-centered organizations which sought to relieve poor and sick members of the society through financial assistance.

The one significant difference between the Irish and German social apostolates was in their attitudes toward the temperance movement. Although German Catholics did not support the temperance movement in New York, they did not come out in favor of intemperance. Mission sermons portrayed its evil consequences, and good German Catholics were told to avoid the disruptive environment of rowdy taverns. At the same time, however, they were called on to support the good taverns and *Biergartens* of Little Germany. A recommended spot, owned by a German Catholic, was located directly opposite the church on Third Street. The newspaper commented on the good quality of the clientele and claimed that they "were always a sober group, mostly people from the community, orderly people"; it was a place "where one can have a good glass of beer or wine and also carry on a Christian discourse."[30] Germans regarded beer "as healthy and nourishing," and unlike the Irish press, German newspapers always printed advertisements for beer and wine, as well as for German *Biergartens*. Among the Irish, however, temperance became a holy crusade.

For Irish Catholics a principal cause of poverty was intemperance. A standard sermon in the parish mission concerned drunkenness; preachers were advised to denounce it in every sermon, but its evil effects demanded that "a special and a most powerful sermon be given on this vice."[31] The spiritual ruin caused by intemperance received special emphasis, since it led to eternal damnation. Equally significant were the social consequences of drunkenness. As a vice it inevitably was denounced as a source of misery and poverty for the family. The preacher claimed that poverty could not exist if temperance and industry prevailed; for the virtuous man material success was possible in this life, but intemperance closed off this possibility. Thus, as a virtue temperance became a means of improving one's position in life. John Hughes pointed out this connection by emphasizing that in those parishes were temperance associations existed "prosperity had been the reward of industry and as a matter of course, more of the comforts of life are enjoyed."[32] With the promise of such material and spiritual blessings, it was not surprising that the temperance movement gained support among Catholics.

Father Varela and Transfiguration parish spearheaded the temperance movement among New York Catholics. In 1840 Varela founded the New York Catholic Temperance Association, and within a year it numbered five thousand members. Evening meetings, which took place in the church, opened with a talk extolling the spiritual and material benefits of a temperate life. At the conclusion of the talk as many as two hundred to four hundred people came forward to take the pledge.[33] The movement continued to spread to other parishes in the city and reached a peak in 1849 with the arrival of the Irish temperance crusader Father Theobald Mathew. While he was in New York, he gave the pledge to more than twenty thousand people.[34] After Mathew's departure the temperance movement lost momentum in the city. Transfiguration and other city parishes continued the crusade, but in an area notorious for its many drinking establishments, whose residents enjoyed the friendship and refreshment offered in the neighborhood pub, the movement met with relatively little success.

Another dimension to the Catholic benevolent apostolate was the organization of charitable institutions. Institutional child care was one aspect of the reform movement in the United States, and Catholics responded to this humanitarian impulse by establishing homes for orphans. The public health movement was making progress in the face of increasing demands, and Catholics characteristically organized their own hospitals. An increasing amount of specialization in welfare work developed at this time, and general indiscriminate care gave way to more specialized treatment. The Catholic response was especially evident in the care of young single women living in the city.[35] The piety that fostered this development did not differ from that which inspired individual Catholics to alleviate the suffering of their neighbors. The only difference was that personal piety was now institutionalized and its efforts extended beyond the narrow confines of the parish. Yet, there was an ingredient in this citywide apostolate that was not so visible in the parish-centered version of social Christianity. Basic to the foundation of these charitable institutions was the fear of Protestant proselytizing; the fear was not unfounded, and as Protestant New Yorkers expanded their benevolent apostolate, Catholics were forced to react in kind or suffer the loss of many coreligionists to Protestant denominations. Another motivating impulse was less reactionary and more typically American. Catholic New Yorkers had a dim view of urban life. Immigrants came to the United States with lurid images of city life fixed in their minds. As one Irish priest put it, "better one meal a day of potatoes and salt in Ireland than face the sin and horror of American city life."[36] To protect young men and women from such "sin and horror" as well as from the missionary zeal of Protestants, the church established a substantial network of charitable institutions throughout the city.

Increasing immigration and periodic epidemics underlined the need for better health facilities in New York City. As early as 1834 Bishop Dubois emphasized the need for a Catholic hospital that would "afford our poor emigrants, particularly from Ireland, the necessary relief, attendance in sickness and spiritual comfort, amidst the disease of a climate new to them."[37] The Protestant atmosphere of public institutions increasingly dramatized this need. Priests were not allowed to visit Catholic patients, and when they did, their anti-Protestant bias often made them unwelcome.[38] In a pastoral letter in 1847, Bishop Hughes attacked the adverse religious atmosphere that Catholics encountered in public hospitals and urged the establishment of a Catholic hospital to care for his immigrant flock. Two years later St. Vincent's Hospital opened in New York under the direction of the Sisters of Charity.[39]

The Sisters of Charity had gained a favorable reputation for their work with the sick poor. Their unselfish service during the cholera epidemic of 1832 captured the attention of many New Yorkers, and in the 1849 epidemic the sisters again achieved public acclaim. During the cholera years "admiration of the Sisters was general and unqualified; their benevolence was of a practical sort, their lives not idled away in the convent's living tomb."[40] The superintendent of a New York hospital described them as a "noble band of women" and sought their services when cholera struck again in 1866.[41] Such singular devotion made the Sisters of Charity a good choice for undertaking the institutional care of Catholics.

In 1849 St. Vincent's had room for thirty patients; by 1861 expanded facilities made room for 150. In comparison with public institutions this was a very limited capacity, and Catholics necessarily frequented other hospitals, where discrimination was gradually disappearing.[42] Though the hospital was open to all New York Catholics, it had one drawback. The English-speaking sisters could not communicate satisfactorily with German Catholics, and as expected, the Germans founded their own hospital.

The language problem was only one reason for the organization in 1865 of St. Francis Hospital on the Lower East Side. As was true in the case of St. Vincent's, the fear of Protestant proselytization exerted a decisive influence, even as late as 1865. In the minds of German Catholics it was "a fact, universally known and felt, that the sick and infirm of the Congregation of the Church of Most Holy Redeemer were not satisfactorily well cared for in the public hospitals not only on account of their language but still more on account of their religion since in those institutions they were surrounded by Infidels, Apostates and even around enemies of religion, circumstances which rendered those institutions anything but desirable for a Catholic who wished to prepare for eternity."[43]

Although the impulse for the establishment of St. Francis Hospital originated in Redeemer parish, it served German Catholics throughout the city and gained their financial support. The German Sisters of the Poor of St. Francis were in charge of the hospital, and within a few years after its foundation they began to care for people of all nationalities and religions.[44] Like St. Vincent's, it was a modest response to the needs of an urban community, but it did illustrate the style of social Catholicism at mid-century.

Another aspect of Catholic benevolence was institutions for the care of a special group of individuals—young single women. Like the hospital, these institutions cared for females from all parishes; the dangers of urban life were a more motivating impulse than fears of Protestant proselytization. Priests did advise single girls to avoid romantic links with Protestant boys, since difference in religion was a source of great unhappiness and a drawback to love and would ultimately raise problems in their children's education. Survival handbooks for Catholic women portrayed the Protestant Bible as an evil book; and if the only employment they could find was with Protestant families, the young ladies were to insist that time be allowed for Sunday Mass.[45] But in addition to this customary anti-Protestant counsel, the city was singled out as a particularly degenerate locale for young immigrant girls.[46] In the opinion of John Hughes, New York needed a special home where "the virtue and innocence of destitute females of good character might be shielded from the snares and dangers to which their destitution exposes them in a wealthy and corrupt metropolis like New York."[47] His successor, John McCloskey, did not think much differently, describing New York as a "vast, and alas, wicked city."[48] It was this ideology that fostered the foundation of special institutions for young women whose aim was to make urban life as virtuous an experience as possible.

Through the personal efforts of John Hughes the Irish Sisters of Mercy came to New York in 1846. In Ireland they had acquired a favorable reputation for their work with "poor women of good character."[49] Hughes wanted them to continue this apostolate in New York, and in 1849 they founded a House of Mercy for the care of recently-arrived immigrant girls. This was their special apostolate: their goal was to teach the girls domestic trades and to find them work in the city. As an employment agency the House of Mercy was quite effective, providing jobs for over eight thousand girls within five years after it opened.[50] The irony was that the sisters had founded the home to protect young women from the dangers of city life, but in the end they sent them forth trained to work in an urban economy. The hope was that the religious formation acquired in the House of Mercy would adequately equip the young women in their struggle with the city devil.

Some girls were not as successful as others in warding off the evils of city life. To respond to the needs of these delinquent females a group of Catholic women sought to establish a special institution. John Hughes approved their plan, though with some hesitation, and the House of the Good Shepherd opened in 1857.[51] The program of reform of the Sisters of the Good Shepherd centered on religion, education, and work. Like the Sisters of Mercy, the Sisters of the Good Shepherd trained the girls in domestic trades needed in the city; spiritually they sought to strengthen the young women so that they could lead a virtuous life in a locale described by one priest as "the Sodom of Atlantic cities."[52]

The negative attitude of Catholics toward the city was shared by most Americans. Underlying this mentality was the idealization of rural life. In the face of increasing urbanization, Americans sought to cling to the pastoral ideals of the recent past. The hallowed traditions of rural origins and a country environment received increased emphasis during this period of transformation. The country was portrayed as a garden of innocence and virtue, while the city remained a den of sin and corruption.[53] Guidebooks for immigrant Catholics reinforced this mentality. They instructed Irish newcomers to settle on the rural frontier, where work was better; there a man could preside over his own homestead and watch his "family grow up prosperous and industrious removed from the pestilential examples and practices of city life."[54] Irish authors idealized the image of the "simple innocent countryman" and extolled the frontier as a place where the immigrant could enjoy "not merely a home, but comfort and independence."[55] In villifying the city, preachers praised agricultural life as "incomparably more wholesome, more happy, and more favorable to virtue and piety than the feverish, comfortless, and unnatural existence to which the mass of the laboring class are condemned in large cities."[56] Catholic fiction also supported this romantic conception of the country. Mary Sadlier wrote *Con O'Regan; or Emigrant Life in the New World* in the 1860s with the explicit intention of urging Irish newcomers to leave the city and take up land in the West. In a typical vignette Con O'Regan and his companion, Andy Dwyer, moralize about the attributes of rural life: In the city a family could lose all its savings through a bank failure. "There's no bank like a good farm," says Andy, "for there's no bank so sure but it may go some day, whereas the farm can never fail, if a man only takes care to till it. The earth will always bring forth its fruit, Cornelius, for the Lord has promised that seed-time and harvest shall never fail."[57] The entire novel repeats this apologia for life on a farm; in every chapter the theme is clothed in moralistic tones. Everything good occurs on the farm, and the city is the scene of all that is evil. In the city young Patsy Bergen skipped catechism class, but on the farm he is converted to a life of virtue. He does not fail to point out that if his former friends in Boston "were out hoeing and weeding in the field or in the garden all day as I am, they wouldn't have half the wickedness in them."[58]

The rural myth was also part of John Hughes's rhetoric. Raised on a farm in rural Ireland and educated in the pastoral setting of the Maryland countryside, he had all the preparation needed to extol the moral values of rural life. He publicly proclaimed that he had always given the immigrant "who came his way the advice rather to seek a home in the West than remain in our cities."[59] To an audience in Cork, Ireland, he extolled the benefits of the frontier in his usual flamboyant style:

> I know there are in this country what are called plains or prairies, where the cottages of the poor man were, and they are now occupied by the ox and the swine. The poor man is not there, but where is he? I can trace him. He is in the west of the United States (cheers) and he is, instead of being the humble cottier afraid of having his cottage taken from him, now the owner of this section of land in America, perhaps of 300 acres or more of what was until lately Government land, and the property of the Government; and even lately he was the proprietor of it under the Government protection, allowed to do what he pleased with it.[60]

Yet coupled with this idyllic prose was a strain of urban boosterism. As a church leader in the city, John Hughes could not gloss over its attributes. For the archbishop the city was a cultural center where immigrants could enjoy the "comparative comforts of a temporary home."[61] In his opinion, New York was a center of education that supported "colleges, seminaries, convents, schools, altogether ranging from the highest education to the very humblest elements of learning."[62] Such a pro-urban attitude was more evident, though more indirect, in his analysis of rural life. Hughes realistically assessed farm life as one which was beset with "discomforts [and] afflictions": "mental and religious evils were frequently the result of rude Western life"; hidden behind the romance of the frontier were hardships "which were untold and could not be foreseen—hardships which were not to be found in a map."[63] Promoters of Irish colonization emphasized the theme of land ownership to immigrants who scarcely knew what it was to own their own land. Hughes opposed such schemes and observed that the rhetoric of colonization "sounded very well in the cities" in the midst of crowded tenements, but "there were many people out West who were much poorer and worse off than if they had never gone there and became owners of the soil."[64] In opposing rural colonization, Hughes chose to support the development of the most famous urban colony in the United States. He was unquestionably a city booster, but his affection for the pastoral ideal obscured his boosterism; like his contemporaries, he exhibited an ambivalence common at a time of transformation, when people moved into a new age carrying baggage from the past.

Other New York Catholics illustrated the same ambivalence. As city dwellers they sought to establish a network of benevolent institutions to care for less fortunate immigrants, and their pioneer work succeeded in making the charitable enterprise a permanent feature of New York Catholicism. Yet, in laying the foundation for a significant urban institution they continued to idealize country life. The one area where this schizophrenia was most evident was in the care of Catholic youth. Like their Protestant contemporaries, Catholics sought to make country boys and girls out of city youth.

Through the initiative of Catholic laymen and with the approval of the bishop, the Roman Catholic Orphan Aslyum was founded in 1817. At that time there was only one other orphanage in New York.[65] The asylum began in simple surroundings on the outskirts of the city, and by the end of the first year, twenty-eight children lived together in an old wooden shanty cared for by three Sisters of Charity. With the growth in population and disruption of family life through sickness, desertion, and death, the need for child care increased. A second orphanage for children of one surviving parent, half-orphans, opened in 1830 to meet these needs. By 1845 the two orphanages were caring for 350 boys and girls.[66] With the passage of time the orphanage expanded its facilities. In 1859 close to eight hundred children lived in the institution, and the number exceeded one thousand during the Civil War, due to the death of many "Catholic fathers, brothers, and guardians in the field of battle."[67]

Catholics throughout the city supported the orphanage, and children from every parish were able to find refuge within its walls; but the parishes that supported the asylum and the people who guided its operations belonged to the predominantly Irish community. As was true in the area of hospital work, ethnic groups sought to establish their own orphanages to meet their particular needs.

In the case of the Germans, once again it was Redeemer parish that provided the necessary impulse to found a benevolent institution for German Catholics. The cholera epidemic of 1849 had left many children homeless or without one parent. The priests of the parish temporarily remedied the situation by placing the children in homes of parishioners. Eventually plans were made to establish a permanent home near the Church of St. Alphonsus: the orphanage opened in 1850 with twenty-three children in residence. Five years later it closed, and the children went to live with German families in New York and Rochester.[68] In 1858 the pastor of the parish reorganized the orphanage, sought financial support for it among the German Catholic community, and reopened the institution in February 1859 in the Yorkville section of the city. The new building had a capacity of 200, and by 1870, 160 boys and girls were living there under the supervision of the School Sisters of Notre Dame.[69]

Parishioners of the French Catholic church opened an orphanage in 1858 which, compared with other homes, sheltered very few children—only sixty girls and twenty-five boys in 1867.[70] The small number of orphans reflected the size of the French community, but the French exhibited the same ethnic consciousness as German and Irish immigrants.

The motivating force behind the organization of these asylums certainly included a genuine desire to care for deprived children. Institutional child care was one aspect of reform in ante-bellum America, and Catholics were not immune to this humanitarian spirit. In fact, increased interest on the part of Protestants in child care impelled Catholics to respond in like manner. With the expansion of Protestant benevolent enterprises and with public welfare institutions still unfriendly to foreign papists, Catholics in New York and elsewhere feared that many children would be lost to the church. The result was the development of a widespread system of child care centered in most of the principal cities of the nation.

In addition to the twofold impulse of charity and self-protection, the myth of the pastoral ideal exercised considerable influence on the child care enterprise. The moral superiority of the country was quite evident in the practice of "binding out" city children to the country, which was a general pattern among reformers and which quite naturally became part of the program of the Roman Catholic Orphan Asylum. The practice of moving children from the institution to a home was present from the very beginning, but such a practice did not always mean that the child was sent to live on a farm in the West. On the contrary, children were often placed in homes in the city to learn a trade useful in the urban economy. Gradually, however, the pattern shifted, and more emphasis was placed on binding out children to the country, preferably to a farm. It is difficult to pinpoint exactly when the shift occurred, but certainly by 1858 the Catholic Orphan Asylum was actively encouraging the removal of city boys and girls to the country. The change in emphasis was due not only to an increasing sense of rural superiority but also to the enthusiastic support given to this practice by the Children's Aid Society. C. Loring Brace had founded the society in 1853, and his success among the city youth not only posed a threat to Catholics but also suggested a way to deal with the problem of homeless children.[71] Another reason for the shift was the lack of acceptable homes in the city. Based on the rural ideal, any home in the city was unacceptable regardless of the virtue of its inhabitants simply because it was surrounded by the perils of the metropolis.

To secure rural homes for city children advertisements were carried in the Catholic press, and circulars were sent to priests on the frontier asking their assistance in placing city youth in their parishes.

The asylum insisted that the applicants be Catholic and that they tend to the religious practice of the child. In addition to this requirement, the authorities added the statement that "applications from farmers, whether for boys or girls, will have preference over all others."[72] The superiority of country life could not have been more clearly implied.

Another benevolent institution founded during the episcopacy of John Hughes was the Catholic Protectory, officially known as The Society for the Protection of Destitute Roman Catholic Children in the City of New York. Organized in 1863 under the impetus of Catholic laymen, principally Levi Silliman Ives, the Protectory sought to rehabilitate delinquent and neglected children, especially Irish youth.[73] A principal motive behind its establishment was the large number of Catholics among the city's vagrant population and the success of Protestant missionaries in drawing these children away from the church. More specifically the Catholic Protectory was a countermovement to the Children's Aid Society and its practice of transporting vagrant youth to the country.[74]

The rural ideal was very evident in the operation of the Protectory. Early in its history two directors of the society made a grand tour of the West to select a suitable site for a rural settlement, after which they submitted a report to the managers of the Protectory recommending several available locations. No further action was taken, however, and the project was dropped. A further indication of the influence of the pastoral ideal was the purchase in 1865 of 114 acres of farmland in the Bronx. The site was to be the new location of the Protectory, since the managers "were convinced that proper care of the children demanded a site outside the city."[75] The Bronx property was transformed into a rural training center where young city boys learned the skills of farming. The plan to make farm boys out of city youth continued throughout the century, but it never achieved its anticipated success. Levi Silliman Ives had quickly recognized the weakness of the project: it was simply too difficult to keep city boys on the farm after they had seen the bright lights of the city.[76] Some boys did learn farming skills, while others mastered trades useful in the city, but the rural training program was eventually abandoned as a failure.

In the operation of both the Catholic Protectory and the Orphan

Asylum the contrast between the city and country ideal was clearly illustrated. Both institutions sought to alleviate the hardships of family life in the city. They were urban institutions, founded and supported by city dwellers, and they served the needs of a special group of Catholics. Each institution upheld the pastoral myth, but this ideal was more symbol than reality. The children of the city simply did not accept the pastoral ideal with the same enthusiasm as adult reformers. When farm placements were made, they were comparatively few in number. In 1860 the Orphan Asylum bound out fifteen boys, only four of whom went to farms; two years later only seventeen out of 114 boys were bound out to farmers.[77] The fact of the matter was that in the case of the Catholic Asylum larger numbers of children were not bound out but were discharged to parents or relatives. In the case of the Protectory, the hesitant policy of training young people in rural trades eventually gave way to advocating occupations suited to the urban economy. New York Catholics, like their contemporaries, were caught in the midst of a changing society: the country was moving to the city, and the trend toward urbanization ultimately undermined their hope of reforming society by a return to the past.

The emphasis on the moral superiority of rural life and the anti-urban bias of Catholics reinforced their social conservatism. Since the city was portrayed as basically evil with few if any redeeming qualities, reformers tended to ignore the possibility of changing it; rather, they sought to reform the individual even if this meant removing him from the city. They accepted the poverty and disorganization present in the city as a natural state of existence and did not dare to challenge what God had ordered. Resigned to His will, they endeavored to ameliorate the condition of the less fortunate through a parochial and citywide benevolent enterprise. It was only later in the century that Catholics, along with Protestants, began to question the social order and challenge the hallowed tradition of laissez-faire economics. Only then did they shift their focus from the individual to the environment and look upon poverty more from an economic point of view than from a moralistic perspective.

Thus, during the middle decades of the century Catholics continued to follow the traditional paths of benevolence. Hospitals, orphanages, and charitable societies had long been a trademark of the church, and what developed in the United States did not differ dramatically from the past. As was true with the Protestant enterprise, American Catholic philanthropy had its roots in Europe, and the church reconstructed a pattern of benevolence that scarcely differed from the practice of the old country.[78] Urbanization and industrialization were changing the social order on both sides of the Atlantic; old problems were intensified, and new ones appeared. The rise of the factory system ushered in a new class of workers who struggled to make ends meet in a fickle economy. The multiplication of large cities and the concentration of Catholics in the city challenged the resources of the church. The response in New York was typical of the reaction elsewhere, and while Catholics succeeded in building up a citywide charitable program, they continued to walk backward along familiar paths in an age that was moving ahead along uncharted routes.

The patterns of the past provided guidelines for the church in the United States. Transplanted from across the ocean, time-honored practices outweighed any attempts at improvisation in the New World. This was especially evident in handing on the faith to immigrant newcomers. A transatlantic voyage did not alter or rearrange the truths of Catholicism: they were packaged and shipped across the ocean to reappear intact in America. A primary means of transmitting them was the sermon, and the preacher, like most Catholics, was looking backward to find his message.

EIGHT

Preaching

COMPARED WITH PROTESTANT preaching, very little is known about Catholic preaching in the United States. One obvious reason is that the nature of Catholic worship has placed the sermon in a position of secondary importance. The stress on the sacramentality of the Mass and the presence of the Lord in the Eucharist inevitably overshadowed the word of the preacher. The style of worship was so fixed that it permitted very little innovation in the form of preaching, and Catholics were so bound to their order of worship that the sermon could never develop beyond a certain point. As part of the Eucharistic liturgy, it occupied a marginal position, and worship without a sermon did not make the Mass any less efficacious. This mentality remains widespread even today and says as much about the quality of preaching as it does about its importance for the man in the pew. For most Protestants, however, the sermon is so necessary an ingredient in worship that it is difficult to imagine a service without it. For this reason Protestant preaching remains an important area of historical inquiry, while the Catholic sermon lies hidden in the pulpit of the past.

Yet preaching has always been an important means of forming the religious consciousness of Catholics, and the church has continually emphasized its pastoral value. The writings of Chrysostom and Augustine guided the course of preaching for ages. Though they did not deny the importance of rhetorical elegance, they abandoned the sophistic spirit of self-display and stressed the need for Christian instruction. The late Middle Ages and the Renaissance witnessed a deterioration in the pulpit, and in the sixteenth century the Council of Trent set out to correct these abuses. In reforming the art of preaching, the Council of Trent reaffirmed the pastoral value of the sermon and charted the course of the pulpit for the next four hundred years.[1]

As an expression of the religious imagination the sermon can serve as a mirror of the past. It was a principal means of transmitting the mysteries of Catholicism from generation to generation; long before the printing press, it was the only catechism available, and the printed word never became a substitute for the spoken word. In fact, in early-nineteenth-century America the sermon was very much in vogue, and a skillful preacher seldom spoke to empty pews.

Catholics as well as Protestants recognized the importance of the pulpit. Writing to an American priest studying in Paris, the archbishop of Baltimore, Ambrose Maréchal, reminded him that "the grand object that the good of religion in this country demands is sacred eloquence."[2] Lay people were eager for good sermons, he said, and a good preacher could render a very important service to the church. "Preaching is an indispensable duty," wrote one priest in 1820, "and the minister who pleases the people in that respect possesses unlimited influence over his flock."[3] The skillful orator was so esteemed that the absence of pulpit eloquence could often lead to a priest's dismissal from the parish. The same situation had prevailed in parts of Ireland, where priests were denied pastorates if they were not capable preachers.[4]

Political oratory underlined the importance and illustrated the potentials of the spoken word; the press publicized the appearance of noted preachers and regularly printed their sermons. Outstanding sermons were even made available in pamphlets. The temper of the times had glamorized the eloquent speaker to the extent that one foreign observer remarked that "in the United States words are everything . . . the newspapers and the parliamentary rostrum perpetuate this idea, attract everyone's attention, decide everyone's merits," and for this reason "a skillful orator is almost indispensable and therefore it is most important that a Bishop be an eloquent man."[5] As a minority religion in a hostile Protestant environment, Catholicism had to measure up to the level of preaching in the United States or suffer the disgrace of public ridicule. Bishop Dubois realized this and admitted that pulpit eloquence was especially necessary in the city, where there were so many good Protestant preachers. The competition was keen, and the urbanity of the people demanded preaching excellence. Since the sermon was the one part of the Mass in English, Dubois believed that it could serve as a means of instruction not only for Catholics but for visiting Protestants;[6] but to be effective it had to "stand the criticism of protestants of the highest class and best information."[7]

With such importance attached to preaching in the early decades of the century, it is not surprising to find priests who were thought to be skillful orators. Father Varela, however, did not fall into this category, though others who worked with him in Transfiguration Church were singled out for their eloquence. Charles C. Pise had briefly served in the parish; a noted novelist and historian, he was also a popular preacher, whose sermons parishioners described as "fervid and purely classical eloquence."[8] The rector of the cathedral parish, Thomas C. Levins, was also a competent orator, and his skill "won for him the esteem of the parish."[9] The founding pastor of Most Holy Redeemer, Gabriel Rumpler, was known as a lively and popular preacher, and clarity was said to be a distinguishing mark of his sermons.[10] One of the foremost preachers in the early decades was the Irish-born pastor of St. Peter's, John Power. His reputation had spread to many Eastern cities, and he traveled up and down the coast preaching in various cities and begging for money to support the Catholic Orphan Asylum in New York. In a letter to the editor of the *Truth Teller*, one contemporary remarked that "in my mind, a more truly eloquent and powerful appeal had seldom emanated from a pulpit, accompanied with a most graceful delivery and a truly evangelical appearance, the recollection of which will not, within a short period, be effaced from my mind."[11]

The most widely known preacher in Catholic New York was John Hughes. As a young priest in Philadelphia he gained acclaim as a skillful orator in his religious debates with the Presbyterian minister, John Breckenridge.[12] As bishop of New York he frequently spoke to large crowds on a variety of religious topics; his talks were well-received and frequently were printed in pamphlet editions that sold out rapidly.[13] His reputation was widespread, and he was frequently invited to speak on behalf of many charitable causes throughout the East; as he himself admitted, "whenever there is money to be collected they call on me."[14] In December 1847 he was invited to speak to Congress, and after hearing his talk one Protestant described him as the "St. Paul of America."[15] In 1860 the graduating class of the University of North Carolina asked him to deliver the baccalaureate sermon, and Hughes did not disappoint them. The local paper noted that "he discoursed on love to God and love to man, as is not often heard in a college chapel. The densely packed audience listened with scarcely a stir for an hour and three quarters."[16]

Despite the oratorical skill of individuals like Hughes and Power, a visible decline in pulpit eloquence had set in by the middle of the century. After touring the United States, Archbishop Bedini of Italy commented that "not many of them [priests] are good preachers."[17] John Hughes made a smiliar observation about the New York clergy in a report to Rome: "If anyone looks for extraordinary eloquence in the pulpit," he said, "he may be prepared for much disappointment."[18] Both Hughes and Bedini agreed that the workload of the clergy was too time-consuming to permit the study necessary to achieve pulpit excellence. As Bedini noted, in the United States "every priest must be a good pastor, a good preacher, a good teacher, a good administrator," and with their time taken up with such diverse responsibilities, few priests became skillful orators.[19] It was an age of rapid expansion; churches and schools had to be built, and the successful administrator, not the talented preacher, was more highly acclaimed.[20]

Another reason for the decline in preaching quality can be traced to seminary education. American seminaries were still in their infant stages at mid-century: talented teachers were rare, and the curriculum was meager. The emphasis was on piety more than learning, and few seminaries included courses in sacred eloquence. In 1866 the Second Plenary Council of Baltimore encouraged homiletic classes in seminaries, and only then did such courses begin to appear in seminary curriculums.[21] The guidelines of 1866 were repeated in the 1884 Plenary Council of Baltimore, but despite the hierarchy's prodding, pulpit oratory was generally unexceptional in Catholic churches. Towards the end of the century a New York priest wrote that there was "a painful mediocrity in preaching"; the sermon and the preacher, he said, had been converted "into veritable cures for insomnia."[22]

Indicative of the lack of preaching excellence was the absence of any indigenous homilectic tradition in American Catholicism.[23] If a priest wanted to learn the art of skillful preaching, he had to search out the works of European writers. Even though the church was able to boast of some exceptional preachers, it could not point to any American writings on the topic. In the early decades priests could turn to American editions of Bousset, Fenelon, Alphonsus Liguori, or noted Irish preachers, and these works shaped their style of preaching.[24] Even at the end of the century the situation was not much different. The writings of Reverend Thomas J. Potter, a professor at All Hallows Seminary in Ireland, dominated the field of homiletics in the United States; but Potter's work was substantially influenced by the treatise of Abbé Hamon, *Traité de la Predication*, published in Paris in 1844.[25] In preaching, then, as in so many areas of religion, American Catholics looked to Europe for their models rather than developing their own. In 1884, when the hierarchy was searching for a homiletic text for seminaries, they inevitably chose a European work, *Sacred Rhetoric*, written by Thomas MacNamara, an Irish Vincentian.[26] It seemed that when Americans, too busy with other tasks, needed a guide, either in catechesis or homiletics, they could always find something written in Ireland suitable for use in the United States.

The sermon delivered at the Sunday Solemn Mass was the most characteristic preaching of the day. Other Sunday services generally featured shorter talks or no sermon at all; Sunday evening devotions also included a sermon, generally an instruction on some point of Christian doctrine. Priests exchanged pulpits for these evening talks and often attracted sizable crowds.[27] Because of its importance and the size of the Catholic population, New York City attracted many visiting preachers of noted ability, and their presence in the city was well publicized. One such orator was Daniel W. Cahill, an Irish priest who visited the United States in 1860 and preached in several New York churches. Both the Irish and the German press commented favorably on his performance; his oratory provided a form of popular entertainment in an age when the spoken word was still highly valued.[28] The dedication of new churches often attracted recognized preachers from out of town, and important feasts, such as St. Patrick's Day, featured special sermons. In fact, one could measure the importance of the event by the length of the sermon. The principal Sunday sermon often went on for one hour or more, and a twenty-minute sermon was considered a short homily; brief five- or ten-minute talks were given at the other Masses. Special events called for longer sermons: at the episcopal consecration of John Hughes the preacher spoke for one and one-half hours.[29]

Sermon books were widely available in the United States, and preachers could use these prepared sermons or model their talks on the eloquence of Liguori, Fenelon, or other celebrated preachers. European works of the seventeenth and eighteenth centuries were regularly advertised in the press in the early decades of the century, and their many editions point to their popularity. Yet, there did emerge a style of preaching by the middle of the century that visibly contrasted with the stylistic and animated sermons of the seventeenth and eighteenth centuries. As one New York priest put it, "French preachers were too lofty and their writings were seldom useful." He believed that one had to preach in a popular style to be effective.[30] This quality of popular, simple sermons best describes the type of homilies that developed in the 1860s. A comparison of earlier European sermon books with American collections that began to appear in the 1860s substantiates this.

Father William Gahan was an acclaimed preacher in late-eighteenth-century Ireland whose sermons were published in Ireland and the United States. Employing an animated and fervid style, he sought to awaken the emotion of his audience. Gahan frequently quoted from the church fathers to reinforce his arguments, and his writing exhibited a literary eloquence that was as impressive as it was moving. Gahan's sermons were available in New York and were quite popular in Ireland as well. They were representative of many other Irish sermon collections and mirrored the style of preaching prevalent at the beginning of the nineteenth century.[31] The literary and classical quality of such sermons, however, did not assure success in the pulpit. In fact some critics claimed that sermons of this type were more literary than religious and "left hearts untouched."[32] In Germany the classical style of Bousset and Massillon was still in vogue at mid-century, but as in America, it was eventually replaced by a more popular style.[33]

From the material available, it can be said that the sermons preached in New York churches were more religious than literary, more colloquial than classical, more ordinary than extraordinary. Even these generalizations, however, must be qualified as one focuses on different parishes. St. Paul's parish served a very poor community, and the sermons preached in this church were very simple in style and used commonplace examples to illustrate the lesson. In St. Ann's, an upper-class parish, the sermons of the pastor, Thomas Preston, were more polished and evidenced more intellectual quality with fewer colloquialisms or familiar examples.[34]

The sermons of John Hughes best represent what pulpit excellence resembled in the middle of the nineteenth century. As bishop he preached many times, and critics said that one of his best sermons was his homily on Good Friday, 1859, in St. Patrick's Cathedral.[35] Hughes began his talk, entitled "The Silence of Christ Before His Judges," with a quote from Scripture followed by a brief introduction. He then developed two themes and ended his talk with a section on Mary at the Cross. Numerous quotes from Scripture embellished the talk, but no references to the church fathers were included; this classical trait of frequently citing the fathers had disappeared by the 1860s. Like his contemporaries, Hughes continually used rhetorical questions to attract the attention of his audience and awaken their emotions. His style was simple and his argument plain, not theologically complicated.[36] This sermon, like others, included doctrinal instruction as well as moral exhortation; one cannot escape the impression that Hughes always sought to instruct his listeners as well as to move their wills. Like many priests, he wrote out his sermons: sentences were long but plain, lacking the vivid imagery and striking vocabulary of a Gahan;[37] it was hardly a literary masterpiece, but delivered with the fiery spirit of Hughes, it was apparently effective, since people still remembered it five years later.[38]

The values transmitted from the pulpit were basically twofold. The aim of every sermon was to emphasize the necessity of personal salvation—a theme of the pulpit for many centuries and a prominent mark of post-Tridentine Catholicism—which reinforced the individual piety of the people and confirmed them in their state of life. A second dominant theme was the primacy of the Roman Catholic church, a theme which was certainly more prevalent in nineteenth-century American preaching than in earlier European sermons. A Protestant culture continually challenged the dogmas of Catholicism, and the preacher was intent to neutralize these attacks; for this reason the sermon tended to be an apologetic defense as well as instructional. The emphasis on salvation impressed it with a moralistic tone, while the stress on instruction gave it a doctrinal quality. Examples from history reinforced the apologetical dimension, and episodes from the gospels and lives of the saints embellished the moralistic parts of the sermons.

The Sunday sermon was the principal opportunity that the clergy had to instruct the adult community, and by reinforcing the lessons learned from the catechism, it strengthened the beliefs of the people and confirmed the work of the church in the world. The national parish set Catholics apart ethnically as well as religiously, which separatist mentality the pulpit supported. American society was Protestant and irreligious in the mind of most clerics, and the preacher confirmed the primacy of Catholicism and the necessity of religion in life. By emphasizing the importance of religion, the sermon necessarily supported the need for religious instruction and ultimately, if not explicitly, the importance of the parochial school. It also strengthened the social conservatism of Catholics by continually reminding them to keep their sights fixed on a heavenly kingdom. The sermon presented the ideals to be sought after, and even though many did not achieve these goals, it confirmed the work of the church and the values it had institutionalized. Preachers were not speaking in a vacuum, but to a community that was rapidly making its presence felt in American society. People could look around them and see churches, schools, hospitals, and orphanages being built; the sermon gave meaning to this work and made it seem necessary and even religious.

The pulpit also became the stage for the parish mission. The parish mission had played an important role in the reform of Catholicism after the Protestant Reformation, reaching its zenith of popularity in the seventeenth century, when preachers traveled the highways of Europe eager to convert dechristianized cities and villages. The eighteenth century witnessed the decline of missions as exaggerated penances, seemingly endless sermons, naive credulity, and grotesque exhibitions corrupted their effectiveness and diminished their usefulness.[39] The mission had all but disappeared in Germany by 1800, and the state had even forbidden them in many places.[40] In Ireland the penal laws outlawed such large public gatherings. Thus, in the early nineteenth century both German and Irish Catholics seldom, if ever, experienced a parish mission. The 1829 campaign for emancipation at times resembled a religious revival, as Irish priests imitated the evangelism of Methodist preachers in delivering "passionate denunciations of their religious grievances and the political system which perpetuated them."[41] The traditional parish mission, however, did undergo a revival in the nineteenth century, and it became an integral part of the Catholic awakening in both Europe and the United States.

The mission began to reappear in Germany after 1848: during the decade of the fifties missions were held in many cities throughout the country. Large missions took place in Cologne in 1850, in Heidelberg in 1851, and in Augsburg in 1853; and Berlin witnessed a spectacular revival in 1858, when more than 18,000 Catholics attended a mission preached by the Jesuits.[42] The Irish Council of Thurles encouraged parish missions, and they eventually became a standard event of Ireland's devotional revolution.[43]

American Catholics underwent a similar awakening at midcentury: parish missions began to flourish in churches from New York to Chicago. Before the formal mission was widespread, priests frequently conducted their own parish revivals by extending the celebration of a particular feast for several days.[44] Along the Kentucky frontier the Catholic priest followed the path of the circuit rider sustaining the faith of scattered settlers with missionary revivals.[45] But in the 1850s the traditional parish mission appeared on the scene with a degree of regularity and organization that paralleled its resurgence in Europe. Religious orders, such as the Jesuits, Redemptorists, and Paulists, organized special groups of trained preachers, who traveled far and wide to conduct missions. By the 1860s they were so popular that the Redemptorists even had to refuse many requests for their services.[46]

Like so many aspects of Catholicism in the United States, the parish mission was directly imported from Europe. The Redemptorists, one of the first groups to incorporate the mission into their apostolate in America, organized their first mission band in 1851. The priests chosen for this work were men who had assisted at similar missions in England. Their mentor and advisor was a Belgian priest, Bernard Hafkenscheid, who had preached missions in Europe, and the pattern the Redemptorists followed in the United States mirrored the parish missions of the old country.[47] Commenting on this point, one of the preachers, describing the first parish mission, wrote that "the mission was conducted fully according to the method observed in Europe and no difficulty was found in introducing every usage at once."[48] Two years later the Redemptorists published a mission book, which was sold at all their parish missions; it proved to be one of the most popular devotional books in use at the time. Like the catechism, it was an American version of an European work: "This little manual of instruction and devotion," the preface stated, "is substantially the same book which has been already so greatly blessed" in European countries.[49] In recommending its use, John Hughes stated that "*The Mission Book* has received the commendation of many distinguished prelates in Europe, as a work eminently fitted for the instruction of the faithful, and the promotion of solid piety."[50]

The mission book, available in German and English versions, also underlined the basic similarity of religion operative in ethnically diverse communities. As a handbook of piety it outlined the essentials of Tridentine Catholicism, which were to be the same in each parish community. The parish mission was a powerful force in establishing this common bond of faith among Catholic immigrants. It created a common world of religious experience in nationally diverse parishes and fostered unity in faith at a time when it was challenged by the variety of nationalities. As a social movement the parish mission also helped to strengthen the self-identity of Catholics in a Protestant environment. It reinforced the group-consciousness fostered in the local parish and was another source of meaning and direction for immigrants coping with the personal and social strains of adjusting to a new homeland. Like a political rally, it brought together people who shared common values and gave them the opportunity to express these convictions publicly and to have them reinforced by the example of others. Such an analysis helps to explain the usefulness of Catholic revivals in mid-nineteenth-century America, but other reasons must be taken into account to explain its widespread popularity.

The very nature of the parish mission helps to explain its resurgence in the 1850s. From its inception it was considered an extraordinary aspect of the church's apostolate. Its purpose was to reclaim the lukewarm, indifferent, and unfaithful Catholics.[51] Although the church always had to seek out such lost sheep, there were certain times when this apostolate was more urgently needed. After the Protestant Reformation the demand was obvious, and the parish mission became an important aspect of the Catholic reform movement. In nineteenth-century Europe, after the challenge of the Enlightenment and with the increasing secularization of traditionally Catholic countries, the demand for a renewal of religion emerged once again and revived the centuries-old tradition of the parish mission. In the United States, other, more indigenous reasons account for the introduction of this extraordinary means of evangelization.

With the beginning of mass immigration Catholicism underwent a rapid expansion, and the church could not keep up with the continual waves of Catholics arriving in America. A sense of urgency began to surface, intensified by the fear that many immigrants were losing their religion. The fear had been present earlier in the century, but it had increased by mid-century and became a topic of public and private debate.[52] Although the fears were exaggerated, they succeeded in dramatizing the issue. In addition to this fear that many newcomers were losing the faith was the more real problem

151

that many had very little faith to lose when they arrived in the country. Mission preachers traveling throughout the country continually noted this in their reports. Areas of Ohio and Michigan had seldom seen a priest, and Catholicism was in a state of decay. One priest in Rhode Island, in asking the Redemptorists to give a mission in his parish, acknowledged the poor spiritual condition of his immigrant flock and wrote that "unless you come and give me a good mission I despair."[53] For the Redemptorists the United States was indeed a mission country in need of much evangelization: they "could not find a better country to evangelize the poor and especially the abandoned souls."[54] Religious ignorance was widespread, and the parish mission became not only a means of religious revival but also an intensified period of instruction in the rudiments of the faith. Catechisms, books of devotion, rosary beads, and religious medals were all sold during the missions, and the distinct impression given in the mission reports was that many Catholics were purchasing such religious material for the first time. The city in particular was viewed as an environment harmful to the progress of religion. Newcomers could disappear in the anonymity of crowded neighborhoods without anyone ever noticing the loss. At St. Joseph's Church in New York's Greenwich Village the people who attended the mission in 1851 were described as "the most abandoned and negligent class of Catholics."[55] In St. Paul's parish a mission was held in 1859 at which "a great many young men received communion for the first time during the mission and many that were not sufficiently instructed came afterwards for instruction and made their communion in a week or two."[56] Such conditions in New York and elsewhere reinforced the fear that Catholics were drifting away from the church, and something extraordinary was needed to correct the situation. The competition from Protestants and their open proselytization only aggravated the problem.

While this climate of alarm was building, the increasing arrival of religious orders from Europe pointed toward a solution. Clergy were scarce, and most were untrained in the techniques of conducting parish missions. Redemptorists and Jesuits had a long tradition in preaching missions; as their numbers multiplied the possibility of combating the loss of faith through parish revivals increased. The revival in Europe demonstrated the effectiveness of the mission, and priests and people arrived in America aware of its popularity and success. Thus, the time was ripe for a Catholic awakening. The church believed it was losing its grip on the immigrants—the United States appeared to be moving toward infidelity and indifferentism in religion. The urban concentration of Catholics heightened the issue, while at the same time the rural isolation of many immigrants only reinforced the fear that the faith was being lost in greater numbers than one would dare to imagine. All these factors, real or imaginary, came together in the 1850s and ultimately succeeded in launching a period of revivalism throughout the country.[57]

The principal aim of the mission was individual conversion. Every mission manual stressed this objective and urged the preacher to reclaim sinners for Christ and to lead them to renounce their sins in confession.[58] For the more virtuous, the mission sought to strengthen their faith and to lead them to a more perfect practice of religion. As one manual put it, "a true mission is that which, after restoring the grace of God to those who have fallen, renews the people in their belief in Christ and the Church, teaches sound principles of morality, and reestablishes the pious frequentation of the Sacraments."[59]

The goals of conversion and renewal were thought to be most necessary in the United States, where "Catholics for want of priests to visit them lose the faith while their children for the most part are borne away by the torrent of infidelity."[60] "The ordinary ministry," one priest observed, "can no longer reach" these wayward souls, and the situation demanded something extraordinary.[61] The city became the focal point of mission preachers, since most revivalists believed that "the great need of missions lay in the cities and large towns where dense masses of Catholics were gathered, and where churches, clergy and religious organizations of all kinds were inadequate to the spiritual wants of the people."[62]

In 1851 New York City witnessed its first formal mission in St. Joseph's Church in Greenwich Village. Two years later a group of Redemptorist preachers conducted a German language mission in Redeemer parish, and German Catholics came from New York and Brooklyn to attend the services; in 1860 the parish held another mission that lasted for two weeks.[63] Transfiguration experienced its first revival in 1860 under the direction of the Jesuits; two years later another one was held in the parish.[64] Revivals took place in other churches with increasing frequency. One of the most memorable was at the Jesuit Church of St. Francis Xavier in 1863: the press reported that more than twenty-two thousand people lined up for confession and that between fifteen and thirty priests were busy from "morning to night in hearing confessions."[65]

The mission usually continued for eight days, but it was not unusual for some to last two weeks—the size of the parish and the schedule of the traveling preachers generally determined the length of the mission. Since parishioners had to work during the day, the exercises were scheduled "in such a manner not to endanger their hours of work."[66] Services with prayers, Mass, and a short thirty-minute instruction began as early as 5 A.M. "In this case punctuality must be strictly observed," one handbook cautioned, "so as to give time to those attending the instructions to go home, take their breakfast, and be on time for their work which begins usually at 7 o'clock."[67] Talks were also given during the day to parishioners who were able to attend. The highlight of the day, however, was the evening service. Well before the appointed hour people filled the church, and music and song together with a litany of prayers warmed up the audience; then the principal sermon of the day was given. It went on for about one hour and treated "the great truths which relate to the eternal destiny of man."[68] The preacher always closed the revival with a spectacular extravaganza featuring processions, singing, and a multitude of lighted candles carried by men and women publicly renouncing Satan and renewing their faith.

The mission's success was measured in terms of the number of confessions and communions—statistics which were proudly included in all mission reports. Another measure of success was the number of conversions from Protestantism, which gains for the church Catholic revivalists enthusiastically reported.[69] How successful the missions actually were is difficult to know. Thousands of people did go to confession and receive communion, but the permanency of their conversion was always questioned. A priest in Redeemer parish noted that of the six hundred youths who attended a revival in 1853, "many were not found among the sheep of Christ" a few years later.[70] The Redemptorists in particular recognized the need for periodical renewals because "the many and extraordinary conversions produced by the Missions are very rarely so permanent as not to be followed by a relapse."[71] Repeated emphasis on the need for missions illustrates the low level of popular fervor. Parish revivals were directed, not only at practicing Catholics, but especially at Catholics who had not attended church for many years. One preacher noted that at a mission "more than one-half of the people would be persons who had not been to confession for five, ten or twenty years, and of these a great number had seldom been at church, and still more rarely heard a sermon."[72] The experience of other preachers also indicated that prior to their arrival large numbers of parishioners had been lukewarm in their religious practice. The need for renewals only confirmed their observations.

The mission sermon was considerably different from the ordinary Sunday homily. Mission preachers were trained in their apostolate, and generally only the best preachers were assigned to this work. The aim of their preaching was to gain conversion of souls, and some orators were more flamboyant and vigorous than others. A noted Jesuit revivalist, Francis X. Weninger, crisscrossed Catholic America. A skillful orator, he often provoked a wail of tears in church. He spent a great deal of money on music and decorations to enhance the atmosphere of the revival, and some parishes refused to invite him because they could not afford the expenses his performance demanded.[73] Joseph Wissel was one of the more popular Redemptorist preachers: his style was vehement, and he often castigated hardened sinners to the embarrassment of his confreres.[74] Another resourceful Redemptorist, Henri Giesen, was so loud and vivid that one time, in describing the fire of Hell, the sound of his voice carried to a nearby firehouse; and within a few moments, the engine crew was rushing to church to put out the fire.[75]

To gain the conversion of souls, preachers appealed to the emotions of their audience and stressed the necessity of confession. In one mission sermon Father Wissel held up the suffering of Christ as an example for his audience and

> he portrayed with such practical conclusions the Scourging, the Crowning with thorns, the Crucifixion; and dwelt especially on the desolation of Christ, 'My God, why hast thou forsaken me'; he drew as conclusions 1. We must never commit another mortal

155

sin which would alone crucify Jesus. 2. we must suffer patiently as Christ suffered.[76]

He delivered the sermon in such a way that "one woman began to cry aloud; twenty others joined in as a chorus; and the whole congregation showed similar symptoms when the preacher said: 'Don't cry now but cry at your confession: then bewail your sins.' "[77]

To dramatize certain points revivalists would use specific props. A note of caution was indicated, however, since in the United States such theatrics might well "excite the ridicule of the people."[78] For the sermon on death, the use of a catafalque surrounded by six candles was recommended; a mournful hymn was to be added, and in the course of the sermon the preacher should point to the symbolic casket and ask the people "where their souls would be if their bodies were lying there ready for burial?" "This ceremony," the manual noted, "never fails to make a very deep impression."[79] Every mission concluded with a public renewal of one's baptismal vows, and to remind the audience of their baptismal innocence, the preacher would hold up a white baptismal robe. Such a simple action performed in an emotionally charged atmosphere produced unusual effects. "Simply holding up the white robe of Baptism," wrote one priest, "set the people almost frantic; all the preacher said after this was drowned in the uproar."[80]

Catholics would not admit it, but the parish mission resembled the Protestant revival in many ways. The preachers were itinerant evangelists especially trained for their work; described as "independent revival preachers," they traveled the country stirring up popular religious fervor. In thirty years Father Weninger logged over two hundred thousand miles, preaching eight hundred missions.[81] William McLoughlin's description of the Protestant revivalist would have fitted Weninger or any other Catholic revivalist:

the revivalist was looked upon as a kind of spiritual masseur employed once a year to tone up the body religious. When he arrived the church was placed in his hands for a thorough overhauling. For a fortnight or so he became the central figure in the religious community and the pastor merely an assistant. As a result of his preaching, church members expected to be whipped back into shape themselves and then to go out and round up those who had strayed from the path since the preceding revival.[82]

One difference between Catholic and Protestant revivals was the use of the anxious bench, where sinners would go to sit and wait for their moment of conversion. Catholics did not feature such a technique, but the confessional was a convenient substitute to which the sinner was directed and where priests were always present ready to aid the penitent through his rite of conversion. Like Catholics, Protestants viewed the city in negative moral tones and realized the need for revivals along the urban frontier. One New Yorker described his hometown to Charles Finney as a "Stupid, Poluted and Perishing City";[83] few Catholic preachers would have challenged his choice of adjectives. Protestants had their manuals on how to make a revival, and Catholics published similar handbooks.

Catholic revivalists appealed to the heart as well as to the head and sought to arouse the emotions of their audience. There was often weeping and crying, but a visible lack of emotional and physical frenzy. Protestant ministers believed that "soul winning was the primary purpose of the clergy," and according to Finney, "preaching was good if it won souls, and bad if it did not."[84] Few priests would have disagreed with him. Protestants used music to warm up the audience and to set the mood for their sermons; Catholics did the same. The techniques used in revivals were an issue of debate in both churches, and they based their revival theology on a similar premise. Protestant revivalists stressed the role of the individual in conversion, while Catholics had always emphasized the human side of this process. The sermon in both churches ended with an exhortation to repentance, and the sinner was told he could repent if he so desired. For Protestants the sawdust trail led to the preacher's platform; for Catholics it was pointed in the direction of the confessional.

The parallels between Catholic and Protestant revivals did not begin in America. Both churches could trace their roots across the ocean to Europe, where revivals were enjoying a similar popularity. Without realizing it, however, Catholics were quickly adapting themselves to American religion. Their sermons reflected the style of the day, and the emphasis on individual piety blended in with the

American Protestant ideal and the philosophy of laissez-faire individualism.[85] As Catholics they developed a separatist mentality in a Protestant society; the alleged rationalism and godlessness in the United States, bemoaned by Protestant and Catholic clergy alike, reinforced this sense of alienation. Catholic and Protestant churches were following similar paths in the United States. Their differences were more striking, but the similarities, though less publicized, were very visible. It was only a matter of time before these became more apparent, and then the charge would be leveled that Catholics were too American and ultimately too Protestant. This would have been an horrendous indictment for a Catholic preacher in the 1850s, but there was a degree of truth to it even then.

NINE

Transformation of the Church

ON SUNDAY, 25 MAY 1879, thousands of New Yorkers filled the streets surrounding St. Patrick's Cathedral. Bright sunshine had attracted an unusually large crowd, and "a dense mass of people in holiday attire crowded the sidewalks." Ushers in formal dress did their best to seat the ticket holders, and Irish policemen held back the crowds, as city and state politicians arrived in force. Over four hundred priests and forty-one bishops marched in procession to the church, where an estimated seven thousand people awaited the arrival of the clerical entourage and the start of the first Mass celebrated in the new Catholic cathedral.[1] It was a day of which Catholics could proudly boast: they had come a long way in the last half-century, and it would not be too long before a Catholic would preside over the city as mayor. This was a dramatic change from earlier years when nativist New Yorkers threatened to burn down the old cathedral and elected as mayor the candidate of the nativist American Republican party. But times had changed: in 1879 Protestants mingled with Catholics inside and outside the church, and such families as the Vanderbilts rubbed shoulders with papist priests and prelates.[2]

As Cardinal McCloskey showered the marble walls of the church with holy water, he was finalizing the dream of John Hughes. The grand cathedral, whose completion he realized he would never see, was the result of his planning.[3] But as was true in so many areas, John Hughes was building for the future; he watched the foundations of the cathedral slowly rise and knew that they were too firmly placed to be moved or altered. As head of the church in New York, he presided over other achievements, and they too provided a pattern for the future that would be slow to change.

Like many of his contemporaries, Hughes sensed that he was living in an age of transformation. In a letter to a foreign mission society in 1845 he said that it was a "time of foundation" for the church,[4] a time when "the tree which has to be brought from Europe, to be planted, to be watered for a time—and all this at great first expenses, will soon find its nutriment in the new soil, it will strike deep its roots, it will spread out its branches on every side, it will be the adornment of the church."[5] For Hughes it was a "period in which religion was taking its catholic form and tone in the United States."[6] A pioneer Catholic historian, John Gilmary Shea, shared a similar belief: in a lecture delivered in 1852 he told his audience that the Catholic church was now "acquiring a more settled form."[7] Both Hughes and Shea sensed a change from earlier years when the church was still groping to find its way in a new environment. Immigration had altered the church as well as the nation, and in the process urbanization was shaping the patterns of the future.

As a church of immigrants concentrated in the cities Catholicism acquired a new identity in the middle decades of the century. The city attracted people from all nations, and each group sought to preserve its unique religious heritage. As one New York priest put it, "the Irish find it difficult to discard their affection for everything that concerns Old Hybernia and thus would like to establish here an

Irish Catholic Church. Germans stay on their own and do not want to have anything to do with the Irish. Frenchmen, in many instances would like indeed a Roman, Apostolic Church, but would like to dress her up *a la francaise.*"[8] The national parish helped to solve this dilemma by reconstructing the religious patterns of the old country, and this made the newcomer's adjustment all the easier. Religion reinforced the cohesion of the group and delayed "the inevitable breakdown and disintegration of most of these groups in the face of the culture demands of the new society."[9] But as the church took on an intensified degree of ethnic diversity, it needed to develop a measure of unity and control lest it split apart into independent national churches. This was the problem confronting the church in the city—unity amidst diversity—but in creating the problem the urban environment would also furnish a solution that would strengthen other, more obvious unifying elements.

One conspicuous bond of unity was the common religion shared by all Catholics; the catechism best illustrates this. Whether it was written by a German Jesuit or an Irish Bishop, the catechism presented the same religious truths to both communities. It was the handbook of Tridentine Catholicism, and in the nineteenth century the mass of Catholics knew no other brand of religion. Irish and German children learned the same prayers, and at Mass they shared in the same Latin liturgy. First communion and confirmation were prized events, and confession was a telling experience for any Catholic. Divergent cultures, symbolized in language differences, separated the groups, but a shared faith provided a fundamental consensus. Even in later years when ethnic conflict intensified, German and Irish remained faithful to a common religion.[10]

The papal flag symbolized another bond of unity—loyalty to a common pope. The pontificate of Pius IX was especially turbulent, and New York Germans did not hesitate to demonstrate their support for the pope in his struggles with Italian nationalists.[11] The Irish were no less enthusiastic. The press supported his crusade against liberalism, while Irish-American seminarians in Rome volunteered to defend Pius IX from armed attack.[12] Ireland was becoming one of the citadels of papal Catholicism; and in America John Hughes gained the reputation of a staunch defender of the beleaguered pope.[13]

A sense of loyalty to an adopted homeland transcended national differences—immigrant Catholics were quick to display their mutual respect for the Stars and Stripes. The national parish aided the newcomers in becoming hyphenated Americans by providing them with a familiar experience in a strange environment. It was not necessary to sever their roots with the old country in order to pledge allegiance to a new flag. The ethnic parish assured them of this, and it helped to facilitate their accommodation to an adopted homeland. The press fostered this sense of patriotism: journalists did not find it inconsistent to be both a loyal American and a triumphal Catholic. The *Freeman's Journal* boasted that its two guiding principles were to be truly American and truly Catholic.[14] Its German counterpart, *Katholische Kirchenzeitung*, carried numerous articles championing American democracy; during the Civil War it repeatedly urged its readers to remain loyal to their country.[15] Meanwhile, Catholic apologists were working overtime to demonstrate the compatibility of their religion with the democratic system.[16] The American and papal flags were at the head of processions in parish churches, and Irish schoolchildren learned the patriotic hymns of the day and recited the speeches of Daniel Webster and Patrick Henry. John Hughes, a foreign-born leader of an ethnic church, told an immigrant audience that "next to God, a man's country has his claim on him," and there was little doubt to what country he referred.[17] During the Civil War the American flag flew from the top of the Cathedral, and in a sermon on the war Hughes told his audience "to be patriotic, to do for the country what the country needs, and the blessing of God will recompense those who discharge their duty."[18] This adopted nationalism proved to be an effective catalyst in uniting the disparate elements of urban Catholicism; and each time the country went to war it tended to increase.

Another obvious cementing force was a common enemy—nativist Americans. "In some respects," wrote John Hughes, "their violence was very serviceable to the Catholic cause." He believed that the anti-Catholic crusades "tended powerfully to unite Catholics," since in attacking their religion as well as their nationality nativists unwittingly united Irish and Germans in a common struggle for survival.[19]

Nativism, patriotism, loyalty to the pope, and a common faith all contributed to unifying the diverse elements of urban Catholicism; but something more was needed to strengthen and preserve such unity. One way the bishops sought to accomplish this was by enacting legislation binding on all Catholics regardless of their nationality. National councils sought this goal for the church throughout the United States, while local diocesan synods reinforced it in smaller geographical areas. In 1842 New York held its first synod, the legislation of which emphasized conformity among Catholics through a common body of laws. In 1850 and again in 1861 Hughes convoked additional councils to strengthen the internal unity of the church.[20]

As legislation increased, ecclesiastical affairs became more complex, and there was a need to centralize and control the administration of diocesan affairs. Hughes recognized this and in 1852 appointed Father Thomas Preston as the chancellor of the diocese.[21] Preston was to establish a chancery office and to organize the administrative aspects of church life. Dispensations from church marriage laws had to pass through his office, and pastors had to submit financial and spiritual reports to the chancery.[22] Gradually the administration of church affairs became centralized around the bishop and his chancellor; episcopal control increased in proportion to the degree of centralization, from which emerged a unifying force that more than anything else bound together the disparate elements of the church in the city.

This trend toward centralization appeared at a time when the church was rapidly expanding. In the early decades of the century church government was often identified with one or two parishes; after 1820 New York witnessed a substantial change, and as city and church expanded, they both outgrew their peculiar forms of government.[23] New churches had to be built, religious education became increasingly necessary, and numerous sick had to be cared for; and such concerns surpassed the resources of a parish-oriented government. These were demands common throughout the city, and they had to be met on a citywide, extra-parochial basis. A decentralized parochial form of government was no longer viable in a city undergoing rapid change: decisions had to be made that transcended parish loyalties, and causes had to be defended that affected all Catholics. The needs of a changing society had to be met as quickly and effectively as possible, and a parochial form of government was not suited to such a task. What ultimately emerged to fill the vacuum was the rule of one man, the church boss.

In New York no one had to ask who ruled the church: John Hughes was boss. He believed that the city demanded a "new mode of government" in the church and that of necessity he had to be both "Bishop and chief."[24] He saw his task as one of molding the diversity of Catholics into "one dough to be leavened by the spirit of Catholic faith and of Catholic union," and he ruled New York's Germans, Irish, French, and Italians with an equally firm hand.[25] If necessary, he would interdict German parishes, dismiss Irish priests with haste, and defend his churches with armed guards.

The school controversy provides a good example of how Hughes exercised this "new mode of government." It was an issue that affected all parishes, and a unified front had to be organized against the city government. Hughes became the rallying point for New York Catholics, and the two-year debate succeeded in strengthening his leadership role. Divisions among Catholics were glossed over as Hughes molded his flock into a united opposition party. His articulate and militant defense gained him national acclaim and enhanced his authority in New York. His struggle with lay trusteeism further reinforced his position: "I made war on the whole system," Hughes said, and he succeeded in breaking the grip of lay trustees on church government.[26] In earlier years such episcopal control was lacking, and the government of the church was centered in local parishes. Aggressive trustee factions challenged weak and aging bishops, but in crossing swords with Hughes they met their match, and he won control over the church in the city. As far as Hughes was concerned, the trustees were handmaids and not decisionmakers; in his opinion, "episcopal authority came from above and not from below and Catholics did their duty when they obeyed their bishop."[27]

The weakening of lay trusteeism shifted decisionmaking to the clergy and ultimately to the bishop. At one time the laity exercised a close control over parochial education and freely hired and fired instructors. By mid-century the administration of Catholic schools was passing rapidly into the hands of the clergy; in 1861 church law made the pastor the parish superintendent of education.[28] Lay men and women remained as teachers, but they no longer exercised the administrative control that their predecessors had enjoyed. The position of the laity had been relocated, and they found themselves at the bottom of the pyramid of church government. The bishop stood at the top and presided over ecclesiastical affairs, while the laity were left to pay, pray, and obey.

Squeezed between bishop and laity was the priest. In earlier years he was able to act quite independently of a distant bishop or a weak superior; if he had to struggle with authority, it was more often with lay trustees. As episcopal control increased, however, the authority of the priest shrunk. "The will of the bishop is the only law," a priest complained, and this was certainly true in New York.[29] But priests did not acquiesce easily. They appealed to tradition and to canon law; the confused state of legal affairs in American Catholicism provided them with some leverage, or so they thought. But in New York John Hughes was law; when some clergy discussed the necessity of priests' rights, Hughes told them "that he would teach them [County] Monaghan canon law; he would send them back to the bogs whence they came."[30]

The emergence of boss rule in the church was a phenomenon fostered by the urbanization of Catholicism. The variety of national groups demanded a degree of control to prevent schism in the church; at the same time the rapid expansion of the city required a "new mode of government" to consolidate church affairs. Boss rule effectively met these needs, and John Hughes was not reluctant to exercise this function. He ruled like an Irish chieftain, and the Irish respect for the hierarchy of power made his task all the easier.[31] When he died, his scepter passed to Archbishop John McCloskey and later to Michael Corrigan; the pattern of government remained the same, more refined perhaps, but no less authoritarian, as the will of the bishop increasingly became the law of the church.[32]

Catholic theology in the nineteenth century certainly encouraged the development of strong episcopal control. Pius IX had consolidated the authority of the church in the papacy, and the First Vatican Council strengthened his position as supreme ruler.[33] This model of monarchical authority became normative on the local level, where each bishop was pope in his own diocese. Urbanization in Europe and America, however, facilitated the role of pope and bishop.[34] Large cities were developing, and the church needed to develop a new style of government to control rapidly expanding communities. Though theology provided the rationale, urbanization emphasized the need for a new mode of government. The rise of the city encouraged the development of monarchical authority, especially in the United States, where Catholicism was taking shape at a time when cities were developing at an unprecedented rate. Since it was predominantly an urban church, the need for control and centralization was even more pronounced. Thus, boss rule appeared at a time when it was theologically justified and culturally necessary, with the happy result that it effectively united the diverse elements of urban Catholicism.

The centralization of government was only one aspect of the transformation of the church in the city. Another dimension of power was developing that was more tangible and more readily perceived: Catholic journalists in the 1870s described it as "ecclesiastical magnificence";[35] in more prosaic words, it was dollar power.

In the early decades of the century the church was financially weak; widespread indebtedness threatened its survival. Bishop Dubois was forced to write letters to European aid societies begging for funds, and despite advancing age, he traveled to Rome and Lyons to plead his case.[36] John Hughes wrote many urgent pleas for aid and also returned to the old country in search of money.[37] But the large increase in the number of Catholics and the rise of middle-class entrepreneurs expanded the resources of the church. Later begging letters became more modest and less urgent. When he was planning St. Patrick's, "a Cathedral," he said, "that may be worthy of our increasing numbers, intelligence and wealth," Hughes sought one hundred Catholics who would contribute a thousand dollars each to the building campaign.[38] Although he was not totally successful, he did collect seventy-three thousand dollars in a short period of time from the more well-to-do members of the church.[39] In 1841 a year-long campaign for funds throughout the city was able to raise only seventeen thousand dollars. Signs of new wealth appeared in parish churches as remodeling and refurnishing embellished the modest achievements of the past. Vestments from France and imported works of art appeared on the scene with greater frequency.[40] In earlier years Catholics were not so ostentatious. In a sermon given at the dedication of St. Nicholas Church in 1835 the speaker pointed out that "its plain construction will furnsh nothing to elicit admiration. It will neither be planned by power nor achieved by wealth."[41] He was not exaggerating either: the small building, which could seat only one hundred people, had no tower, no bells, and only one altar, and the priest lived in the basement.[42] The new German church of Most Holy Redeemer, built in 1851, elicited an entirely different response. Catholics boasted of its size and grandeur, and its bell tower proudly stood out along the skyline of the Lower East Side. St. Patrick's was the ultimate sign of arrival and financial stability. Rivaling cathedrals in Europe, its grandeur appeared worthy of the "numbers, intelligence and wealth" of New York Catholics.

In 1820 the church owned very little property in New York, and it could claim only two modestly built churches. Forty years later thirty Catholic churches were scattered throughout the city, and their combined property value totaled over a million and a half dollars ($1,505,600); only the Presbyterians and the Episcopalians surpassed the Catholics in landed wealth.[43] By 1858 the educational enterprise represented almost a two-million-dollar investment.[44] Thus, in a relatively short period of time the church had moved from borderline bankruptcy to landed wealth. Pride had replaced modesty, and architectural grandeur and financial resources were signs of success that all Americans understood.

One reason for the growth in financial resources was the emergence of a large middle class. Though many Catholics were poverty-stricken immigrants, there is no doubt that many others enjoyed a modest degree of financial security. In a moment of literary exaggeration a Catholic journalist observed that most Catholics "are well to do; some considerable number are rich."[45] Indeed, there was some foundation for this burst of Catholic pride. Irish and Germans were well-represented in the middle classes of society and were able to finance the building of churches, hospitals, and schools. The multiplication of private academies and colleges with high tuitions and increasing enrollment pointed to a segment of urban Catholics who cannot be labeled as poverty-stricken immigrants. Many were old-time New Yorkers who were making their way in the city well before the famine migration, and by the 1860s social class defined some parishes more accurately than religious affiliation. The clergy took on similar characteristics as refined tastes, European vacations, and holidays at Saratoga Springs became a style of life for more than a few.[46] By the 1870s upper-class Catholics were repudiating their lower-class brethren, and the New York Irish were already living in "lace-curtain" apartments, as well as run down, "shanty" homes.[47]

This concentration of large numbers of middle- and lower-class Catholics furnished the resources necessary to build up the church in the city. In the process the church acquired an internal strength measurable in financial figures that was not present in earlier days. Equally significant was the mentality that shaped this transformation.

The Protestant tone of ante-bellum New York, reinforced by a hostile nativist crusade, forced the church to back away from any accommodation with urban institutions. Separate schools, hospitals, and orphanages became necessary as far as Catholics were concerned, and defensive, apologetic sermons strengthened this separatist stance; the pervasive presence of Protestant missionaries, seemingly eager to gain converts, tended to justify the withdrawal. The city government, rooted in a Protestant past, could not meet the needs of an expanding Catholic community, and so Catholics developed their own institutions. Their large numbers, their financial resources, and a strong authoritarian leader eventually made the church a citadel in the city that politicians learned to reckon with and Protestants could not ignore.

In withdrawing from an unfriendly society and concentrating on its own internal development, the church had few models to follow except those of the old country. In looking to the past for their response to current needs Catholics inevitably adopted a conservative social program. A similar pattern appeared when the Irish captured control of urban politics. "They never thought of politics as an instrument of social change," Daniel Moynihan has observed, and "their kind of politics involved the processes of a society that was not changing."[48] The church's social apostolate followed the same trend. Catholics lived in crowded tenements; children gathered rags on school holidays; and the poor and the sick crowded the city's institutions. But for Catholics this was all part of God's plan, and what had worked in the past was adequate for the present. This mentality was nurtured by the catechism and reinforced by the pulpit. As an immigrant institution, the church's task was to conserve the old order and to strengthen the self-identity of Catholics in a predominantly Protestant culture. In this situation religion could not function as a catalyst for social change: it was forced to serve as a link with the past; and as long as the church ministered to the immigrants, its basic stance toward society remained conservative.

In a sense the conservatism of the church was its greatest strength: by remaining faithful to the past it succeeded in preserving the faith of the immigrants. To achieve this goal it chose to become an island community, and as the immigrants were slowly becoming more American, the church was also building walls of separation isolating them from the rest of society. In subsequent decades, as more newcomers settled in the city, the church acquired a degree of diversity and organization unimagined in 1870. Yet, the features of urban Catholicism remained intact. The "time of foundation" had charted the course of the future, and the success of the church in the city continued to be the measure of its achievement in the nation.

Essay on Sources

When this study was first envisioned, one of the critical problems I
had to resolve was the availability of pertinent sources. American
Catholic historiography includes many outstanding studies, but a
large majority of these writings view the church from the top down,
with the result that episcopal biographies dominate the field. In
attempting to write a more social and thus more representative history of one aspect of American Catholicism, I chose to look at the
church from the bottom up. After considerable research I am convinced that such an approach is more feasible than previously
acknowledged. I have included this essay as an aid for those who
might be inclined to follow a similar path in their search for a
better understanding of the American Catholic experience. While it
is not exhaustive, it is suggestive in the hope that it will encourage
others to undertake a study of American Catholicism from a perspective too long ignored.

A variety of sources are available for the study of the city. A
primary requirement is good maps: New York has an abundance of
maps depicting the ante-bellum city, which are available at the New
York Historical Society and the New York Public Library. The maps
that proved most useful for the study of city neighborhoods were
those done under the direction of William Perris, *Maps of the City
of New York Surveyed Under the Directions of Insurance Companies of Said City* (1852–53), which graphically portray the type of
neighborhood buildings and illustrate the variety of land use. Wil-

liam Perris also directed a similar project in 1867–68, the maps from which can serve as a useful index of the development of the city from 1852 to 1868. Continual walking and browsing around city neighborhoods helped to stimulate the historical imagination. Old churches still remain in their nineteenth-century location, and a visit to them helps to enliven the inanimate data of history. To visit the streets where tenements once stood also provides a sense of proportion and understanding to one-dimensional maps and drawings.

Each age writes its own history in a variety of ways. A most valuable source for my purposes was *The Citizens Association of New York. Report of the Council of Hygiene and Public Health* (New York, 1865), an account of housing and living conditions for the entire city of New York; the history of the report and the method used in compiling it are explained by Stephen Smith in *The City That Was* (New York, 1911). Another useful social history of the city was presented in the Annual Reports of the New York Association for Improving the Condition of the Poor, 1845–65. The Association also conducted one of the first housing studies of New York, *First Report of a Committee on the Sanitary Condition of the Laboring Classes in the City of New York with Remedial Suggestions* (New York, 1853). Four years later the state legislature sponsored a similar report, *New York State Assembly. Documents. Report of a Select Committee Appointed to Examine into the Condition of Tenant Houses in New York and Brooklyn 1857*, vol. 3, report no. 205. John H. Griscom, *The Sanitary Condition of the Laboring Population of New York* (New York, 1845), was also helpful.

Immigrant aid societies frequently published annual reports of their activities. Particularly valuable for a study of the New York Germans were the reports of the German Society of the City of New York, *Jahres-Bericht der Deutschen Gesellschaft der Stadt N.Y.*, 1846–65.

Population figures and many other social statistics are available in state and federal censuses. Though they are not infallible, they do provide information that is not available elsewhere. The decennial *New York State Census*, 1835–65, and the *U.S. Census*, 1850–80, in both printed and manuscript editions are essential for a study of New York. Another important source is *New York State Assembly*.

Documents. Report of the Tenement House Committee 1894. Report No. 37, which contains information on population growth and density as well as on the housing conditions of the city.

City directories also provide a variety of information about urban life. As an index of population mobility they must be used with discretion, but their listing of names, occupations, and home addresses can be correlated with parish baptismal records to provide a social profile of families living in a city parish. A complete bound set of New York City Directories is available at the New York Historical Society.

Nineteenth-century urban history includes many valuable studies. For New York, Benson J. Lossing, *History of New York City* (New York, 1884); and James G. Wilson, ed., *Memorial History of the City of New York*, 4 vols. (New York, 1892–93), were most helpful.

A wide variety of resources are available for the study of the church in the city. An unlikely place to begin is the University of Notre Dame. Notre Dame has a rich collection of manuscript and printed material related to the history of American Catholicism. Included in this collection are microfilm copies of diocesan reports sent by American bishops to mission societies in Europe; written with a view toward solliciting financial aid for a diocese, these reports provide a general picture of the church in the city as well as in the diocese. The condition of German Catholics in the United States is described in the Annals of the Leopoldine Society, located in Vienna, Austria—*Berichte der Leopoldinen-Stifung im Kaiserthume Oesterreich*. In addition to this printed work, the University has a microfilm collection of unpublished letters and reports to the society, English translations of which, in summary form, are available at the archives. Another unpublished manuscript collection contains letters and reports to the Ludwig-Missionsverein in Munich, Germany. Theodore Roemer, O.F.M. Cap. has written two useful studies of these mission societies: *The Leopoldine Foundation and the Church in the United States, 1829–1839* (New York, 1933), and *The Ludwig-Missionsverein and the Catholic Church in the United States, 1838–1918* (Washington, D.C., 1933). Microfilm copies of diocesan reports to the Society for the Propagation of the Faith at Paris and Lyons, France, also provide valuable information on the life of the church. The most valuable materials, however, were the microfilm copies of letters and reports sent by bishops, priests, and laity to the Congregation of Propaganda Fide in Rome, which documents are essential for anyone studying the history of American Catholicism in the nineteenth century. A guide to this collection, has been compiled by Anton Debevec and edited by Finbar Kenneally, O.F.M.: *United States Documents in the Propaganda Fide Archives: A Calendar*, 1st series, 5 vols. (Washington, D.C., 1966–74). This guide is an indispensible index to the thousands of letters contained in the collection and also provides a summary of the contents of each document.

The Archives of the Archdiocese of New York, located at St. Joseph's Seminary in Yonkers, contain a large collection of material related to the history of New York Catholicism. The major portion of the collection is the correspondence of New York bishops, chief among which is the correspondence of John Hughes. Included in the Hughes collection are a letterbook of the archbishop, containing copies of letters sent by Hughes to different persons, and the diaries of his secretaries, Rev. James R. Bayley and Rev. Thomas Preston. One of the most valuable sources in the archives is the diary of Rev. Richard L. Burtsell, covering the period from 1865 to 1905. Burtsell was actively involved in church affairs, and his diary records a view of New York Catholicism not often included in published materials. The archives also contain the financial and spiritual reports of New York parishes. Mention should also be made of the personal collection of Dr. Henry J. Browne of Rutgers University. Dr. Browne spent several years preparing a definitive biography of John Hughes and has gathered together a wealth of material related to the life of Hughes. I was able to consult this material, as well as Dr. Browne's unpublished biography of the archbishop.

Most religious orders manifest an historical consciousness and record and preserve the events of their community's past. For my purposes the Archives of the Baltimore Province of the Redemptorists, located in Brooklyn, New York, were most useful. These archives contain the chronicles of Most Holy Redeemer and St. Alphonsus parishes; these chronicles are a continuous history of the parishes, written by a priest or brother assigned to this task by the community. The archives also include a multivolume history by Joseph Wuest, C.SS.R.: *Annales Congregationis S.S. Redemptoris*

Provinciae Americae, 5 vols. (vols. 1–3: Ilchester, Md., 1888–99; vols. 4–5: Boston, 1914–24). This collection contains diaries, parish chronicles, and mission reports of the community throughout the United States; it provides valuable material related to German Catholics, since they represented the special apostolate of the Redemptorists in the nineteenth century. The Rev. Michael J. Curley, C.SS.R., now deceased, was most helpful in assisting me during this phase of my research. The archives of the Paulist Fathers, located on West Fifty-ninth Street in New York City, also contain valuable material on parish missions. In particular, it includes in its collection unpublished mission chronicles recording the activities of the Paulist mission band, which offer very useful information about the history of the church in all parts of the United States.

Catholic parishes do not have archives in the technical sense of the word, but they do possess valuable sources in the registers of baptism and marriage. These registers contain the name, age, and often place of residence and place of birth of the individuals involved in the sacraments of marriage and baptism. Transfiguration Church did have in its possession the Trustee Minutes of the parish from 1836 to 1844, and these provided a good description of the 1837 depression and the financial crisis that struck the parish community.

Parish histories also provide useful information, but one has to be judicious in the use of such works. Many are not very scholarly and tend to portray a very superficial picture of parochial life. Yet, several good histories of New York parishes are available. Chief among these are, Henry J. Browne, *St. Ann's on East Twelfth Street New York City, 1852–1952* (New York, 1952); idem, *The Parish of St. Michael, 1857–1957* (New York, 1957); Georg Dusold , C.SS.R., *Goldenes Jubiläum der Kirche zum Allerheiligsten Erlöser* (New York, 1894); and Francis X. Murphy, C.SS.R., *The Centennial History of St. Alphonsus Parish* (New York, 1947). The most valuable work on Catholic parishes in New York is the comprehensive study of John Gilmary Shea: *The Catholic Churches of New York City* (New York, 1878).

Catholic newspapers provided a valuable insight to the community. Bound copies of the New York Irish paper, *Truth Teller,* are available at the American Irish Historical Society in New York City.

Bound copies of the *Freeman's Journal* are available at St. Joseph's Seminary in Yonkers, N.Y., and at the Dominican College of the Immaculate Conception in Washington, D.C. The Catholic University of America in Washington, D.C., has an extensive microfilm collection of American Catholic newspapers, which I consulted for the *Metropolitan Record* and the *New York Weekly Register and Catholic Diary*. The German Catholic newspaper, *Katholische Kirchenzeitung*, was located at the Redemptorist Provincial Archives in Brooklyn, N.Y. A useful guide to the Catholic press is the work of Eugene P. Willging and Herta Hatzfeld, *Catholic Serials of the Nineteenth Century in the United States: A Descriptive Bibliography and Union List*. The first series of this bibliography was published serially in the *Records of the American Catholic Historical Society of Philadelphia, 1954–63*; the second series was published by the Catholic University of America Press, Washington, D.C., during the years 1962–67.

The published legislation of the New York synods and councils indicates the concerns of an immigrant church and its plans for organization. I consulted *Synodus Dioecesana Neo-Eboracensis Prima Habita Anno 1842* (New York, 1842); *Concilium Neo-Eboracense Primum Habitum Anno 1854* (New York, 1855); and *Concilium Provinciale Neo-Eboracense III Mense Julii, Anno 1861 Celebratum* (New York, 1862).

Catholic Directories were published during the ante-bellum period and contain a wealth of material related to American Catholicism. The first directory appeared in 1822: *The Laity's Directory to Church Services* (New York, 1822); the next directory was published in 1833, *United States Catholic Almanac or Laity's Directory* (Baltimore, 1833), and it appeared annually until 1838. The next series was entitled *Metropolitan Catholic Almanac and Laity's Directory* (Baltimore, 1839–57). In 1860–61 the *Metropolitan Catholic Almanac and Laity's Directory for the United States* (Baltimore) was published. In 1864 *Sadlier's Catholic Almanac and Ordo* (New York) appeared, and it continued publication until 1896.

The history of Catholic Education has been written about in great detail, but surprisingly little work has been done on the values passed on in Catholic schools. In order to understand this aspect of education the study of nineteenth-century textbooks and principally the catechism is indispensable. Two guides to this vast area of literature are: A. H. Songe, "A Bibliographical Survey of Catholic Textbooks Published in the United States from 1764 Through 1865" (M.A. thesis, Catholic University of America, 1956); and M. A. Foohey, "Bibliographical Survey of Catholic Textbooks Published in the United States from 1866–1900" (M.S.L.S. diss., Catholic University of America, 1961). Many other guides to Catholic publications were done at the Catholic University of America as Master's theses in Library Science, and they furnish a useful index to Catholic Literature.

The Catholic Directory regularly advertised textbooks, catechetical manuals, and novels; such advertisements were useful in determining the popularity of certain books and often indicated in what schools particular books were used. The books consulted in this study, indicated in the footnotes to chapter six, were obtained from the University of Notre Dame library. The Archives of the American Catholic Historical Society of Philadelphia, located at St. Charles Seminary in Philadelphia, Pennsylvania, also has a large collection of catechisms used in the nineteenth century.

Another neglected area in American Catholic historiography is preaching. For many Catholics the pulpit was the principal source of instruction and confirmation in their religious beliefs. While it is true that many sermons were never recorded for history, a substantial number were. These sermons, available in published form, provide the principal key to understanding the values transmitted from the pulpit. Lawrence Kehoe, ed., *Complete Works of the Most Rev. John Hughes, D.D.*, 2 vols. (New York, 1865), contain many of Hughes's sermons, and the Archives of the Archdiocese of New York has a collection of his sermons in manuscript form. The parish sermons of religious order priests are frequently available, such as *Sermons Preached at the Church of St. Paul the Apostle, New York* (New York, 1862–67). This type of sermon book became more plentiful in subsequent decades. The sermons of noted European preachers were widely advertised in the Catholic Directory and were used by priests in the United States as ready-made source material. The work of Joseph M. Connors, S.V.D., "Catholic Homiletic Theory in Historical Perspective" (Ph.D. diss., Northwestern University, 1962), is a very helpful guide to these works and especially to the nature of pulpit oratory operative in the United States. For the study of parish missions before 1870 the following works were most useful: Gilbert J. Garraghan, S.J., *The Jesuits of the Middle United States,* 3 vols. (New York, 1938); Joseph Wissel, C.SS.R., *The Redemptorist on the American Missions,* 3 vols., 3d rev. ed. (n.p., 1920); and Wuest, *Annales.* A. F. Hewit, *Sermons of the Rev. Francis A. Baker, C.S.P. with a Memoir of His Life,* 6th ed. (New York, 1865), also contains the mission sermons as well as Sunday sermons of a noted New York preacher.

Additional sources used in this study are indicated in the footnotes to each chapter.

Notes

INTRODUCTION

1. George Rogers Taylor, *The Transportation Revolution* (New York, 1968), p. 388; and *idem*, "American Urban Growth Preceding the Railway Age," *Journal of Economic History* 27 (September 1967): 309–69.

2. Martin E. Marty, *The Modern Schism* (New York, 1969), p. 98.

3. Archives of the Paulist Fathers (hereinafter to be cited as APF), Mission Chronicle, vol. 2, p. 382; similar descriptive comments about Maryland-type Catholics are found throughout the Chronicles.

4. Peter Guilday, *The Life and Times of John Carroll* (New York, 1922), p. 832.

5. Donna Merwick, *Boston Priests, 1848–1910* (Cambridge, Mass., 1973), p. 4.

6. Gerald Shaughnessy, *Has the Immigrant Kept the Faith?* (New York, 1925), p. 72.

7. *Ibid.*, pp. 153–54.

8. John Gilmary Shea, *The History of the Catholic Church in the United States*, 4 vols. (New York, 1886–92).

9. Ray Allen Billington, *The Protestant Crusade, 1800–1860* (New York, 1938).

10. *Ibid.*, p. 33.

11. Oscar Handlin, *Boston's Immigrants, 1795–1865* (Cambridge, Mass., 1959).

12. James F. Connelly, *The Visit of Archbishop Gaetano Bedini to the United States of America* (Rome, 1960), p. 241.

13. See John Bossy, "The Counter-Reformation and the People of Catholic Europe," *Past and Present* 47 (May 1970): 52; and L.-J. Rogier, G. De Bertier De Sauvigny, and J. Hajjar, *Siécle des Luminiéres Révolutions Restaurations*, vol. 4 of *Nouvelle Histoire de L'Église*, ed. L.-J. Rogier, R. Aubert, and M. D. Knowles (Paris, n.d.), pp. 107–8, 122–23.

14. *Ibid.*

15. See Eugenio Correcco, *La Formazione Della Chiesa Cattolica Negli Stati Uniti D'America Attraverso L'Attività Sinodale* (Brescia, 1970).

16. "Religion in New York," *Catholic World* 3 (June 1866): 387.

17. Henry DeCourcy, *The Catholic Church in the United States*, trans. and enlarged by John Gilmary Shea, 2d rev. ed. (New York, 1857), p. 449.

18. APF, Rev. Isaac Hecker to Cardinal Barnabo, New York, February 9, 1864.

ONE. THE CITY AND THE CHURCH

1. Henry Têtu, ed., *Journal des Visites Pastorales par Mgr. Joseph-Octave Plessis, Evêque de Quebec* (Quebec, 1903), p. 161; and Mary Peter Carthy, *Old St. Patrick's: New York's First Cathedral* (New York, 1947).

2. Robert G. Albion, *The Rise of the New York Port: 1815–1860* (New York, 1939), p. 386.

3. *New York State Census 1865*, p. xxv; and Thomas Adams *et al., Population, Land Values, and Government*, vol. 2 of *Regional Survey of New York and Its Environs* (New York, 1929), p. 53.

4. This population is based on figures given in a letter of Bishop Hughes to the Society for the Propagation of the Faith, Paris, 27 November 1839, f. 104, Archives of the University of Notre Dame (hereinafter to be cited as AUND); and *Truth Teller*, 27 March 1841.

5. John Gilmary Shea, *The Catholic Churches of New York City* (New York, 1878), pp. 564–66.

6. Joseph Salzbacher, *Meine Reise nach Nord Amerika in Jahre 1842* (Vienna, 1845), pp. 297–99.

7. *Truth Teller*, 24 October 1840.

8. *New York State Census 1865*, p. xxv; and Adams, *Population, Land Values, and Government*, p. 53.

9. James G. Wilson, ed., *Memorial History of the City of New York*, 4 vols. (New York, 1892–93), vol. 3, p. 518.

10. "Religion in New York," *Catholic World* 3 (June 1866): 386–87.

11. Joseph W. Greene, Jr., "New York City's First Railroad: The New York and Harlem, 1832–1867," *New York Historical Society Quarterly Bulletin*, January 1926, pp. 1–19.

12. Edward Ruggles, *A Picture of New York in 1846* (New York, 1846), p. 23; Wilson, *Memorial History*, vol. 3, p. 446.

13. Patrick J. Dooley, S.J., *Fifty Years in Yorkville or Annals of the Parish of St. Ignatius Loyola and St. Lawrence O'Toole* (New York, 1917), pp. 12–13.

14. Ruggles, *A Picture of New York in 1846*, p. 23.

15. Shea, *The Catholic Churches of New York City*, pp. 165 and 462.

16. Howard B. Woolston, *A Study of the Population of Manhattanville* (New York, 1909), pp. 24–29.

17. The phrase "suburban churches" was in use in the 1860s, for example, in *Freeman's Journal*, 7 April 1866.

18. John Anderson Miller, *Fares Please! From Horse Cars to Steamliners* (New York, 1941), pp. 1–2.

19. "Omnibus Lines In New York City in 1855," *New York Historical Society Quarterly* 22 (October 1938): 125–29; and Bayrd Still, *Mirror for Gotham: New York As Seen by Contemporaries From Dutch Days to the Present* (New York, 1956), p. 154.

20. I. T. Williams, *Broadway Railroad: Speech of Mr. I. T. Williams in Opposition before the Railroad Committee of the Assembly March 5, 1862* (New York, 1862), pp. 3–7; *New York City Directory 1860*, p. 17; and Still, *Mirror For Gotham*, p. 138.

21. State of New York, *Report of a Special Commission Designated by the Senate to Ascertain the Best Means for the Transportation of Passengers in the City of New York* (Albany, 1867), no. 28, p. 3.

22. Wilson, *Memorial History*, vol. 3, pp. 446 and 519.

23. *Historical Records Survey: Inventory of the Church Archives in New York City: The Roman Catholic Church*, 2 vols. (New York, 1941), vol. 2, pp. 50–68.

24. *New York State Census 1865*, p. xxv.

25. *Metropolitan Record*, 28 March 1863.

26. Archives of the Archdiocese of New York (hereinafter to be cited as AANY), Diary of the Rev. Richard L. Burtsell, 29 November 1865.

27. AUND, *Scritture Riferite nei Congressi: America Centrale* (hereinafter to be cited as *Scritture*), vol. 18, letter 1316, Louis Binsse to Prefect of Propaganda Fide, 9 April 1858, f. 216; and James D. McCabe, Jr., *Lights and Shadows of New York Life* (Philadelphia, 1872), p. 494.

28. AANY, Diary of the Rev. Richard L. Burtsell, 22 June 1865.

29. Walt Whitman, "City of Ships," in *Leaves of Grass*, ed. John Kouwenhoven (New York, 1950), p. 233.

30. Cf. Robert D. Cross, ed., *The Church and the City* (New York, 1967), pp. xxi–xxv; AUND, *Scritture*, vol. 19, letter 1841, Rev. I. T. Hecker to Prefect of the Propaganda Fide, 26 June 1861, f. 231; and *The Citizens Association of New York. Report of the Council of Hygiene and Public Health* (New York, 1865), hereinafter to be cited as the *Report of the Council of Hygiene*, pp. 291–93.

31. Woolston, *A Study of the Population of Manhattanville*, p. 27.

32. Cf. Henry J. Browne, *St. Ann's on East Twelfth Street* (New York, 1952); and Edmund T. Delaney, *New York's Greenwich Village* (Barre, Mass., 1968), p. 77.

33. AUND, *Scritture*, vol. 19, letter 2102, Rev. E. McGlynn to Prefect of Propaganda Fide, 4 November 1861, f. 980.

34. AANY, Rev. Richard Burtsell to Cardinal Prefect of Propaganda, 1 May 1867 (copy of letter).

35. AANY, Diary of the Rev. Richard L. Burtsell, 24 June 1865.

36. *Annual Report of the New York Association for Improving the Conditions of the Poor 1867* (hereinafter to be cited as A.I.C.P.), p. 42.

37. Cross, *The Church and The City*, pp. xx–xxi; cf. also Francois Houtart,

Aspects Sociologiques du Catholicisme Américain (Paris, 1957), pp. 49 ff.; *idem,* "A Sociological Study of the Evolution of the American Catholics," *Sociaal Kompass,* January/April 1955, pp. 189–216; and C. J. Nuesse and Thomas J. Harte, eds., *The Sociology of the Parish* (Milwaukee, 1951).

38. See, for example, *Synodus Diocesana Neo-Eboracensis Prima 1842* (New York, 1842), pp. 11–12.

39. *Ibid.,* p. 12, where the concept of the "national parish" is evident in the diocesan statutes; also AANY, Archbishop John Hughes to Rev. Anthony Sanguinetti, 25 March 1861.

40. Cf. Leo R. Ryan, *Old St. Peter's: The Mother Church of Catholic New York, 1785–1935* (New York, 1935), pp. 61 ff., for history of early New York Catholicism.

41. Richard J. Purcell, "Immigration from the Canal Era to the Civil War," *History of the State of New York,* ed. A. C. Flick, 10 vols. (New York, 1933–37), vol. 7, p. 43.

42. *U.S. Census 1860, Population,* p. 609.

43. Salzbacher, *Meine Reise,* p. 298; *Katholische Kirchenzeitung,* 1 October 1857, also for the expression "Irish churches."

44. AUND, *Scritture,* vol. 15, letter 307, Rev. Jeremiah Cummings to Prefect of Propaganda Fide, 29 May 1849.

45. AUND, Bishop John Hughes to Society for Propagation of the Faith, Paris, 23 January 1845, f. 104.

46. See *St. Nicholas Church in Second Street* (New York, 1932), for the early history of German Catholics in New York.

47. *U.S. Census 1860, Population,* p. 609; see *Historical Records Survey,* vol. 2, for summary of the organization of different parishes in New York.

48. The German Catholic population for 1869 was 49,000. Cf. Ernst A. Reiter, *Schematismus der katholischen deutschen Geistlichkeit in den Ver. Staaten Nord-Amerika's* (New York, 1869), pp. 97 ff. This was a conservative estimate; a more accurate figure appears to be around 70,000, based on the relative German Catholic population in ante-bellum New York (cf. Jay P. Dolan, "Urban Catholicism: New York City, 1815–1865" [Ph.D. diss., University of Chicago, 1970], pp. 152–55).

49. *U.S. Census 1860, Population,* p. 609.

50. Henry Binsse, "The Church of Saint Vincent de Paul (The French Church), New York," *Historical Records and Studies* 12 (June 1918): 102–14.

51. AUND, *Scritture,* vol. 18, letter 1685, f. 1475; the U.S. Census in 1860 recorded only 1,464 foreign-born Italians in New York, (*Population,* p. 609).

52. Robert Ernst, *Immigrant Life in New York City, 1825–1863* (Port Washington, N.Y., 1949), p. 195; and Howard A. Marraro, "Italians in New York During the First Half of the 19th Century," *New York History* 26 (July 1945): 291.

53. AUND, *Scritture,* vol. 17, letter 1080, Louis Binsse to Prefect of Propaganda Fide, 16 March 1857(?), f. 873; vol. 18, letter 1281, Louis Binsse to Prefect of Propaganda Fide, 6 February 1858, f. 118.

54. *Ibid.,* vol 18, letter 1703, Rev. Antonio Sanguinetti to Prefect of Propaganda

Fide, 27 October 1860; letter 1704, Sanguinetti to Prefect, 5 November 1860; letter 1685, Appeal of Italian Community to Holy Father, 7 July 1860; letter 1681, D. Lucciardi, Cardinal Bishop to Prefect of Propaganda Fide, 18 August 1860.

55. *Ibid.*, letter 1701, Petition of Italians to Archbishop John Hughes, 16 August 1860, f. 1522.

56. *Ibid.*, letter 1703, ff. 1532–36; and AANY, Hughes to Sanguinetti, 25 March 1861.

57. AUND, *Scritture*, vol. 18, letter 1685, f. 1476.

58. Rhoda G. Freeman, "The Free Negro in New York City in the Era Before the Civil War" (Ph.D. diss., Columbia University, 1966), pp. 412–13, 422.

59. *Catholic Mirror*, 16 February 1867.

60. AUND, *Scritture*, vol. 16, letter 715, Harriet Thompson to Holy Father, 29 October 1853, f. 772; and AANY, Diary of the Rev. Richard L. Burtsell, 12 May 1867.

61. New York Public Library, Pierre Toussaint Mss. Collection, Prospectus for the Schools, 22 August 1846; and Binsse, "Church of St. Vincent de Paul," p. 106.

62. Thomas F. Meehan, "Mission Work Among Colored Catholics," *Historical Records and Studies* 8 (1915): 122–23; AANY, Diary of the Rev. Richard L. Burtsell, 2 February 1865; Archives of Josephite Fathers, Canon Peter L. Benoit, Diary of a Trip to America, 6 January–8 June 1875, p. 328; cf. also John T. Gillard, *The Catholic Church and the American Negro* (Baltimore, 1929), pp. 67 ff.; Edward J. Misch, "The American Bishops and the Negro from the Civil War to the Third Plenary Council of Baltimore, 1865–84" (Ph.D. diss., Gregorian University, Rome, 1968), p. 367; and Freeman, "The Free Negro," pp. 375 ff.

63. Misch, "The American Bishops," pp. 44–45, 74, and *passim*.

64. AUND, *Scritture*, vol 16, letter 715, f. 773.

65. Gilbert Osofsky, *Harlem: The Making of a Ghetto* (New York, 1968), p. 45.

66. *Freeman's Journal*, 5 June 1869.

67. Letter of Father F. X. Weninger to American Bishops, 19 March 1874, cited in Misch, "The American Bishops," p. 616.

68. William Osborne, *The Segregated Covenant* (New York, 1967), p. 128.

69. James R. Bayley, *A Brief Sketch of the Early History of the Catholic Church on the Island of New York*, 2d ed. (New York, 1870), p. 160.

TWO. THE ETHNIC VILLAGE

1. *Katholische Kirchenzeitung*, 19 August 1858; and *New York Times*, 16 August 1858.

2. *U.S. Census 1860, Population*, pp. 345 and 609; and Kate Claghorn, "The Foreign Immigrant in New York City," *Reports of the Industrial Commission on Immigration and on Education*, 19 vols. (Washington, D.C., 1901), vol. 15, pp. 449–92.

3. *Truth Teller*, 29 November 1834; and George W. Potter, *To the Golden Door* (Boston, 1960), p. 231.

4. *New York State Census 1855*, p. 110; and *New York State Census 1865*, pp. xxv and 130.

5. Maldwyn Allen Jones, *American Immigration* (Chicago, 1960), p. 110; *Jahres-Bericht der Deutschen Gesellschaft der Stadt N.Y.* 72 (1855): 7; and *U.S. Census 1860, Population*, pp. 345 and 609.

6. Still, *Mirror for Gotham*, p. 161.

7. *New York State Census 1865*, p. 130.

8. Charles Dickens, *American Notes and Pictures from Italy* (London, 1887), p. 88.

9. Vols. 1 and 3 of William Perris, *Maps of the City of New York Surveyed Under Directions of Insurance Companies of Said City*, 4 vols. (New York, 1852–53), were used in determining the type of land use in Wards Four, Five, and Six.

10. Alvin F. Harlow, *Old Bowery Days: The Chronicles of a Famous Street* (New York, 1931), p. 319; and *Report of the Council of Hygiene*, pp. lvi and 147.

11. *Report of the Council of Hygiene*, p. 160.

12. Samuel Gompers, *Seventy Years of Life and Labor*, 2 vols. (New York, 1925), vol. 1, p. 24.

13. *Report of the Council of Hygiene*, p. 95.

14. Charles D. Shanly, "Germany in New York," *Atlantic Monthly* 19 (May 1867): 559; and Harlow, *Old Bowery Days*, pp. 184–85.

15. *Report of the Council of Hygiene*, p. 81.

16. *Ibid.*, p. 106.

17. Alexander B. Callow, Jr., *The Tweed Ring* (New York, 1969), p. 42.

18. Raymond A. Mohl, *Poverty In New York, 1783–1825* (New York, 1971), p. 62.

19. Douglass T. Miller, *Jacksonian Aristocracy: Class and Democracy in New York, 1830–1860* (New York, 1967).

20. John H. Griscom, *The Sanitary Conditions of the Laboring Population of New York* (New York, 1845), p. 13; and *A.I.C.P. Report, 1845*, p. 14, and *1854*, p. 29.

21. Ernst, *Immigrant Life in New York City*, p. 201; and *A.I.C.P. Report, 1853*, p. 25.

22. *A.I.C.P. Report, 1855*, p. 22.

23. *A.I.C.P. Report, 1857*, p. 44.

24. Allan Nevins and Milton H. Thomas, eds., *The Diary of George Templeton Strong*, 4 vols. (New York, 1952), vol. 2, p. 367.

25. *A.I.C.P. Report, 1852*, p. 25; and Ernst, *Immigrant Life in New York City*, p. 201.

26. AUND, Bishop John Hughes to Society for the Propagation of the Faith,

Paris, 26 June, 1849, f. 104; and *Scritture,* vol. 18, letter 1417, Hughes to Propaganda, 23 March 1858, f. 514.

27. Mohl, *Poverty in New York,* p. 46; and Mack Walker, *Germany and the Emigration, 1816–1885* (Cambridge, Mass., 1964), pp. 74 and 160–61.

28. Salzbacher, *Meine Reise,* p. 367.

29. *Jahres-Bericht der Deutschen Gesellschaft der Stadt N.Y.* 75 (1858): 25; and Rudolf Cronau, *Denkschrift zum 150. Jahrestag der Deutschen Gesellschaft der Stadt New York, 1784–1934* (New York, 1934), pp. 72–73.

30. Chronicle of the Most Holy Redeemer Convent, p. 115; for further indications of the poverty of German Catholics see *Katholische Kirchenzeitung,* 23 July 1857 and 26 November 1853.

31. Mohl, *Poverty in New York,* p. 21.

32. Quoted in R. W. DeForest, "Tenement House Reform in New York City, 1834–1900," in *The Tenement House Problem,* ed. R. W. DeForest and L. Veiller, 2 vols. (New York, 1903), vol. 1, p. 71.

33. *First Report of a Committee on the Sanitary Condition of the Laboring Classes in the City of New York with Remedial Suggestions* (New York, 1853), p. 6.

34. New York State Assembly, *Report of a Select Committee Appointed to Examine into the Condition of Tenant Houses in New York and Brooklyn, 1857,* vol. 3, no. 205, p. 14.

35. *A.I.C.P. Report, 1863,* p. 38.

36. DeForest, "Tenement House Reform," pp. 94–95.

37. *Report of the Council of Hygiene,* pp. lxxx and 349.

38. James McCague, *The Second Rebellion: The New York City Draft Riots of 1863* (New York, 1968), p. 25; and New York State Assembly, *Report of a Select Committee,* p. 28.

39. *First Report of a Committee,* p. 10; *Report of the Council of Hygiene,* p. 84; and Charles E. Rosenberg, *The Cholera Years* (Chicago, 1962), pp. 104–7.

40. *Report of the Council of Hygiene,* pp. lxxvi–lxxvii.

41. New York State Assembly, *Report of a Select Committee,* p. 25.

42. *Ibid.,* pp. 28–29.

43. *Report of the Council of Hygiene,* pp. 177–79.

44. *A.I.C.P. Report, 1854,* p. 27.

45. *Report of the Council of Hygiene,* pp. 47–49.

46. *Ibid.,* p. 56; and New York State Assembly, *Report of a Select Committee,* pp. 17–18.

47. New York State Assembly, *Report of a Select Committee,* p. 29.

48. *Ibid.,* p. 19.

49. *Ibid.,* pp. 19–20.

50. *Ibid.,* p. 25.

51. *Report of the Council of Hygiene,* p. 58.

52. DeForest, "Tenement House Reform," p. 72.

53. Lawrence Kehoe, ed., *Complete Works of the Most Rev. John Hughes, D.D.*, 2 vols. (New York, 1865), vol. 2, p. 692.

54. Ladies of the Mission at Five Points, quoted in James Ford, *Slums and Housing: With Special Reference to New York City*, 2 vols. (Cambridge, Mass., 1936), vol. 1, pp. 116–17.

55. Still, *Mirror for Gotham*, p. 161.

56. See Walker, *Germany and the Emigration*, pp. 47 ff., for living conditions in Germany; also Marcus Hansen, *The Atlantic Migration*, ed. Arthur M. Schlesinger (New York, 1961), pp. 243 ff.

57. See Peter R. Knights, *The Plain People of Boston* (New York, 1971); Stephan Thernstrom and Richard Sennett, eds., *Nineteenth Century Cities: Essays in the New Urban History* (New Haven, 1969); and Stephan Thernstrom, *The Other Bostonians: Poverty and Progress in the American Metropolis, 1880–1970* (Cambridge, Mass., 1973).

58. Knights, *Plain People*, p. 103.

59. The Irish sample represented 13 percent and the German sample 20 percent of the families with children baptized in 1850. The sample was taken according to the principles explained in W. Allen Wallis and Harry V. Roberts, *Statistics: A New Approach* (New York, 1956), pp. 334–39. The Parish baptismal registers and the city directories from 1845 to 1875 were used to cross-check one another and to locate any family that may not have appeared in the city directory for a given year. Although the number of families in the sample was small, it does reflect the pattern of mobility arrived at in more comprehensive studies.

60. *Truth Teller*, 28 January 1832.

61. *Katholische Kirchenzeitung*, 13 November 1862 and 2 July 1863.

62. *Jahres-Bericht der Deutschen Gesellschaft der Stadt N.Y.* 72 (1855): 9 and 15.

63. AANY, J. G. Schwarz to Bishop John Hughes, Vienna, 12 June 1847.

64. *A.I.C.P. Report, 1854*, p. 21.

65. *Report of the Council of Hygiene*, p. 54.

66. Quoted in "The Sanitary and Moral Condition of New York City," *Catholic World* 7 (July 1868): 555.

67. Municipal Archives and Records, New York City, Death Records, 1853–54.

68. *A.I.C.P. Report, 1854*, p. 21.

69. Ernst, *Immigrant Life in New York City*, pp. 53–54; and John Duffy, *A History of Public Health in New York City, 1625–1866* (New York, 1968), pp. 582 ff.

70. Knights, *Plain People*, pp. 103 ff.

71. *Jahres-Bericht der Deutschen Gesellschaft der Stadt N.Y.* 72 (1855): 14; and Ernst, *Immigrant Life in New York City*, p. 54.

72. *Katholische Kirchenzeitung*, 21 January 1858.

73. James P. Shannon, *Catholic Colonization on the Western Frontier* (New Haven, 1957), pp. 103 ff.; and Stephan Thernstrom, "Urbanization, Migration

and Social Mobility in Nineteenth Century America," in *Towards a New Past*, ed. Barton J. Bernstein (New York, 1967), p. 160.

74. Shannon, *Catholic Colonization*, pp. 151–53.

75. Colman Barry, *The Catholic Church and German Americans* (Washington, D.C., 1953), pp. 9 ff.

76. Emmet H. Rothan, *The German Catholic Immigrant in the United States, 1830–1860* (Washington, D.C., 1946), p. 77.

77. Daniel Boorstin, *The Americans: The National Experience* (New York, 1967), p. 95.

78. Still, *Mirror for Gotham*, p. 114.

79. *Ibid.*

80. AUND, Bishop John Dubois to Society for the Propagation of the Faith, Paris, 9 May 1836, f. 104.

81. New York State Assembly, *Report of a Select Committee*, pp. 9–10.

82. *Ibid.*

83. Miller, *Jacksonian Aristocracy*, pp. 161 ff.; and McCague, *The Second Rebellion*, p. 15.

84. Samuel Osgood, *New York in the Nineteenth Century* (New York, 1867), p. 123.

85. Griscom, *The Sanitary Condition*, p. 7.

86. The intra-urban mobility of the 1850 sample groups was based on tracing the addresses of the families in the city directories from 1850 to 1870.

THREE. THE IRISH PARISH

1. Kenneth H. Connell, *Irish Peasant Society* (Oxford, 1968), p. 152; R. B. McDowell, ed., *Social Life in Ireland, 1800–1845* (Dublin, 1957), pp. 10 and 18; and Thomas P. Kennedy, *Church Building*, vol. 5, pt. 8 of *A History of Irish Catholicism*, ed. Patrick J. Corish, 6 vols. (Dublin, 1967–), pp. 1–8.

2. Emmet Larkin, "The Devotional Revolution in Ireland, 1850–75," *American Historical Review* 77 (June 1972): 625–52.

3. James A. Reynolds, *The Catholic Emancipation Crisis in Ireland, 1823–1829* (New Haven, 1954); *Oeuvres de M. Le Comte de Montalembert*, 6 vols. (Paris, 1860–61), vol. 4, p. 161; and Alexis De Tocqueville, *Journeys to England and Ireland*, ed. J. P. Mayer (New Haven, 1958), pp. 168–69.

4. *Decreta Synodi Plenariae Episcoporum Hiberniae Apud Thurles* (Dublin, 1851); and Terence P. Cunningham, *Church Reorganization*, vol. 5, pt. 7 of *A History of Irish Catholicism*, ed. Patrick J. Corish, 6 vols. (Dublin, 1970) p. 1.

5. Peter Guilday, *A History of the Councils of Baltimore, 1791–1884* (New York, 1932), pp. 179 ff.

6. See Kennedy, *Church Building*, pp. 13 ff.

7. Joseph and Helen McCadden have written the most recent biography of Father Varela, *Father Varela: Torch Bearer from Cuba* (New York, 1969);

previously the only other biography was that of José Ignacio Rodriguez, *Vida del Presbitero Don Félix Varela* (New York, 1878).

8. McCadden and McCadden, *Father Varela*, pp. 165 and 167.

9. *Ibid.*, pp. 99 ff.

10. Archives of St. Peter's Church, Report of the Board of Trustees, 12 April 1841.

11. Ryan, *Old St. Peter's*, pp. 186–89.

12. AANY, Financial Report of St. James Church, 10 July 1835.

13. *Freeman's Journal*, 31 October 1841.

14. *Ibid.*, 26 November 1842; cf. also John R. G. Hassard, *Life of the Most Reverend John Hughes, D.D.* (New York, 1866), pp. 254 ff.

15. AANY, Bishop John Hughes to Rev. DeSmet, 22 July 1843; Hassard, *Life of Hughes*, pp. 268–71; and AUND, Bishop John Hughes To Society for Propagation of the Faith, Lyons, 28 January 1842, f. 104.

16. Printed Certificate of Agreement between the board of trustees and Joseph Bouchaud, 7 March 1837, in Transfiguration Church Archives (hereinafter to be cited as ATC). The certificate stated in part: "Whereas, it hath been determined to create a Fund to pay the purchase money of The Transfiguration Church and Premises in Chamber-street, New York, which is to be secured inviolably as a lien on the same.

"And whereas, Mr. Joseph Bouchaud has contributed, by way of Loan to said Fund, the sum of one hundred dollars, which will be repaid by the Corporation of 'The Transfiguration Church' to him or his legal representative, upon ten days' previous notice being given to the President of said Corporation, together with interest on said sum so loaned, at the rate of 7 percent, per annum from the date of Loan, interest payable semi-annually on the first days of March and September in each year. . . ."

17. ATC, Trustees' Minutes, 8 October 1840.

18. *Ibid.*

19. *Ibid.*

20. *Ibid.*, 23 October and 31 October 1843.

21. Patrick J. Dignan, *A History of the Legal Incorporation of Catholic Church Property in the United States, 1784–1932* (New York, 1935), pp. 52 and 64.

22. ATC, Trustees' Minutes, 8 October 1840.

23. *Ibid.*, 10 March 1836 and *passim*; *Truth Teller*, 23 November 1839 and 23 May 1840.

24. ATC, Trustees' Minutes, 1 April 1844.

25. *Freeman's Journal*, 24 November 1849.

26. AANY, Letterbook of Bishop John Hughes, copy of letter of J. Hughes to Rev. Felix Varela, 25 January 1853.

27. Dignan, *History of Legal Incorporation*, p. 64; cf. Trustees' Minutes for the period.

28. AUND, Bishop John Dubois to Society for Propagation of the Faith, Paris, 1836, f. 104.

29. The sacramental index is an instrument of relative parish population based on the number of baptisms and marriages in a parish in a single year; cf. Houtart, *Aspects Sociologiques*, pp. 227 ff.

30. Carthy, *Old St. Patrick's*, pp. 67 and 99; and John Dubois, "Bishop Dubois on New York in 1836," *Historical Records and Studies* 10 (January 1917): 127.

31. Cf. *Freeman's Journal*, 25 July 1857, on mobility of population in relation to pew rents.

32. Jean Blanchard, *The Church in Contemporary Ireland* (Dublin, 1963), pp. 47 ff.; cf. K. S. Inglis, *Churches and the Working Classes in Victorian England* (London, 1963), for a discussion of pew rents among English Protestants and Catholics.

33. ATC, Trustees' Minutes, 17 May 1838 and 26 May 1843.

34. ATC, Financial Reports, 1836–42; Archives of St. Peter's Church, Trustees' Report, 12 April 1841; and AANY, St. Joseph Church, Financial Report, December 1840.

35. AANY, Diary of the Rev. Richard L. Burtsell, 27 December 1866 and 7 January 1867.

36. The trustees were listed in the minutes of the board, and their occupations and addresses were derived from the *City Directory.*

37. *Truth Teller*, 11 December 1841.

38. Lately Thomas [Robert V. P. Steele], *Delmonico's: A Century of Splendor* (Boston, 1967), pp. 5–8.

39. ATC, Trustees' Minutes, 28 February 1836.

40. *Ibid.*; also the financial records of the period in ATC.

41. Thomas, *Delmonico's*, p. 47.

42. ATC, Financial Records of the period.

43. Thirty people were selected (i.e., a six percent sample) in 1845, and their occupations were derived from the *City Directory*. The selection was made according to the principles of random sampling outlined in Wallis and Roberts, *Statistics*, pp. 334–39. The occupation categories were derived from Stephan Thernstrom, *Poverty and Progress* (Cambridge, Mass., 1964) pp. 90–94.

44. See chapter 2 for the use of the 1850 sample group.

45. *A.I.C.P. Report, 1852*, p. 22.

46. *Ibid.*

47. Cf. Ernst, *Immigrant Life in New York City*, pp. 76–77.

48. Jeremiah O'Donovan, *A Brief Account of the Author's Interview with His Countrymen* (Pittsburgh, 1864), pp. 94–95.

49. Thomas N. Brown, *Irish-American Nationalism* (Philadelphia, 1966), p. 35; and Potter, *To the Golden Door*, pp. 102–3.

50. *Metropolitan Record*, 14 March 1863.

51. Henry J. Browne, "The Archdiocese of New York A Century Ago: A Memoir of Archbishop Hughes, 1838–1858," *Historical Records and Studies* 39–40 (1952): 179.

52. Robert F. Hueston, "The Catholic Press and Nativism, 1840–1860" (Ph.D. diss., University of Notre Dame, 1972), pp. 139–41.

53. Larkin, "The Devotional Revolution," p. 649; see Connell, *Irish Peasant Society*, p. 151, for a similar evaluation.

54. Thomas D'Arcy McGee, *A History of the Irish Settlers in North America From the Earliest Period to the Census of 1850* (Boston, 1855), p. 193.

55. Handlin, *Boston's Immigrants*, p. 128.

56. Roger Aubert, *Le Pontificat de Pie IX* (Paris, 1963), pp. 359 ff.

57. John Milner, *The End of Religious Controversy* (New York, n.d.), pp. 243 and 122, respectively; this book was an apologetical exposition of the Catholic religion by an English Bishop and was very popular in the United States as a handbook for debate with Protestants and a defense of the Catholic religion. Its theology is very representative of the day. Cf. Robert Gorman, *Catholic Apologetical Literature in the United States, 1784–1858* (Washington, D.C. 1939), pp. 53 ff.

58. AUND, *Scritture*, vol. 18, letter 1417, Hughes to the Prefect of Propaganda Fide, 23 March 1858, f. 509.

59. Milner, *The End of Religious Controversy*, p. 245.

60. *The Mission Book* (New York, 1859), p. 30.

61. AUND, *Scritture*, vol. 18, letter 1417, Hughes to Prefect of Propaganda Fide, 23 March 1858, f. 509; and James Parton, "Our Roman Catholic Brethren," *Atlantic Monthly* 21 (1868): 432 ff., for a description of Sunday Mass at St. Stephen's Church.

62. Larkin, "The Devotional Revolution," p. 636; cf. P. K. Egan, *The Parish of Ballinasloe* (Dublin, 1960), pp. 158 ff., for further evidence of popular religious fervor and church attendance.

63. AUND, *Scritture*, vol. 18, letter 1417, Hughes to Prefect of Propaganda Fide, 23 March 1858, f. 507.

64. Dolan, "Urban Catholicism," pp. 313 ff.

65. Andrew M. Greeley and William C. McCready, "Drop in churchgoing 'catastrophic,'" *National Catholic Reporter*, 16 November 1973.

66. Sheridan Gilley, "The Roman Catholic Mission to the Irish in London," *Recusant History* 10 (October 1969): 123–45.

67. Joseph Wuest, C.SS.R., *Annales Congregationis SS. Redemptoris Provinciae Americae*, 5 vols. (vols. 1–3: Ilchester, Md., 1888–99; vols. 4–5: Boston, 1914–24), vol. 5, pt. 2, p. 225.

68. APF, Mission Chronicles, vol. 1, p. 174.

69. AANY, Diary of the Rev. Richard L. Burtsell, 27 March 1865.

70. APF, Mission Chronicles, vol. 1, p. 16.

71. *Ibid.*, vol. 1, p. 3.

72. *Freeman's Journal*, 25 July 1857.

73. *Ibid.*; AANY, Diary of the Rev. Richard L. Burtsell, 31 May 1865.

74. AANY, Diary of the Rev. Richard L. Burtsell, 12 July 1865.

75. *Ibid.*, 31 May 1865.

76. Shea, *The Catholic Churches of New York City, passim.*

77. John Talbot Smith, *The Catholic Church in New York,* 2 vols. (New York, 1908), vol. 1, p. 179; and Frances Trollope, *Domestic Manners of Americans* (London, 1832), p. 273.

78. Most Rev. Michael A. Corrigan, "Register of the Clergy Laboring in the Archdiocese of New York from Early Missionary Times to 1885," *Historical Records and Studies* 5 (November 1907): 398.

79. Parton, "Our Roman Catholic Brethren," p. 434; also *Freeman's Journal,* 10 February 1855.

80. ATC, Trustees' Minutes, 24 June 1840 and 28 September 1843.

81. AANY, Diary of the Rev. Richard L. Burtsell, 17 December 1865; Carthy, *Old St. Patrick's,* p. 50; and *St. Stephen's Parish: Centennial Journal 1848–1948* (New York, 1948).

82. *Metropolitan Record,* 7 June 1862.

83. See, for example, *Battersby's Catholic Directory* (Dublin, 1860), p. 170.

84. AANY, Diary of the Rev. Richard L. Burtsell, 25 January 1867.

85. *Ibid.*, 26 November 1865, and 5 August 1866.

86. Shea, *The Catholic Churches of New York City,* gives many accounts of the dedication of new churches.

87. *Freeman's Journal,* 14 November 1868.

88. Milner, *The End of Controversy,* p. 119.

89. Constantia Maxwell, *Country and Town in Ireland under the Georges* (Dundalk, Ireland, 1949), p. 348; James Macaulay, *Ireland in 1872* (London, 1873), pp. 3–4; and J. Brady, "Funeral Customs of the Past," *Irish Ecclesiastical Record* 78 (November 1942): 330–39.

90. *New York Weekly Register and Catholic Diary,* 21 December 1833.

91. *Truth Teller,* 21 September 1844; see also New York City, Municipal Archives and Records, Death Records, for the period, where the name of John Dillon is listed frequently as the undertaker of deceased Irishmen.

92. AUND, *Scritture,* vol. 9, letter 1015, Pastoral Letter of Bishop John Dubois, 6 July 1827, f. 25; *New York Weekly Register and Catholic Diary,* 21 December 1837; and *Freeman's Journal,* 25 September 1858.

93. *Metropolitan Record,* 8 June 1861; cf. Carl Wittke, *We Who Built America* (New York, 1945), p. 142, about Boston Irish funerals.

94. AUND, *Scritture,* vol. 9, letter 1015, Pastoral Letter of Bishop John Dubois, 6 July 1827.

95. Maxwell, *Country and Town,* p. 344; and De Tocqueville, *Journeys,* p. 159.

96. De Tocqueville, *Journeys,* p. 191.

97. Egan, *Parish of Ballinasloe,* p. 264; and W. J. Fitzpatrick, *The Life, Times and Correspondence of Rt. Rev. Dr. Doyle,* 2 vols. (Dublin, 1880), vol. 1, pp. 116–17.

98. AUND, *Scritture*, vol. 15, letter 307, Rev. Jeremiah Cummings to Prefect of Propaganda Fide, 29 May 1849, f. 205.

99. *Ibid.*; and AANY, Diary of the Rev. Richard L. Burtsell, 7 March 1867.

100. AANY, Diary of the Rev. Richard L. Burtsell, 16 June 1866.

101. *The Mission Book*, p. 87.

102. Pastoral Letter of Bishop John Hughes, *Freeman's Journal*, 20 February 1847.

103. *Truth Teller*, 24 March 1832.

104. *Metropolitan Record*, 14 February 1863; and *Truth Teller*, 29 February 1840.

105. AUND, *Scritture*, vol. 18, letter 1362, Rev. Isaac Hecker to Cardinal Barnabo, 25 June 1860.

106. *Freeman's Journal*, 31 May 1856.

107. Shea, *The Catholic Churches of New York City*, p. 696.

108. Egan, *Parish of Ballinasloe*, pp. 263 ff.; see, e.g., *Battersby's Catholic Directory*, pp. 163 and 173.

109. *Truth Teller*, 1 June 1833.

110. Oliver MacDonagh, "The Irish Catholic Clergy and Emigration During the Great Famine," *Irish Historical Studies* 5 (1946–47): 288; cf. Potter, *To the Golden Door*, p. 81; and Connell, *Irish Peasant Society*, pp. 144–45.

111. Potter, *To the Golden Door*, p. 81.

112. Rodriguez, *Don Felix Varela*, p. 302.

113. Both Hughes and Dubois had problems with "strange clergymen" who came to the diocese to work and later proved to be "unworthy" of the bishop's confidence (for example, AUND, John Hughes to Society for the Propagation of the Faith, Paris, 27 November 1839, f. 104).

114. *Freeman's Journal*, 19 February 1848.

115. *Ibid.*; and AANY, Diary of John Hughes, where these type of deaths are mentioned and no others merit notice.

116. *Freeman's Journal*, 19 February 1848.

117. *Ibid.*, 18 August 1855.

118. *Truth Teller*, 1 June 1833; and AUND, *Scritture*, vol. 11, letter 1574, Bishop Dubois to Prefect of Propaganda Fide, 13 March 1835, f. 486.

119. *Freeman's Journal*, 28 March 1846.

120. Connelly, *The Visit of Archbishop Bedini* p. 244.

121. *Ibid.*, p. 213.

122. AUND, *Scritture*, vol. 18, letter 1417, Hughes to Prefect, 23 March 1858, f. 496.

123. Corrigan, "Register of the Clergy Laboring in the Archdiocese of New York from Early Missionary Times to 1885," p. 398.

124. Potter, *To the Golden Door*, p. 362; as an indication of this concern cf. William Strang, *Business Guide for Priests* (New York, 1899).

125. Circular Letter of Bishop John Hughes to the Clergy in *Freeman's Journal,* 5 July 1845; and AANY, financial reports of various parishes.

126. AANY, Diary of the Rev. Richard L. Burtsell, 25 May 1865; priests were also urged to draw up wills so that their estates would go to the poor and the church (*Concilium Provinciale Neo-Eboracense III* [New York, 1862], decretum 6): such a decree would suggest that some priests had the means to accumulate an estate.

127. AANY, Diary of the Rev. Richard L. Burtsell, 12 May 1865.

128. Stephen Bell, *Rebel, Priest and Prophet* (New York, 1937).

129. AUND, *Scritture,* vol. 10, letter 1270, Bishop John Dubois to Prefect of Propaganda Fide, undated (c. 1829), f. 280.

130. See chapter one for population figures; and *Metropolitan Catholic Almanac and Laity's Directory* (Baltimore, 1840), pp. 146–47, and *Sadlier's Catholic Almanac, 1865* (New York, 1865), pp. 89–91, for the number of priests working in the city parishes.

131. Shaughnessy, *Has the Immigrant Kept the Faith?* p. 262; and Larkin, "The Devotional Revolution," p. 644.

132. Philip Schaff, *America: A Sketch of Its Political, Social and Religious Character,* ed. Perry Miller (Cambridge, Mass., 1961), p. 178.

FOUR. THE GERMAN PARISH

1. Franz Schnabel, *Deutsche Geschichte im neunzehnten Jahrhundert: Die Katholische Kirche in Deutschland* (Freiburg, 1965), p. 20.

2. *Ibid.,* p. 65 and *passim.*

3. J. D. Mansi, *Sacrorum Conciliorum Nova et Amplissima Collectio,* 53 vols. (Paris, 1901–27), vol. 43, col. 86.

4. Smith, *The Catholic Church in New York,* vol. 1, p. 42; *St. Nicholas Church in Second Street,* p. 25.

5. Theodore Roemer, *The Leopoldine Foundation and the Church in the United States, 1829–1839* (New York, 1933), p. 200; and Salzbacher, *Meine Reise,* p. 300; see chapter one for the 1865 figure.

6. Barry, *The Catholic Church and German Americans,* p. 9.

7. Walker, *Germany and the Emigration,* p. 69.

8. See Heinrich Brück, *Geschichte der katholischen Kirche in Deutschland im neunzehnten Jahrhundert,* 4 vols. (Mainz, 1887–1901), vols. 1–3, for the history of this struggle.

9. Barry, *The Catholic Church and German Americans,* p. 10.

10. *Ibid.*

11. Connelly, *The Visit of Archbishop Bedini,* p. 241.

12. Anton Walburg, "The Question of Nationality," in *The Church and the City,* ed. Robert D. Cross (New York, 1967), p. 122.

13. *Synodus Dioecesana Neo-Eboracensis Prima,* chaps. 12 and 14.

14. The parish baptismal registers of 1850 used in the study of mobility and

social status showed no ethnically mixed marriages. The marriage records of Most Holy Redeemer parish indicated very few Irish-German unions, the highest percentage in any one year between 1850 and 1870 being 4 percent.

15. See Albert Kleber, *Ferdinand, Indiana, 1840–1940* (St. Meinrad, Ind., 1940).

16. Charles G. Herbermann, "The Rt. Rev. John Dubois, DD, Third Bishop of New York," *Historical Records and Studies* 1 (1899): 337.

17. AUND, Bishop Hughes to Society for Propagation of the Faith, Paris, 24 January 1844; and *Scritture*, vol. 18, letter 1417, Hughes to Prefect of Propaganda Fide, 23 March 1858, f. 511.

18. AANY, Diary of the Rev. Richard L. Burtsell, 25 June 1865.

19. *St. Nicholas Church in Second Street*, p. 34.

20. *Katholische Kirchenzeitung*, 28 January 1858.

21. *Ibid.*, 19 August 1858.

22. Wuest, *Annales*, vol. 1, p. 130; John F. Byrne, C.SS.R., *The Redemptorist Centenaries* (Philadelphia, 1932), p. 141; and John L. Obendorfer, C.SS.R., *Portrait of a Mother: Church of the Most Holy Redeemer* (New York, n.d.), p. 18.

23. Wuest, *Annales*, vol. 1, p. 151; and Chronicle of the Most Holy Redeemer Church, March 1859, pp. 127–28.

24. Baptismal registers of the parish indicated the parents' place of birth.

25. *U. S. Census 1860, Population*, p. 609.

26. These individuals were mentioned in the Chronicle of the Parish or in the Chronicle of the Convent, and their occupations were listed in the *City Directory*.

27. Wuest, *Annales*, vol. 2, p. 161.

28. The sample group was the same as that used in the study of mobility in chapter two; the occupational categories are found in Thernstrom, *Poverty and Progress*, pp. 90–94.

29. *Report of the Council of Hygiene*, p. 174.

30. Ernst, *Immigrant Life in New York City*, p. 69.

31. *Report of the Council of Hygiene*, p. 174.

32. Theo. Griesinger, *Leiben und Treiben in Amerika* (New York, 1874), p. 10. See Ernst, *Immigrant Life in New York City*, for the concentration of immigrant groups in various trades; and Shanly, "Germany in New York," pp. 555 ff.

33. Aubert, *Le Pontificat de Pie IX*, pp. 463 ff.

34. Georg Dusold, C.SS.R., *Goldenes Jubiläum der Kirche zum Allerheiligsten Erlöser* (New York, 1894), p. 28.

35. *Constitutiones et Regulae Congregationis Sacerdotum sub titulo Sanctissimi Redemptoris* (Rome, 1861), p. 69.

36. Franz X. Buchner, *Volk und Kult* (Dusseldorf, 1936), pp. 26–27.

37. *Freeman's Journal*, 12 March 1870.

38. Wuest, *Annales*, vol. 4, pt. 2, p. 55; and Dusold, *Goldenes Jubiläum*, p. 83.

39. Buchner, *Volk und Kult*, p. 38.

40. Joachim Meisner, *Nachreformatorische Katholische Frommigkeitsformen in Erfurt* (Leipzig, 1971), p. 90; and Aubert, *Le Pontificat de Pie IX*, pp. 466–67.

41. Chronicle of the Most Holy Redeemer Convent, p. 28.

42. *Constitutiones et Regulae*, p. 5.

43. Alphonsus Liguori, *The Glories of Mary* (New York, 1852); and Aubert, *Le Pontificat de Pie IX*, pp. 461–62.

44. Liguori, *The Glories of Mary*, p. 11.

45. Dusold, *Goldenes Jubiläum*, p. 22; and Wuest, *Annales*, vol. 2, p. 262; and *Constitutiones et Regulae*, p. 66.

46. Wuest, *Annales*, vol. 2, p. 297.

47. Meisner, *Nachreformatorische*, pp. 88–90; and *Allgemeine Kirchen-Zeitung*, 1845, pp. 445–47.

48. Dusold, *Goldenes Jubiläum*, pp. 62–63.

49. Chronicle of St. Alphonsus Church, p. 76.

50. Obendorfer, *Portrait of a Mother*, p. 62.

51. Dusold, *Goldenes Jubiläum*, p. 22; and *Constitutiones et Regulae*, pp. 5 and 68.

52. *Katholische Kirchenzeitung*, 10 June 1858; and Obendorfer, *Portrait of a Mother*, pp. 16 ff.

53. Still, *Mirror for Gotham*, p. 163.

54. Shea, *The Catholic Churches of New York City*, pp. 361–62.

55. *Ibid.*, pp. 363–64.

56. Abbelen Memorial, quoted in Barry, *The Catholic Church and German Americans*, p. 294.

57. Dusold, *Goldenes Jubiläum*, p. 26.

58. Buchner, *Volk und Kult*, p. 41; and *Katholische Kirchenzeitung*, 15 July 1858.

59. Obendorfer, *Portrait of a Mother*, pp. 37 ff.; and *Katholische Kirchenzeitung*, 29 April and 3 June 1858; 10 December 1867.

60. *Ibid.*

61. See August Hagen, *Geschichte der Diözese Rottenburg*, 3 vols. (Stuttgart, 1956–60), vol. 2, pp. 260 ff.

62. *Freeman's Journal*, 21 April 1866; and Dusold, *Goldenes Jubiläum*, p. 61.

63. *Katholische Kirchenzeitung*, 10 December 1857; and Chronicle of the Most Holy Redeemer Convent, p. 48.

64. Aubert, *Le Pontificat de Pie IX*, pp. 145–47; and Brück, *Geschichte*, vol. 3, pp. 511–13.

65. *Katholische Kirchenzeitung*, 17 September 1857 and 2 September 1858.

66. *Ibid.*, 2 September 1858.

67. *Ibid.*

68. Dusold, *Goldenes Jubiläum*, pp. 68 ff.

69. Hagen, *Geschichte*, vol. 2, pp. 260 ff.

70. Dusold, *Goldenes Jubiläum*, pp. 68 ff.

71. Obendorfer, *Portrait of a Mother*, p. 62.

72. *Katholische Kirchenzeitung*, 7 September 1857.

73. Dusold, *Goldenes Jubiläum*, p. 60.

74. ·Wuest, *Annales*, vol. 2, p. 216.

75. *Katholische Kirchenzeitung*, 1 October 1857.

76. Michael J. Curley, C.SS.R., *The Provincial Story* (New York, 1963), p. 3.

77. Byrne, *The Redemptorist Centenaries*, pp. 41 and 141.

78. Dusold, *Goldenes Jubiläum*, pp. 29 ff.

79. Wuest, *Annales*, vol. 2, p. 103; the Chronicle of the Most Holy Redeemer Parish also gives the names of priests and brothers assigned to the church.

80. Edgar Alexander, "Church and Society in Germany," in *Church and Society*, ed. Joseph Moody (New York, 1953), pp. 341 ff.

81. AANY, Diary of the Rev. Richard L. Burtsell, 20 November 1867; and Connelly, *The Visit of Archbishop Bedini*, p. 255.

82. Thomas Meehan, "Notes and Comments," *Historical Records and Studies* 10 (1917): 184.

83. *Katholische Kirchenzeitung*, 3 September and 17 September 1857.

84. *Ibid.*, 10 December 1857.

85. Wuest, *Annales*, vol. 2, pp. 219–33.

86. *Constitutiones et Regulae*, pp. 127 and 165.

87. Archives of Redemptorist Province of Baltimore (hereinafter to be cited as APB), Report of Superior, 1 August 1860.

88. *Ibid.*

89. *Constitutiones et Regulae*, pp. xiii ff.

90. Wuest, *Annales*, vol. 2, pp. 214–15.

91. *Ibid.*

92. Curley, *The Provincial Story*, p. 160.

93. Schnabel, *Deutsche Geschichte*, pp. 19–36.

94. Hagen, *Geschichte*, vol. 2, p. 182.

95. Aubert, *Le Pontificat de Pie IX*, p. 142.

96. *Ibid.*

97. Rogier, De Bertier De Sauvigny, and Hajjar, *Siécle des Luminiéres*, p. 502, n. 21.

98. Mansi, *Sacrorum Conciliorum*, XLIII, cols. 59 ff.

99. Wuest, *Annales*, vol. 1, pp. 124 and 204; vol. 4, pt. 2, p. 388; vol. 5, pt. 1, p. 208.

100. Quoted in *St. Nicholas Church in Second Street*, p. 30; cf. Salzbacher, *Meine Reise*, p. 371.

101. Dusold, *Goldenes Jubiläum*, p. 69.

102. APB, Quoted in Rev. Mullaney, Manuscript History of St. Alphonsus Church, p. 46.

103. Schnabel, *Deutsche Geschichte*, pp. 156 ff.; and Mansi, *Sacrorum Conciliorum*, XLIII, cols. 89–90.

104. Wuest, *Annales*, vol. 3, p. 236; the relatively small number of marriages in the parish confirmed his observation.

105. Wuest, *Annales*, vol. 4, pt. 2, p. 388; vol. 5, pt. 1, p. 208.

106. APB, *Berichte der Leopoldin-Stiftung im Kaiserthume Oesterreich, Heft XXXI* (1861), A Canonical Visitation in 1860 of the Redemptorist Houses in the United States; see report by Rev. L. Coudenhove, C.SS.R., p. 4, for observation on capacity of the church and crowds at Mass.

107. *Freeman's Journal*, 10 February 1855, where four Masses were listed for the parish; see Reiter, *Schematismus*, p. 97, for the estimated size of the parish.

108. *Freeman's Journal*, 12 March 1870.

109. Curley, *The Provincial Story*, p. 160.

FIVE. CONFLICT IN THE CHURCH

1. E. B. O'Callaghan, *Documentary History of the State of New York*, 4 vols. (Albany, 1849–51), vol. 4, p. 15; and Whitman, in *Leaves of Grass*, p. 233.

2. See Benson J. Lossing, *History of New York City* (New York, 1884), p. 375 and *passim*.

3. Lewis A. Coser, *The Functions of Social Conflict* (Glencoe, Ill., 1956), pp. 95–103.

4. Peter Guilday, "Trusteeism," *Historical Records and Studies* 18 (1929): 7–73; and Ryan, *Old St. Peter's* p. 151.

5. AUND, Bishop John Dubois to Bishop John Purcell, 2 July 1835.

6. Peter Guilday, *The Life and Times of John England*, 2 vols. (New York, 1927), vol. 2, p. 343.

7. Barry, *The Catholic Church and German Americans*, p. 13.

8. AUND, Microfilm copy of letters to Leopoldine Society, reel 2, no. 16, John Neumann to Father Dichtl, Prague, 27 June 1836.

9. AANY, Archbishop John Hughes to Pastor and Congregation of Most Holy Redeemer Church, 5 August 1849.

10. Wuest, *Annales*, vol. 2, pp. 35–37, 375.

11. AANY, Bishop John Hughes to Catholics of the Church and Congregation of St. Francis Church, 24 August 1850; and John Hughes to Congregation of St. Francis Church, 25 October 1850.

12. AUND, *Scritture*, vol. 18, letter 1417, Hughes to Prefect of Propaganda Fide, 23 March 1858, f. 511.

13. Quoted in Sister M. Mileta Ludwig, F.S.P.A., "Sources for the Biography of Michael Heiss, Bishop of LaCrosse 1868–1880 and Archbishop of Milwaukee

1881–1890," *Records of American Catholic Historical Society of Philadelphia* 79 (December 1968): 210.

14. Rev. Raymond Knab, C.SS.R., "Father Joseph Prost, Pioneer Priest in the United States," *Historical Records and Studies* 22 (1932): 51; and Wuest, *Annales*, vol. 1, p. 129.

15. Wuest, *Annales*, vol. 3, pp. 224–25.

16. *Ibid.*, vol. 1, p. 130.

17. *Ibid.*, vol. 1, p. 151; and Chronicle of the Most Holy Redeemer Church, March 1859, pp. 127–28.

18. *St. Nicholas Church in Second Street*, p. 35; and Adalbert Callahan, O.F.M., *Medieval Francis in Modern America* (New York, 1936), pp. 80–81.

19. Wuest, *Annales*, vol. 2, p. 160.

20. *Ibid.*

21. *Ibid.*, pp. 214–15.

22. Joshua A. Fishburn, *Language Loyalty in the United States* (The Hague, 1966), p. 223; and Coser, *The Functions of Social Conflict*, pp. 37 ff. and 87 ff.

23. Ryan, *Old St. Peter's*, pp. 47 ff.

24. Brown, *Irish-American Nationalism*, pp. 40–41.

25. *Ibid.*, p. xvii.

26. Ernst, *Immigrant Life in New York City*, p. 193; and *U. S. Census 1870, Statistics of Population*, p. 212.

27. *U. S. Census 1860, Population*, p. 337.

28. Ernst, *Immigrant Life in New York City*, p. 193.

29. U.S. Manuscript Census 1860, 8th Ward, 1st District.

30. Francis X. Murphy, C.SS.R., *The Centennial History of St.. Alphonsus Parish* (New York, 1947), pp. 11–14.

31. APB, Mullaney, Manuscript History, p. 40.

32. *Ibid.*, p. 42.

33. *Ibid.*

34. *Ibid.*, p. 45.

35. *Ibid.*, pp. 41–43.

36. *Ibid.*, p. 46.

37. *Ibid.*, p. 49.

38. Chronicle of St. Alphonsus Church, p. 41; and *Synodus Dioecesana Neo-Eboracensis Tertia* (New York, 1868), p. 13.

39. Chronicle of St. Alphonsus Church, p. 2.

40. *Ibid.*, pp. 2–3.

41. *Ibid.*

42. Wuest, *Annales*, vol. 5, pt. 1, pp. 199–200; pt. 2, pp. 190 and 404; such activities were also listed in the Chronicle of the parish.

43. Wuest, *Annales*, vol. 5, pt. 1, p. 163.

44. AANY, Diary of the Rev. Richard L. Burtsell, 25 June 1865.

45. APB, Mullaney, Manuscript History, p. 73.

46. *Ibid.*

47. Murphy, *The Centennial History*, pp. 27 and 33.

48. *Ibid.*, p. 35.

49. *New York State Census 1855*, pp. 110–11; *1865*, pp. 130–31; *1875*, pp. 37–38.

SIX. HANDING ON THE FAITH

1. See Catholic directories for advertisements of such material, e.g., *The Metropolitan Catholic Almanac and Laity's Directory, 1844* (Baltimore, 1844).

2. Aubert, *Le Pontificat die Pie IX*, pp. 245 ff.

3. *Freeman's Journal*, 2 February 1856.

4. Quoted in Edward M. Connors, *Church-State Relationships in Education in the State of New York* (Washington, D.C., 1951), p. 47.

5. See Bernard J. Meiring, "Educational Aspects of the Legislation of the Councils of Baltimore, 1829–1884" (Ph.D. diss., University of California, Berkeley, 1963), pp. 18 ff., for a discussion of the origin of Catholic schools.

6. Bernard Bailyn, *Education in the Forming of American Society* (Chapel Hill, 1960).

7. Quoted in R. Freeman Butts and Lawrence A. Cremin, *A History of American Education in American Culture* (New York, 1953), p. 215.

8. Rev. Robert T. Mulligan, "The Status and Role of the Lay Teacher in the Catholic Elementary Parochial School in the Nineteenth Century" (Ph.D. diss., Catholic University of America, 1967), pp. 159 ff.

9. *Metropolitan Record*, 14 May 1859; Meiring's study presents an excellent view of the hierarchy's position on religion in education.

10. Timothy L. Smith, "Protestant Schooling and the American Nationality, 1800–1850," *Journal of American History* 53 (March 1967): 679–95.

11. See William Bourne, *History of the Public School Society of the City of New York* (New York, 1870), pp. 168 and 529; also Vincent P. Lannie, "Alienation in America: the Immigrant Catholic and Public Education in Pre-Civil War America," *The Review of Politics* 32 (October 1970): 503–21.

12. Cf. J. Mol, *Churches and Immigrants* (The Hague, 1961), pp. 27–28.

13. Ryan, *Old St. Peter's*, pp. 236 ff.

14. *Freeman's Journal*, 2 July 1842.

15. Mulligan, "The Status and Role of the Lay Teacher," p. 33.

16. Smith, *The Catholic Church in New York*, vol. 1, p. 188.

17. Vincent P. Lannie, *Public Money and Parochial Education: Bishop Hughes, Governor Seward and the New York School Controversy* (Cleveland, 1968), p. 32.

18. *Ibid.*, p. 21.

19. See Lannie, *Public Money*, for the history of the controversy.

20. *Freeman's Journal*, 11 July 1840.

21. *Address of the Roman Catholics to their Fellow Citizens of the City and State of New York* (New York, 1840), p. 8.

22. Lannie, *Public Money*, pp. 67 ff.

23. *Ibid.*, p. 247.

24. Donald Akenson, *The Irish Education Experiment* (Toronto, 1970), p. 2; cf. Hagen, *Geschichte*, vol. 1, pp. 300–309; vol. 2, pp. 248–96.

25. *Truth Teller*, 30 November 1841; and Akenson, *The Irish Education Experiment*, pp. 86–94, for a background of the Kildare Street society.

26. James A. Burns, C.S.C., *The Growth and Development of the Catholic School System in the United States* (New York, 1912), p. 124.

27. *Address of the Roman Catholics*, p. 8.

28. Quoted in Mulligan, "The Status and Role of the Lay Teacher," p. 38.

29. *The New York Morning Herald*, 22 January 1857, quoted in Connors, *Church-State Relationships*, p. 46.

30. Catholic school population figures were taken from the Catholic press and Catholic directories; the public school figures were taken from Bourne, *History of the Public School Society*; Thomas Boese, *Public Education in the City of New York* (New York, 1869); and *Annual Reports of the Board of Education of New York City*; which sources confirmed the figures of the Catholic press. See table 3 on the growth of Catholic schools.

31. AUND, *Scritture*, vol. 17, letter 1038, L. Binsse to Prefect of Propaganda Fide, 1 November 1856, f. 738. In 1858 Hughes wanted to resign (AUND, *Scritture*, vol. 18, letter 1370, John Hughes to B. Smith, 10 September 1858, f. 357; also *Freeman's Journal*, 9 January 1864).

32. See table 3.

33. "Conversations of Our Club," *Brownson's Quarterly Review*, October 1858, p. 430; and AANY, Diary of the Rev. Richard L. Burtsell, 14 February 1867.

34. *Freeman's Journal*, 9 August 1845.

35. *Ibid.*, 27 October 1849.

36. Rodriguez, *Don Félix Varela*, pp. 65–67.

37. *Truth Teller*, 9 August 1828; and Thomas Meehan, "Some Schools in Old New York," *Historical Records and Studies* 2 (1900): 440.

38. *Freeman's Journal*, 4 January 1851.

39. Mulligan, "The Status and Role of the Lay Teacher," p. 69.

40. *Truth Teller*, 17 June 1843.

41. See *Freeman's Journal*, 9 August 1845 and 10 September 1859; and Connors, *Church-State Relationships*, pp. 55 ff., for a discussion of Bible reading in New York schools.

42. *Truth Teller*, 17 June 1843.

43. The school in Nativity parish closed, and the reason given was the number

of public schools in the area; see *Souvenir Journal of Centennial Year of Nativity Parish, 1842–1942.*

44. Shea, *The Catholic Churches Of New York City*, p. 693; and *Metropolitan Record*, 18 October 1862.

45. *Truth Teller*, 17 February 1844.

46. Wuest, *Annales*, vol. 2, pp. 274 and 478; and Obendorfer, *Portrait of a Mother*, p. 26.

47. Chronicle of the Most Holy Redeemer Convent, pp. 1 and 37; and Wuest, *Annales*, vol. 2, pp. 160–61.

48. Meiring, "Educational Aspects," pp. 152–53.

49. Cf. Connors, *Church-State Relationships*, p. 49.

50. AANY, Diary of the Rev. Richard L. Burtsell, 14 February 1867; and Connors, *Church-State Relationships*, pp. 106–7.

51. Smith, *The Catholic Church in New York*, vol. 1, p. 187.

52. Cf. Mrs. J. Sadlier, *Blakes and Flanagans* (New York, 1855).

53. *Katholische Kirchenzeitung*, 13 November 1862; there were many pro-Catholic education editorials in this paper.

54. Wuest, *Annales*, vol. 2, pp. 160–61; Chronicle of the Most Holy Redeemer Convent, p. 1; and APB, Mullaney, Manuscript History of St. Alphonsus Church, p. 32.

55. Chronicle of the Most Holy Redeemer Convent, p. 1; and Kleber, *Ferdinand, Indiana*, p. 116.

56. *27th Annual Report of the Board of Education for the Year ending Dec. 31, 1868* (New York, 1869), pp. 71 ff.

57. *Ibid.*, pp. 78 and 85; and Obendorfer, *Portrait of a Mother*, pp. 28–29.

58. See Bayrd Still, *Milwaukee: The History of A City* (Madison, 1948), pp. 260–61, where he discusses the issue of the Bennett law in Wisconsin; also Barry, *The Catholic Church and German Americans*, pp. 184 ff.

59. Howard Weisz, "Irish-American Attitudes and the Americanization of the English-Language Parochial School," *New York History* 53 (April 1972): 157–76.

60. Sebastian A. Erbacher, O.F.M., *Catholic Higher Education for Men in the United States, 1850–1866* (Washington, D.C., 1931), p. 116; Edmund J. Goebel, *A Study of Catholic Secondary Education During the Colonial Period Up to the First Plenary Council of Baltimore, 1852* (New York, 1937), pp. 223–25; and X. J. Harris, "Education, I (History of)," *New Catholic Encyclopedia* (New York, 1967), vol. 5, pp. 138–39, for a map of Catholic schools.

61. *The Metropolitan Catholic Almanac and Laity's Directory, 1840* (Baltimore, 1840), pp. 149–51; and *Sadlier's Catholic Almanac, 1864* (New York, 1864), pp. 88–90.

62. Sister Mary A. O'Brien, S.C., *History and Development of Catholic Secondary Education in the Archdiocese of New York* (New York, 1949), pp. 68–70; and Francis X. Curran, "Archbishop Hughes and the Jesuits," *Woodstock Letters* 97 (1968): 5–56.

63. Erbacher, *Catholic Higher Education for Men*, pp. 15–17.

64. Hassard, *Life of Hughes*, p. 215; AUND, Memorial of Hughes to Society for Propagation of the Faith, Paris, 5 February 1845, f. 104; and O'Brien, *History and Development of Catholic Secondary Education*, p. 70.

65. *Freeman's Journal*, 21 August 1847; and Erbacher, *Catholic Higher Education for Men*, p. 86.

66. *Metropolitan Record*, 13 September 1862.

67. Brother Angelus Gabriel, F.S.C., *The Christian Brothers in the United States, 1848–1948* (New York, 1948), p. 417.

68. O'Brien, *History and Development of Catholic Secondary Education*, pp. 66–67; AUND, Memorial of Hughes to Society for the Propagation of the Faith, Paris, 5 February 1845, f. 104; and AANY, Diary of the Rev. Richard L. Burtsell, 27 June 1866.

69. O'Brien, *History and Development of Catholic Secondary Education*, pp. 66–67; and *Sadlier's Catholic Almanac, 1864*, p. 88.

70. O'Brien, *History and Development of Catholic Secondary Education*, p. 143; an example of the classical curriculum is given in Thomas G. Taaffe, *A History of St. John's College, Fordham, N.Y.* (New York, 1891), pp. 72–74; also, Harold A. Buetow, *Of Singular Benefit* (New York, 1970), pp. 52 and 56.

71. Mulligan, "The Status and Role of the Lay Teacher," pp. 110–11; and Weisz, "Irish-American Attitudes."

72. Burns, *The Growth and Development of the Catholic School System*, p. 13; A. H. Songe, "A Bibliographical Survey of Catholic Textbooks Published in the United States from 1764 Through 1865" (Master's Thesis, Catholic University of America, 1956), p. 98; and Charles Carpenter, *History of American School Books* (Philadelphia, 1963), pp. 97 and 151.

73. Ruth M. Elson, *Guardians of Tradition* (Lincoln, Nebr., 1964), pp. 46 ff.; and Meiring, "Educational Aspects," p. 53 *passim*.

74. Burns, *The Growth and Development of the Catholic School System*, p. 140; Martin J. Kearney, *A Compendium of Ancient and Modern History*, 26th ed. (Baltimore, 1866); and Songe, "A Bibliographical Survey," pp. 106 ff.

75. Songe, "A Bibliographical Survey," pp. 96–97; and M. A. Foohey, "Bibliographical Survey of Catholic Textbooks Published in the United States from 1866–1900," (M.S.L.S. diss., Catholic University of America, 1961), p. 157. I am very grateful to Mrs. Christa Klein for her assistance and use of research material that she compiled in her study of Catholic books and catechisms.

76. Songe, "A Bibliographical Survey," p. 27; and Richard Challoner, *The Catholic Christian Instructed* (New York, n.d.).

77. Buetow, *Of Singular Benefit*, pp. 198–99; and *An Abridgment of Christian Doctrine in Which Each Question and Answer is taken, word for word, from the Most Rev. Dr. James Butler's Catechism, Lately Revised, enlarged, approved and commended as a general catechism for the Kingdom by the four Roman Catholic Archbishops of Ireland* (St. John, N.B., 1824). There were numerous versions of Butler's Catechism, but this was the one consulted. It was pocket-size and sold for two cents in the United States.

78. Songe, "A Bibliographical Survey," pp. 99–100; and *A Short Abridgment of Christian Doctrine* (Washington City, 1801).

79. Songe, "A Bibliographical Survey," pp. 82 and 78; Michael J. Curley, C.SS.R., *Venerable John Neumann C.SS.R., Fourth Bishop of Philadelphia* (Washington, D.C., 1952), p. 161; and John Neumann, *Katholischer Katechismus* (Baltimore, 1853).

80. Francis L. Keene, "Joseph Deharbe," *The Catholic Encyclopedia* (New York, 1908), vol. 4, p. 678; and Joseph Deharbe, S.J., *A Full Catechism of the Catholic Religion* (New York, n.d.).

81. Some manuals consulted were Francis X. Weninger, S.J., *A Manual of the Catholic Religion for Catechists, Teachers and Self-Instruction* (New York, 1861); Rev. Dr. J. Cummings, *Definitions and Aids to Memory for the Catechism; being a Catechism in Rhyme* (Boston, 1862); idem, *Songs for Catholic Schools and the Catechism in Rhyme* (New York, 1862); and Christian Brothers, *Catholic Anecdotes: or The Catechism in Examples* (New York, 1885).

82. *Freeman's Journal*, 12 March 1870.

83. *Butler's Catechism*, p. 66; and Neumann, *Katholischer Katechismus*, p. 144.

84. Cummings, *Definitions and Aids*, p. 19.

85. See Weninger, *A Manual of the Catholic Religion*, p. 324; and Michael Muller, C.SS.R., *Catechism of Christian Doctrine for Parochial and Sunday Schools* (New York, 1875), pp. 23 and 276.

86. *Ibid.*

87. Challoner, *The Catholic Christian Instructed*, p. 155; and Deharbe, *A Full Catechism*, p. 307.

88. See Willard Thorp, *Catholic Novelists in Defense of Their Faith, 1829–1865*, reprinted from the Proceedings of the American Antiquarian Society, 1968.

89. Christian Brothers, *The Third Book of Reading Lessons* (Montreal, 1860), p. 4; and Songe, "A Bibliographical Survey," p. 102.

90. Christian Brothers, *The Third Book*, p. 11.

91. The readers consulted were: *ibid.*; idem, *The Literary Class-Book or Fourth Series of Select Reading Lessons in Prose and Verse* (New York, 1855); Member of the Order of Holy Cross, *The Metropolitan Second Reader, The Metropolitan Third Reader, The Metropolitan Fourth Reader, and The Metropolitan Fifth Reader* (New York, 1871–80); and J. S. Denman, *Fifth Book or Rhetorical Reader* (New York, 1856).

92. Christian Brothers, *Fourth Series*, pp. 248–50; this essay appeared in many readers.

93. Member of the Order of Holy Cross, *Metropolitan Fifth Reader*, p. 269.

94. Cummings, *Songs for Catholic Schools*, pp. 35 and 78.

95. *Metropolitan Record*, 14 May and 30 July 1859.

96. *Freeman's Journal*, 23 September 1854.

SEVEN. SOCIAL CATHOLICISM

1. The best analysis of Catholic social thought is James E. Roohan, "American Catholics and the Social Question" (Ph.D. diss., Yale University, 1952).

2. Quoted in Roohan, "American Catholics and the Social Question," p. 242.

3. "The Church and the Republic," *Brownson's Quarterly Review*, July 1856, p. 303.

4. De Tocqueville, *Journeys*, p. 164.

5. *Ibid.*, p. 170.

6. Connell, *Irish Peasant Society*, pp. 131–33.

7. Alexander, "Church and Society," pp. 410 ff.

8. Roohan, "American Catholics and the Social Question," pp. 55–57; see also C. J. Nuesse, *The Social Thought of American Catholics, 1634–1829* (Westminister, Md., 1945).

9. Kehoe, *Works of Hughes*, vol. 1, p. 527.

10. *Truth Teller*, 21 December 1833.

11. William Gahan, O.S.A., *Sermons and Moral Discourses for all the Sundays and Principal Festivals of the Year, on the Most Important Truths and Maxims of the Gospel* (Dublin, 1846), p. 254. This book of sermons was popular in Ireland and in the United States; see the Diary of the Rev. Richard L. Burtsell, 4 March 1866, and advertisements in the Catholic Directories.

12. *New York Times*, 12 November 1852.

13. "Charities of New York," *Catholic World* 8 (November 1868): 285.

14. Kehoe, *Works of Hughes*, vol. 1, p. 529.

15. Anna H. Dorsey, *The Oriental Pearl, or The Catholic Emigrants* (Baltimore, 1848), pp. 8, 38, and 48.

16. Mary Sadlier, *Willy Burke; or the Irish Orphan in America* (Boston, 1850).

17. *Ibid.*, p. 263.

18. *Butler's Catechism*, p. 7; see Christopher von Schmid, *Angelica* (New York, 1848), *The Lamb* (New York, 1848), and his other works written in German and translated into English.

19. Christian Brothers, *The Third Book*, p. 93.

20. Cummings, *Songs for Catholic Schools*, pp. 48–50.

21. Rodriguez, *Don Félix Varela*, p. 142.

22. *Ibid.*, pp. 255 and 302.

23. *Ibid.*, p. 304.

24. Bayley, *A Brief Sketch*, p. 123; and Shea, *The Catholic Churches of New York City*, p. 691.

25. Obendorfer, *Portrait of a Mother*, pp. 34 ff.

26. Wuest, *Annales*, vol. 2, pp. 219–33.

27. *New York Weekly Register and Catholic Diary*, 24 May 1834; *Truth Teller*, 23 November 1839 and 11 January 1840; and *Metropolitan Record*, 26 November 1859.

28. *Freeman's Journal*, 20 May 1848.

29. Daniel T. McColgan, *A Century of Charity: The First One Hundred Years of the Society of St. Vincent de Paul in the United States*, 2 vols. (Milwaukee, 1951), vol. 1, pp. 114 ff.; and Aaron I. Abell, *American Catholicism and Social*

Action (Notre Dame, Ind., 1963), pp. 22–23. See also *Metropolitan Record*, 8 October 1859 and 4 May 1861, for membership in the society.

30. *Katholische Kirchenzeitung*, 30 July 1857 and 23 September 1858.

31. Joseph Wissel, C.SS.R., *The Redemptorist on the American Missions*, 3 vols., 3d rev. ed. (n.p., 1920), vol. 1, p. 230.

32. Kehoe, *Works of Hughes*, vol. 1, p. 438; and "The Sanitary and Moral Condition of New York City," *Catholic World* 7 (July 1868): 560.

33. *Truth Teller*, 5 September 1840 and 9 January 1841.

34. Potter, *To the Golden Door*, pp. 522–23; see Joan Bland, *Hibernian Crusade: The Story of the Catholic Total Abstinence Union of America* (Washington, D.C., 1951).

35. See David M. Schneider, *The History of Public Welfare in New York State, 1609–1860* (Chicago, 1938); and Duffy, *A History of Public Health in New York City*.

36. Connell, *Irish Peasant Society*, p. 135; cf. Arnold Schrier, *Ireland and the American Emigration, 1850–1900* (Minneapolis, 1958), p. 62.

37. AUND, *Scritture*, vol. 11, letter 1510, Pastoral letter of Bishop John Dubois, 1834, f. 263.

38. *Freeman's Journal*, 5 February 1848; Alvin W. Skardon, *Church Leader in the Cities: William Augustus Muhlenberg* (Philadelphia, 1971), pp. 145–46; and Smith, *The Catholic Church in New York*, vol. 1, p. 130.

39. *Freeman's Journal*, 20 February 1847; Sister Marie de Lourdes, *With a Great Heart: The Story of St. Vincent's Hospital and Medical Center of New York, 1849–1964* (New York, 1965).

40. Rosenberg, *The Cholera Years*, pp. 139–40; and *Truth Teller*, 3 August 1833.

41. AANY, James Fagan, Superintendent of State Emigrant Refuge and Hospital Ward's Island to Archbishop J. McCloskey, 3 August 1866.

42. *Metropolitan Record*, 29 June 1861 and 21 March 1863; for the size of public hospitals, see Duffy, *A History of Public Health in New York City*, p. 487.

43. AANY, Claims of the Fathers and the Congregation of the Church of the Most Holy Redeemer, New York, to the St. Francis Hospital, Fifth Street, New York, 20 July 1868.

44. Obendorfer, *Portrait of a Mother*, p. 37; and "Who Shall Take Care of Our Sick?" *Catholic World* 8 (October 1868): 45–46.

45. George Deshon, *Guide for Catholic Young Women, Especially for those who Earn Their Own Living* (New York, 1863), pp. 61 ff. and 293 ff.

46. Dorsey, *Oriental Pearl*, pp. 39–40.

47. AUND, Archbishop John Hughes to Society for Propagation of the Faith, Paris, 13 May 1851, f. 104.

48. *Freeman's Journal*, 17 September 1870.

49. George P. Jacoby, *Catholic Child Care in Nineteenth Century New York* (Washington, D.C., 1941), p. 193.

50. *Freeman's Journal*, 4 November 1854.

51. Jacoby, *Catholic Child Care*, p. 199.

52. *Metropolitan Record*, 26 December 1863.

53. See Leo Marx, *The Machine in the Garden* (New York, 1967).

54. John O'Hanlon, *The Irish Emigrant's Guide for the United States* (Boston, 1851), pp.. 166–67.

55. John F. Maguire, *Irish in America* (London, 1868), pp. 249–50.

56. A. F. Hewit, *Sermons of the Rev. Francis A. Baker, C.S.P. with a Memoir of His Life*, 6th ed. (New York, 1865), p. 179.

57. Mary Sadlier, *Con O'Reagan; or Emigrant Life in the New World* (New York, 1885), p. 276.

58. *Ibid.*, p. 368.

59. Kehoe, *Works of Hughes*, vol. 2, p. 751.

60. Quoted in Henry J. Browne, "Archbishop Hughes and Western Colonization," *Catholic Historical Review* 36 (October 1950): 282.

61. Kehoe, *Works of Hughes*, vol. 2, p. 692.

62. *Ibid.*

63. *Ibid.*, p. 754.

64. *Ibid.*, p. 753.

65. Schneider, *The History of Public Welfare*, p. 190.

66. Jacoby, *Catholic Child Care*, pp. 92 and 97; and *Truth Teller*, 11 January 1834.

67. Jacoby, *Catholic Child Care*, pp. 111–12; and *Metropolitan Record*, 25 November 1862.

68. Obendorfer, *Portrait of a Mother*, p. 30; and Wuest, *Annales*, vol. 2, p. 35, and vol. 3, p. 131.

69. Wuest, *Annales*, vol. 4, p. 40; and Jacoby, *Catholic Child Care*, p. 212.

70. Jacoby, *Catholic Child Care*, p. 215.

71. *Ibid.*, pp. 115–17; *Freeman's Journal*, 4 September 1858; and Miriam Z. Langsam, *Children West: A History of the Placing-Out System of the N.Y. Children's Aid Society, 1853–1890* (Madison, Wis., 1964), pp. 45–55.

72. Jacoby, *Catholic Child Care*, p. 118; *Freeman's Journal*, 4 September 1858; and *Metropolitan Record*, 26 March 1859.

73. John O'Grady, *Catholic Charities in the United States* (Washington, D.C., 1930), p. 111.

74. Schneider, *The History of Public Welfare*, p. 335.

75. Jacoby, *Catholic Child Care*, p. 129; and O'Grady, *Catholic Charities*, p. 115.

76. *Ibid.*, pp. 114–15.

77. Jacoby, *Catholic Child Care*, p. 117; and *Metropolitan Record*, 15 February 1862.

78. See William G. McLoughlin, "Changing Patterns of Protestant Philanthropy," in *Religious Situation, 1969*, ed. Donald Cutler (Boston, 1969), pp. 538–614.

EIGHT. PREACHING

1. Joseph M. Connors, S.V.D., "Catholic Homiletic Theory in Historical Perspective" (Ph.D. diss., Northwestern University, 1962), pp. 76 ff.

2. Quoted in John Tracy Ellis, "The Formation of the American Priest: An Historical Perspective," in *The Catholic Priest in the United States: Historical Investigations*, ed. John Tracy Ellis (Collegeville, Minn., 1971), p. 19.

3. Guilday, *The Life and Times of John England*, vol. 1, p. 25.

4. Ryan, *Old St. Peter's*, p. 48; and Fitzpatrick, *The Life, Times and Correspondence of Rt. Rev. Dr. Doyle*, vol. 1, p. 140.

5. Connelly, *The Visit of Archbishop Bedini*, p. 211.

6. AUND, *Scritture*, Bishop John Dubois to Prefect of Propaganda Fide, vol. 10, letter 1270, *ca.* 1830, f. 280.

7. Guilday, *The Life and Times of John England*, vol. 1, pp. 25–26.

8. *Truth Teller*, 22 February 1844.

9. Carthy, *Old St. Patrick's*, p. 48.

10. Obendorfer, *Portrait of a Mother*, pp. 32–33.

11. *Truth Teller*, 30 November 1839.

12. Hassard, *Life of Hughes*, pp. 134 ff.

13. *Freeman's Journal*, 23 December 1843; and *Metropolitan Record*, 9 January 1864.

14. Henry J. Browne, Manuscript History of Archbishop Hughes (unpublished), chap. 2, p. 35.

15. *Ibid.*, chap. 8, p. 27; and *Freeman's Journal*, 18 December 1847.

16. Hassard, *Life of Hughes*, p. 430; the text is in Kehoe, *Works of Hughes*, vol. 2, pp. 316–25.

17. Connelly, *The Visit of Archbishop Bedini*, p. 243.

18. AUND, *Scritture*, vol. 18, letter 1417, Hughes to Prefect of Propaganda, 23 March 1858, f. 512.

19. Connelly, *The Visit of Archbishop Bedini*, p. 243.

20. *Ibid.*, p. 244.

21. Theodore Heck, O.S.B., *The Curriculum of the Major Seminary in Relation to Contemporary Conditions* (Washington, D.C., 1935), pp. 27 ff.; the annual Catholic Directories also listed the professors in seminaries and their fields of instruction.

22. John Talbot Smith, *Our Seminaries* (New York, 1896), p. 122.

23. See Connors, "Catholic Homiletic Theory," pp. 15–16.

24. *Ibid.*, pp. 193 ff.; these books were regularly advertised in the Catholic Directories.

25. Connors, "Catholic Homiletic Theory," pp. 242 ff.

26. *Ibid.*, pp. 237 ff.

27. *Truth Teller*, 4 May 1844.

28. *Metropolitan Record*, 16 February 1861; *Katholische Kirchenzeitung*, 6 January 1860; and Leslie Stephen and Sidney Lee, eds., *The Dictionary of National Biography* (London, 1917), vol. 7, p. 800.

29. Meehan, "Notes and Comments," pp. 184–85; AANY, Diary of the Rev. Richard L. Burtsell, 17 June 1866; and *Truth Teller*, 13 January 1838.

30. Wuest, *Annales, Supplementum*, pt. 2, pp. 167–68.

31. Gahan, *Sermons and Moral Discourses*; and P. Ó Súilleabháin, O.F.M., "Catholic Sermon Books Printed in Ireland, 1700–1850," *Irish Ecclesiastical Record* 99 (1963): 31–36.

32. P. Ó Súilleabháin, O.F.M., "Sidelights on the Irish Church 1811–1838," *Collectanea Hibernica: Sources for Irish History* (Dublin) 9 (1966): 77.

33. Hagen, *Geschichte*, vol. 2, pp. 239–40. One Austrian preacher whose works were in circulation in the United States was Johann E. Veith; the following works were located in APB: *Homilienkranz für das katholische Kirchenjahr* (Vienna, 1838), *Das Vater Unser* (Vienna, 1842), and *Die Heilung des Blindgeboren* (Vienna, 1846). See Aubert, *Le Pontificat de Pie IX*, p. 134.

34. See *Sermons Preached at the Church of St. Paul the Apostle, New York, During the Year 1862* (New York, 1862) (similar volumes were published each year—those consulted were between 1862 and 1866); and Thomas Preston, *Christ and the Church* (New York, 1869), and *The Sacred Year: Sermons for the Principal Sundays and Holydays from the Feast of St. Andrew to the Nineteenth Sunday after Pentecost*, 3d ed. (New York, 1885).

35. *Metropolitan Record*, 9 January 1864.

36. The sermon is in Kehoe, *Works of Hughes*, vol. 2, pp. 275–83.

37. Hassard, *Life of Hughes*, p. 325, stated that Hughes rarely wrote a sermon, but the AANY contain numerous sermons in Hughes's handwriting; the Diary of Rev. Richard Burtsell in many places speaks of this custom among priests and bemoans the fact that more do not follow it.

38. *Metropolitan Record*, 9 January 1864.

39. E. Kretz and P. Hitz, C.SS.R., *Missions Paroissiales et Liturgie* (Bruges, 1957), pp. 13–14; and Jerome G. Stowell, C.P., "The Object of the Parish Mission" (M.A. thesis, University of Notre Dame, 1964), pp. 3–10.

40. Brück, *Geschichte*, vol. 3, p. 540; and Aubert, *Le Pontificat de Pie IX*, p. 144.

41. Reynolds, *The Catholic Emancipation Crisis in Ireland*, p. 50.

42. Aubert, *Le Pontificat de Pie IX*, p. 144; and Karl Matthes, *Allgemeine Kirchliche Chronik 1858* (Leipzig, 1859), p. 151.

43. *Decreta Synodi Plenariae*, p. 14; see *Battersby's Catholic Directory 1860*, pp. 208 ff., for examples of frequent parish missions.

44. Varela followed this practice in Transfiguration. Shea, *The Catholic Churches of New York City*, p. 689; and Rodriguez, *Don Félix Varela*, pp. 42–43.

45. Gilbert J. Garraghan, S.J., *The Jesuits of the Middle United States*, 3 vols. (New York, 1938), vol. 2, p. 52.

46. Michael J. Curley, C.SS.R., *Cheerful Ascetic: The Life of Francis Xavier Seelos, C.SS.R.* (New Orleans, 1969), p. 260.

47. P. Claessens, *La Vie du Père Bernard* (Paris, 1873), p. 81; and APF, Mission Chronicles, vol. 1, p. 2.

48. APF, Mission Chronicles, vol. 1, p. 3.

49. *The Mission Book*, p. 5; also Wuest, *Annales*, vol. 4, pt. 2, pp. 112–13.

50. *The Mission Book*, p. 4.

51. The best historical survey of parish missions is M. Van Delft, C.SS.R., *La Mission Paroissiale: Pratique et Theorie*, trans. Fr. Van Groenendael (Paris, 1964).

52. See Shaughnessy, *Has the Immigrant Kept the Faith?*

53. Wuest, *Annales*, vol. 4, pt. 2, p. 119.

54. *Ibid.*, vol. 2, p. 356.

55. APF, Mission Chronicles, vol. 1, p. 3.

56. *Ibid.*, vol. 1, p. 238.

57. Cf. Kehoe, *Works of Hughes*, vol. 2, pp. 127 and 693; and *Freeman's Journal*, 14 April 1866. The theme of America's infidelity appeared frequently in sermon books of the Paulists and also in D. A. Merrick, S.J., *Sermons for the Times, Delivered in St. Francis Xavier Church, N.Y., 1870–71* (New York, 1872).

58. P. Hitz, C.SS.R., *To Preach the Gospel*, trans. Rosemary Sheed (New York, 1963), pp. 113–14.

59. Wissel, *The Redemptorist on the American Missions*, vol. 1, p. 4.

60. Garraghan, *The Jesuits of the Middle United States*, vol. 2, p. 70.

61. Wissel, *The Redemptorist on the American Missions*, vol. 1, pp. 7–8.

62. Hewit, *Sermons of the Rev. Francis A. Baker*, p. 122.

63. *Freeman's Journal*, 5 May 1851; Byrne, *The Redemptorist Centenaries*, pp. 261–62; and Wuest, *Annales*, vol. 4, pt. 1, pp. 89–90.

64. Shea, *The Catholic Churches of New York City*, pp. 693–94.

65. *Metropolitan Record*, 9 May 1863; and Garraghan, *The Jesuits of the Middle United States*, vol. 2, pp. 91–92.

66. AUND, *Scritture*, vol. 19, letter 1841, Rev. Isaac Hecker to Prefect of Propaganda Fide, 26 June 1861, f. 229–30; this letter contains a good description of the parish mission.

67. Wissel, *The Redemptorist on the American Missions*, vol. 1, p. 41.

68. Hewit, *Sermons of the Rev. Francis A. Baker*, p. 117.

69. *Metropolitan Record*, 9 May 1863; and Wuest, *Annales*, vol. 3, pt. 2, pp. 408 ff.

70. Wuest, *Annales*, vol. 2, p. 262.

71. Wissel, *The Redemptorist on the American Missions*, vol. 2, p. 4.

72. Hewit, *Sermons of the Rev. Francis A. Baker*, p. 125.

73. Garraghan, *The Jesuits of the Middle United States*, vol. 2, p. 62.

74. Curley, *Cheerful Ascetic*, p. 254.

75. *Ibid.*, p. 252.

76. AANY, Diary of the Rev. Richard L. Burtsell, 18 November 1867.

77. *Ibid.*

78. Wissel, *The Redemptorist on the American Missions*, vol. 1, p. 114.

79. *Ibid.*, vol. 1, p. 115.

80. APF, Mission Chronicles, vol. 1, p. 53.

81. AANY, Diary of the Rev. Richard L. Burtsell, 24 November 1867; and Garraghan, *The Jesuits of the Middle United States*, vol. 2, p. 57.

82. William G. McLoughlin, *Modern Revivalism* (New York, 1959), p. 160.

83. *Ibid.*, p. 51.

84. *Ibid.*, pp. 87 and 124.

85. See Robert Baird, *Religion in America*, ed. Henry Warner Bowden (New York, 1970), pp. 179 ff.

NINE. TRANSFORMATION OF THE CHURCH

1. *New York Times*, 26 May 1879.

2. *Ibid.*; and Billington, *The Protestant Crusade*, pp. 232 and 247.

3. John M. Farley, *History of St. Patrick's Cathedral* (New York, 1908), pp. 114 ff.

4. AANY, Copy of letter of Bishop John Hughes to Society for the Propagation of the Faith, 23 January 1845.

5. AUND, Bishop John Hughes to the Society for the Propagation of the Faith, Paris, 5 February 1845, f. 104.

6. AANY, Copy of letter of Bishop John Hughes to Society for the Propagation of the Faith, 23 January 1845.

7. *New York Times*, 10 December 1852.

8. AUND, *Scritture*, vol. 14, letter 226, Rev. Jeremiah Cummings to Prefect of Propaganda Fide, 24 November 1847, f. 639.

9. Mol, *Churches and Immigrants*, p. 73.

10. See Barry, *The Catholic Church and German Americans*.

11. *Katholische Kirchenzeitung*, 12 July 1860, where it is noted that one thousand parishioners of Most Holy Redeemer Church sent a letter to Pius IX pledging loyalty to him; St. Alphonsus Parish sent a similar letter in September 1866, (Chronicle of St. Alphonsus Church, 1866).

12. Smith, *The Catholic Church in New York*, vol. 2, pp. 379 ff.

13. See Kehoe, *Works of Hughes*, vol. 2, pp. 9–69, where the papal views of Hughes are clearly indicated; and Larkin, "The Devotional Revolution."

14. *Freeman's Journal*, 23 February 1889.

15. *Katholische Kirchenzeitung*, 6 August 1857; and Sister M. Thomas Johan-

nemann, "Max Oertel, Convert and Journalist" (M.A. thesis, Catholic University of America, 1939), pp. 29 and 51.

16. Dorothy Dohen, *Nationalism and American Catholicism* (New York, 1967).

17. *Freeman's Journal*, 27 May 1854.

18. Hassard, *Life of Hughes*, pp. 439 and 487.

19. AUND, *Scritture*, vol. 18, letter 1417, Hughes to Prefect, 23 March 1858, f. 525.

20. John J. Considine, "The History of Canonical Legislation in the Diocese and Province of New York, 1842–1861" (M.A. thesis, Catholic University of America, 1947), is a general study of the New York councils during Hughes's episcopacy.

21. AANY, Diary of Archbishop's Secretary, 24 December 1852; also Diary of the Rev. Richard L. Burtsell, 17 November 1866, for a description of Preston's work; see John Tracy Ellis, *Perspectives in American Catholicism* (Baltimore, 1963), p. 152, for the position of the First Plenary Council of Baltimore on the organization of the chancery.

22. AANY, Circular Letter of Archbishop Hughes to Pastors, 5 November 1857.

23. Cf. Callow, *The Tweed Ring*, p. 4.

24. AUND, *Scritture*, vol. 18, letter 1417, Hughes to Prefect, 23 March 1858, ff. 527–28.

25. *Ibid.*

26. Browne, "The Archdiocese of New York a Century Ago," p. 139.

27. AANY, Diary of Archbishop's Secretary, 12 May 1850; see Smith, *The Catholic Church in New York*, vol. 1, pp. 38 ff., for a history of early New York Catholicism.

28. *Concilium Provinciale Neo-Eboracense III*, decretum 1; and Sister M. Patricia Ann Reilly, O.P., "The Administration of Parish Schools in the Archdiocese of New York, 1800–1900," *Historical Records and Studies* 44 (1956): 45 ff.

29. Quoted in Barry, *The Catholic Church and German Americans*, p. 17; cf. Connelly, *The Visit of Archbishop Bedini*, p. 223.

30. AANY, Diary of the Rev. Richard L. Burtsell, 26 July 1865.

31. Cf. Nathan Glazer and Daniel P. Moynihan, *Beyond the Melting Pot* (Cambridge, Mass., 1963), pp. 226–27.

32. See Robert Trisco, "Bishops and Their Priests in the United States," in *The Catholic Priest in the United States*, ed. John Tracy Ellis, pp. 111–292, for the history of this problem.

33. See Aubert, *Le Pontificat de Pie IX*.

34. Adna F. Weber, *The Growth of Cities in the Nineteenth Century* (New York, 1899).

35. James P. Rodechko, "Patrick Ford and His Search for America: A Case Study of Irish-American Journalism, 1870–1913" (Ph.D. diss., University of Connecticut, 1967), p. 164.

36. Herbermann, "The Rt. Rev. John Dubois, D.D.," p. 318.

37. Hassard, *Life of Hughes*, pp. 206 ff.

38. Farley, *History of St. Patrick's Cathedral*, p. 120.

39. *Ibid.*, pp. 127 and 235–36.

40. AANY, Diary of the Rev. Richard L. Burtsell, 15 October 1865; many parish histories witness to this transformation, e.g., *Souvenir of the Golden Jubilee of St. Bridgid's Church, 1849–1899* (New York, 1899), pp. 15–17.

41. Shea, *The Catholic Churches of New York City*, pp. 538–39.

42. Wuest, *Annales*, supplement to vols. 1–3, p. 399.

43. *U. S. Census 1860: Statistics of the U.S. in 1860* (Washington, D.C., 1866), pt. 2, pp. 431–33.

44. Connors, *Church-State Relationships*, p. 46, n. 137.

45. *Freeman's Journal*, 14 April 1866.

46. AANY, Diary of the Rev. Richard L. Burtsell, 17 November 1865 and *passim* for an image of the priest's life at this time.

47. Florence E. Gibson, *The Attitudes of the New York Irish Towards State and National Affairs, 1848–1892* (New York, 1951), pp. 247 ff.

48. Glazer and Moynihan, *Beyond the Melting Pot*, p. 229.

Index

213

This book was composed in Linotype Caledonia text and
Caslon Bold display type by the Maryland Linotype
Composition Co., Inc., from a design by Susan Bishop.
It was printed on 60-lb. Perkins and Squire Litho R paper
and bound in Joanna Arrestox cloth by The Murray
Printing Company.

LIBRARY OF CONGRESS CATALOGING IN PUBLICATION DATA

Dolan, Jay P.   1936–
  The immigrant church.

  Includes bibliographical references and index.
  1. Catholics in New York (City).   2. Catholics, Irish.
3. Catholics, German.   I. Title.
BX1418.N5D64   282'.747'1   75–12552
ISBN 0-8018-1708-0

803620

282
DCL

Dolan, Jay P.

The immigrant church

DATE			

© THE BAKER & TAYLOR CO